HAPPIER THAN A

Billionaire

The Sequel

NADINE HAYS PISANI

Copyright © 2012 Nadine Hays Pisani

All rights reserved.

ISBN-13: 978-1481098229

DEDICATION

To the Readers

CONTENTS

*P*art II

*P*art III

ACKNOWLEDGMENTS

I'd like to thank the following people: A. Pawlowski for writing about my story and making an author's dream come true, Cheryl Bradshaw for her thoughtful corrections and funny side notes, Denio and Ewa at Villa Bougainvillea, Eddie Belaval for taking the beautiful cover shot of my book, and Teresa Minue who loves an em dash almost as much as I do.

To my sister, who thought no one reads the acknowledgments, and has since learned many do. I have hundreds of emails asking me to tell her just that. I'm lucky to have her in my life.

Thanks to my dear nieces Diana, Veronica, and Anastasia. The world is a lovely place. Go explore.

Without Rob, I would never have gone on this journey, and the stories would never have been so funny. Thank you, Sweetie.

And finally, I want to thank everyone who enjoyed *Happier Than A Billionaire* and shared it with their friends. This book is dedicated to you.

Dear Mom and Dad,

I'm not coming home just yet. There's so much more to see.

Love,

Nadine

Part I

A Little Green Light

Gray ash rains down like confetti as my husband pulls into the driveway. This is a normal occurrence when you live at the base of a volcano. Occasionally, the crater releases pressure by ejecting ash three hundred feet into the air. It's quite the sight. On some mornings, the ash is so white it reminds me of snowflakes; I could almost stick my tongue out and catch one. That's until I get a whiff of the accompanying sulfuric gas. I'm quickly reminded that Poas Volcano is my neighbor, one that can be as cantankerous as a grumpy old man.

I can't help but think of my mortality on days like this. Let's face it. I live near a volcano, on a fault line, in a country where mudslides can wash away entire villages. And because I want to make sure Rob is taken care of in the unfortunate event I find myself tobogganing down the side of this mountain, I spend an unusual amount of time deciding on who will become his second wife.

If I kick the bucket, Giada de Laurentiis, the Italian-American chef, is my lucky replacement. She has it all: beauty, culinary skills, and apparently a very good dentist. I have never seen such white teeth. I'm positive Rob would be in good hands; this woman cooks everything he loves and does it all with a perky disposition. The only problem I see with Giada is that you can't be too picky with her food. If she gives you a sausage sandwich in a purple paper bag, you better just eat it and not ask any questions. She'll smack it right out of your hands if you complain. That sparkly smile of hers hides an Italian temper. I'm sure of it.

"I need to ask you something, Nadine," Rob says after walking through the front door. He's just met with our architect in town, and by the look on his face I'm suspecting it didn't go well. "When you practice your Spanish on Rosetta Stone, do you actually speak into the microphone or do you just skip that part and move on to the next lesson?"

"I try to repeat the phrases, and if I say them correctly, the little green light turns on."

"And does that little green light ever go on?"

"Hmm, nah. But it's not my fault. I can't roll my r's and practically every word in this language is pronounced that way. It's a disability, Rob. I have a lazy tongue."

When I was in elementary school, I had four years of speech therapy for a lisp and a lazy R. I was repeatedly pulled out of class by Mrs. Cohen, the speech therapist. I then sat for hours in a room where I had to repeat phrases—like the presumptuous *Sally rides red roller coasters on Saturday*—over and over again for hours. It was even more glamorous than you're imagining. I was also required to stare at pictures of tongues, and was frequently reminded of how mine was defective, flopping around in my mouth like an unmanned fire hose.

Rob informs me I've been teaching him the incorrect word for "pay." It's actually the word for "punch." Unfortunately, our architect didn't find the humor in this when Rob asked to punch him at the end of the meeting.

"Nadine, I must have mispronounced this to everyone from the gasoline attendant to cashiers in the hardware store. I've even threatened the nine-year-old boy who sells us mangos at the farmers market. Basically, I've been bullying half of Costa Rica when all I want to do is pay them."

"It's not my fault that those two words, pagar and pegar, sound the same. Tomato, Tah-mato, what's the difference?" I ask.

"One will get me arrested for assault. That's the difference," he grunts. It looks like Rob might be shopping for a second wife sooner than I anticipated.

I suppose this creates quite the problem. By the end of any given day, Rob is threatening the baker, cracking the egg vendor, and even the old man at the butcher shop is getting a smack. I'm surprised we ever made it out of there alive.

It's true. I've failed Rosetta Stone, an honor bestowed on only a select group of idiots. If I could just get those little green lights to appear, waving me onto the next lesson, it would do wonders for my self-esteem.

At least I'm not like those people who come here bragging about the four years of Spanish they took in high school. *I'm fluent,* they boast at a restaurant as they repeat words like El Salvador and burrito like they interned in a Chilean mining camp. But when the waiter comes over discussing the specials, they freeze up realizing they haven't heard or spoken the language in twenty years. I feel vindicated during these encounters, even if Rob has been telling the waiters he's going to beat them up after dessert.

When I go back to the states to visit my family, they love to tease me about my horrible Spanish. To get them off my back, I've decided to make up words since they don't know what I'm saying anyway. Only my twelve-year-old niece is on to me. She takes Spanish in school and knows that her aunt is a fraud. That's okay, I keep her quiet by taking her to *Claire's* to buy headbands and sunglasses. Then to top it off, we end the day with a frothy Starbucks beverage that her mother would never let her drink. I'm being extorted by an accessorized and—thanks to me—highly caffeinated middle schooler.

I should probably amp up the lessons since we're finally working with an architect and are one step closer to building our house. Knowing the words for door and window could come in handy. While Rob sits at our kitchen table and looks over the architect's drawings, I go back to working on my blog. Lately I've been getting a lot more comments. They are mostly positive except for this one guy who greets me every morning with:

Hey happier, you sound like an idiot. Drop dead.

It's like eighth grade homeroom all over again.

I like posting all the funny things we do. It seems like this mountaintop in Grecia makes me more creative. Besides the occasional kinkajou jumping at my window, I have very few distractions. I now understand why so many writers go on retreats to wintery bed and breakfasts to finish manuscripts. Just take that guy from *Misery*. Having his legs bashed in by Kathy Bates was probably the best thing for his writing career. Where else can you get that kind of focus?

But my quiet life on the volcano is about to be uprooted. If we are seriously going to build this house we have to move to the beach. I just finished *Under the Tuscan Sun* (for the third time), and it gives me hope that my story will turn out like hers. If she can have a beautiful home overlooking fields of olive trees in Italy, how hard can it be to build my ocean-view home in Costa Rica?

Scented Oils & Golden Hues

We'll be saying goodbye to our dear little town of Grecia. I love this place but it is time to go and build on our property. Although we decided not to build at our original location, we have found the perfect spot for us at the beach and it's clear that starting the permit process is impossible to do when you live five hours away. A part of me wants to stay; it's wonderful here, and I don't know if building a house is going to add any more happiness to my life. The time I've spent in Costa Rica has calmed my compulsive urge to always think bigger is better. I have since learned bigger usually means a lot more indigestion.

"It doesn't make sense to keep renting when we have a beautiful ocean-view property," Rob says.

"But I really like it in Grecia. Our friends are here."

"Yeah? So is the Dog Lady. Wouldn't it be nice to have a day where we don't have to entertain her five dogs?" It would be great getting away from Dolores. It appears that I might be the only one left she is allowed to visit anymore. Her crew of dogs keeps changing, but they all continue to pee on my yoga mat, new sneakers, and our barbecue. Sometimes she joins them, always wanting to be closer to nature by whizzing behind my azalea bush. Every morning I pray she sleeps in. Even the Luftwaffe took an occasional day off.

I can easily envision a life without her, but it will be sad to leave Frankie and Darlene. We've grown close and I will miss our lovely dinners out on their terrace. They've been so kind to us; Darlene has even begun calling us her "kids." Now we are moving across the country and I'm falling back into one of my cranky moods. It's hard enough for me to make friends and I will have to do it all over again at the beach. I can already feel my old introverted personality battling to take over.

It's not that this is the worst idea. We have ocean-view property that I could never have afforded in the states. And being many hours away makes it difficult when we have to get brush cleared or even pay the taxes at the local municipality. It's time to go. I know it's the right thing to do, but I'm longing to stay in my cute little mountaintop rental. It's the most peaceful place I know. I don't have as much anxiety anymore and can finally appreciate each moment. There is nothing about my life now that resembles my former one; I'm not always worrying about the next big thing but just grateful for each day as it comes. I'm even doing yoga every morning on the patio in-between Dolores' daily urine assault.

So how do you know when you are supposed to change it up again? Wasn't this enough? Selling everything I owned and moving to another country? I try to shift my adventurous spirit back into drive, but my mind wants to rev in neutral for a little while longer. I'm not sure if I am ready for this yet.

Living close to Tamarindo is totally different than living in the mountains. Grecia is a quiet community, whereas Tamarindo is a very popular tourist area. People come from all over the world to not only surf but to enjoy the incredible beaches. There are a lot of fun things to do and plenty of restaurants to enjoy. However, I'm not looking forward to living near a tourist town. I like the solitude, the cool weather, and the comfy couch I'm sitting on in Grecia. I don't want to move.

Our budget is already fragile and we need much of our savings to build this house. I explained my concerns to Rob a few months back when we started discussing it. "You know rentals will be more expensive there. How are we going to afford a thousand dollars a month rent? It's not in our budget."

"Listen, we need to be closer. Just have some faith. We need to look around and take our time finding the right home for us. We have to try. We've gotten this far haven't we? And we didn't do it by playing it safe."

I check out rentals on Craigslist, but they are very expensive and are for short-term tenants only. This was the same problem we encountered when I first moved to Costa Rica. You can't get good deals this way. You have to get your feet on the ground and do your own investigating. We set aside three days to see if we can make that happen.

The road trip is uneventful except for my somber attitude. Even though it's a gorgeous day, I have a pit in my stomach knowing I'm moving again. We stop at a few cheaper hotels but they are booked. We call the more pricey ones, but they only have the most expensive rooms available. Rob decides to stop at a property manager's office. She goes through her listings and finds a beautiful condominium she is willing to rent to us for one hundred and seventy-five dollars a night. With a little persuasion, Rob talks her down to one hundred dollars, but we have to stay at least three nights. It's pricey, but we figure we can eat most of our meals there which will help save a little money. At this point, I'm too tired to find something else so we book it.

"I'm starving. Let's get a bite to eat. Afterwards we can go to the supermarket and pick up some groceries," Rob suggests. We remember passing a cute restaurant situated right on the beach in Brasilito, a small town located ten minutes outside Flamingo. It seems like the perfect place to unwind before we dive into our hectic mission of finding a house.

We walk into the restaurant where tables and chairs are arranged in the sand ten feet from high tide. They are covered with vibrant fabrics in orange and lavender colors that wave in the breeze like Buddhist flags. I watch as a waiter brings a seafood platter to a neighboring table. The dish is full with shrimp, mussels, and a small lobster. "Pescado fresco. Fresh fish, right from these waters. Enjoy."

After we place our order, a woman approaches the table with a bowl of ice water filled with floating flowers. *Is that scented oil I smell?* She instructs me to dip my hands into the bowl; my fingers relax in the coolness. After I remove them, she dries my hands with a soft, white towel. I smell my perfumed fingertips and try to distinguish the scent. It could be orange blossoms. Or is it passion fruit?

"What's in there?" I ask.

"We don't tell. It's a secret."

The smell lingers in the air as a mischievous breeze blows through the restaurant and billows the table fabric like a bridal gown. Folded napkins take flight, as does the staff chasing them to the water's edge. I look up as a V formation of pelicans approach, the last light of day at their backs. Suddenly, the leader breaks ranks and dive bombs into the sea. The rest spread out and alternately descend, crashing into the water, hoping to ambush a wary fish. Some come up with dinner, while others fly back and repeat their maneuvers. This orchestrated production continues until each bird catches its prey. Finally they all rest and float on the surface, most likely enjoying the sensation of a belly full of fish. Soon, I'll be feeling the same way.

I watch a couple a few yards away lock hands and walk into the ocean. They pause and passionately kiss each other under a setting sun. I glance over at Rob where the light casts a soft, golden glow on the side of his face. I realize once again there is so little time to do all the things we wish to do. I can't go back to thinking that this opportunity will always be here for us. I take a deep breath and feel my worries gently slip off me like a silk robe. I was so anxious about moving here I almost missed this wonderful night. It's clear what is right in front of me; it's another adventure.

A Little Bit of Luck

The next day we're busy going from one house to the next. A couple of the places aren't even worth getting out of the car. Some are fixer-uppers offering low rent in exchange for repairs. But these repairs include a new roof, electrical system, and indoor plumbing. We are not up to the task. A few look nice but are in low-lying areas with a lot of mosquitos. It seems we can't find the right place, and start thinking once again that it might not be the right decision to move. However, Rob doesn't give up, and in a last ditch effort, he calls the property manager back and asks if she knows anyone who would be willing to lower their rent for very responsible tenants. It just so happens that she has the perfect place in mind that will be available in six weeks.

Elizabeth and Henry are a retired couple from New Mexico and own a beautiful three-bedroom, four-bathroom house that they only use one month out of the year. Their son and his family come for another four weeks in July. The house is divided by two floors, with the lower level functioning as a two-bedroom, two-bathroom apartment. For ten months out of the year, the renter has the whole house. For the other two months, the renter must stay in the apartment downstairs.

Unfortunately for them, they haven't had the best luck with tenants. The last one owned a Rottweiler that scratched apart their custom wood doors. To make matters worse, his latest girlfriend was a smoker and she left her cigarettes unattended, consequently burning holes in all of their furniture. Their dream vacation home is turning into a nightmare—it's time for a Pisani intervention.

I feel bad for this couple. As a past landlord, I know what it is like when someone takes advantage of you. Rob and I do our best to reassure them that we are good people, professionals who just need a cheap place to live while we try to sort out our building permits. They both like us and Henry offers the house for two hundred dollars a month. Rob then negotiates it down to one hundred and fifty dollars; we will have a more expensive electric bill because the house is so large. In addition, the climate is hotter, and we will be using the air conditioning for at least part of the day. Henry tilts his head, thinks about it for a few moments, and agrees. I once read the definition of luck was when preparation meets opportunity. If that's the case, this is one of our luckiest days. The universe has just aligned in our favor and we have no choice but to seize this opportunity before it passes.

After speaking some more, we learn Henry and Elizabeth were once in the insurance business and are now enjoying their retirement. They are adventurous people and don't want to spend the rest of their years sitting at home. They want to explore the world and do all the things that they couldn't do while raising a family. I like them already.

As they take us on a tour of the house, I notice a man under the sink in their master bathroom.

"That's Jackson, our handyman," Henry says. "We are trying to get this on-demand hot water heater to work. When my son was here, the appliance actually exploded and shot a piece clear into the living room. When he brought the hot water heater back to the hardware store, the guy said he sees this all the time. He then sold him the exact same model. Now we can't seem to regulate the water in the shower, it's either burning hot or completely cold." Between the suicide showers and the SCUD missile hot water heaters, the bathroom may be the most dangerous place in this country. This might explain why there is no army in Costa Rica; they just need to cram all their enemies into a bathroom to achieve certain victory.

"There are so many things that are screwy with the house, I actually made a list," Henry continues.

"Does it get you angry, do you want to complain to the builder?" I ask.

"No. Actually, I don't get angry at all. It's just amazing all the things that go wrong in here. When I read over this list, I just have to laugh. Like this one, the garbage disposal. It actually just goes out to a bucket in the front yard. Do you know how disgusting it is to clean out a month's worth of organic waste? So now we don't even bother using it. And the dishwasher hasn't worked since the day we moved in."

It's this type of attitude one has to have to be happy living in Costa Rica. Things go wrong, and if every bit of it bothers you, it can make you nuts. Instead, Henry just jots down these troublesome predicaments in his diary.

As I'm listening to Henry tell his house stories, I notice a large scorpion running along the baseboard. "Do you get a lot of scorpions here?"

"What do you consider a lot?" Elizabeth asks.

"More than one."

"Why… yes… the answer to that would be yes," she says before taking a broom and sweeping him out the door. I've seen scorpions in Grecia, but this one is huge, and even as he is being swept out of the house, he's going down fighting. His stinger points straight up, his front pincers snapping wildly. He doesn't want to go.

Scorpions are well traveled little critters. Their prehistoric bodies are found on almost every continent. And boy can these guys take a licking and keep on ticking. Just for fun, scientists pulled a Han Solo on a lucky few, freezing them only to watch as they thawed out and miraculously shuffled away with one hell of a brain freeze. Saying these guys are durable is an understatement. They mostly get a bad rap since twenty-five species have venom strong enough to kill you. People assure me that the dangerous kinds don't reside in Costa Rica, but you wouldn't know by the one that just got evicted to the front yard. He looks as dangerous as they come.

The longer we talk with Henry and Elizabeth, the more we like them. It's not that common to run into people as laid back as this. There have been a number of people we've met that can't get past these inconveniences. It bugs them to the point that they want to leave the country and start blogging daily on how terrible Costa Rica is. I would much rather have temperamental appliances than sit in rush hour traffic. It's a matter of what you are looking for in life; this country is not for everyone.

"But I can't complain," Henry adds. "Look out the window." In the far distance, I see a family of monkeys high in the trees. "They come much closer than that. Sometimes we see them in this tree over here." He points to one that stands right next to the house. Since we are on the second floor, we are an arm's reach away from the branches. "I can't believe how close they get, many times only a few feet away. They'll howl at us in the morning, and later, fall asleep in the same spot. How can I possibly complain about living here when I get to witness that?"

He has the same attitude we do. You have to overlook the negative and concentrate on the blessings surrounding us. There are few places in the world where you can live like this, and I'm already excited thinking about the possibility of waking up to the sound of howler monkeys. I'm a little disappointed that they don't have a pool, but it's nice that we won't have that added expense. I'm sure we can find an incredible one to swim in at one of the resorts at the beach. I see a lot of pool hopping in my future.

It's crazy how we landed this deal and met one of the nicest couples. It turns out I am already making friends here. I don't know why I always think I won't. Maybe I just use that as an excuse not to move on to the next big thing. But "next" has been pretty good to me so far and meeting Henry and Elizabeth are living proof of it.

We have another day left at the beach and this one is dedicated to having fun. I recently bought a new phone that can access my email, so before heading out I check my inbox. There are a dozen emails from my dad, each subject heading reads: URGENT.

Japan-
Tsunami Tsunami Tsunami Tsunami
Take Necessary Precautions, Love Daddy

Rob turns on CNN and we watch the catastrophe unfold. We talk to neighbors in the condominium complex and there is a precautionary warning in the area. I call my mother and promise her I'll go to higher ground, but not to worry since another tsunami is unlikely to happen here.

We spend the afternoon a few miles away, high on top of a mountain. We have a beautiful ocean view and luckily the sea doesn't show any signs of danger. I am so grateful to be on this side of the world at this moment. However, I can't help but think what an ominous day it is to make a move to the coast.

Osa Peninsula

When I left the states, I was periodically informed by my friends and family of the many ways I was going to perish in Central America. Sandinistas will rip me from Rob's clutching arms in the middle of the night or a bacteria saturated ice cube will have me longing for a twenty-four hour Rite Aid.

However, despite the naysayers I am enjoying myself and don't plan on moving back any time soon. This has raised a good amount of curiosity with my friends back home; they now want to visit. Somehow, my ability to stay alive has them purchasing two coach tickets and Hawaiian shirts.

Scott and Marie were the first to visit. In fact, I think they would have come even if I did get kidnapped. They have two small children, run their own business, and are overwhelmed with their many responsibilities. On their first trip away from their kids, the only request Marie had was that she wanted to take a nap at some point during the trip.

"I haven't had a nap in five years. I want to know that they still exist," she said.

We took them to the Caribbean where we enjoyed snorkeling all morning and hiking through the national forests. They saw so many monkeys and sloths that they decided to return this year. They're coming at the perfect time since we will be busy packing for our move in a couple weeks. Marie never did get that nap during her first trip, so this time I promise her that we will fit it in.

"Oh, no. Forget about the nap, I want to see a crocodile," she says over the phone. "But one in the wild."

I could totally get behind this if Marie was in graduate school studying the homing instincts of the Central American saltwater variety, or if she had a life-long fascination with the species. But I remind her of the more sensible request she'd made last year: to take a nap.

"Marie, do you value all your extremities?" I ask.

"Of course I do."

"Then why on earth do you want to do that? I came face to face with one in a bat cave and it was the scariest day of my life. I consider that my first strike and I don't think people get two with a crocodile. Can't we go back to the nap idea?"

"Who am I kidding? I'm too excited when I'm down there to take a nap. And I've always wanted to see a crocodile in the wild. I don't want to put us at risk, but if we have the opportunity to see one, it would be great."

Rob and I decide that we should visit the Osa Peninsula, a beautiful stretch of unspoiled land on the southern Pacific side of the country. It could be a lot of fun to go with our friends, and since Scott is a mechanic, it would be great to have him along on such a long ride. I like knowing that if we break down, Scott will most likely be able get us going. I don't want to be stuck in the jungle, in ninety-degree weather, searching for a tow truck. Rob thinks I'm being neurotic and should just "wing it" every so often. He's one of those guys who would hike a snowy mountain with only a protein bar and be surprised when a blizzard suddenly rolls in. *Oh shoot, I should have brought a sweater*, he'd casually say as he attempts to dig a snow cave with his wallet.

15

There are wonderful places to travel in Costa Rica. Ones that will make your jaw drop and wish you never had to leave. The Osa Peninsula is one of those places. It is home to The Corcovado National Park, an area abundant with a variety of wildlife: tapirs, ocelots, monkeys, sloths, and pumas. It is also home to many venomous snakes, poisonous frogs, and crocodiles. This area is so biologically diverse because it's part of the "land bridge", the area that connects North and South America. We are only seven hours away from one of the most spectacular places on earth.

After picking our friends up at the airport, Rob immediately asks Scott's opinion on all the little sounds coming from our car, especially the one that has been bugging us for months.

"What kind of noise is it?" Jeff asks.

"I'm getting a clicking noise from the left front wheel. When I take it to the mechanic, he can't find anything wrong."

"Does it go click-click? Or clickety-click, bang bang, clickety-click?"

"No, just the click-click. It hasn't done it in a week so I'm sure it fixed itself."

I want to interject and ask Rob how a car fixes itself and why are we going on a seven hour drive with a bad wheel. But I don't bother. There's not much we can do about it now and Marie doesn't seem concerned in the least. She is the type of person who stays calm in every situation. She reminds me a lot of Rob. Scott, on the other hand, is more like me. Moments of frustration sometimes take over, but then he quickly cools down. This makes us great traveling companions. I always find it comforting when someone expresses the same amount of hysteria during a challenging situation as I do.

The next morning we head out on our trip. We decide to stay at a hotel outside of Puerto Jiménez. It's on the beach overlooking the Golfo Dulce, a pristine body of water popular with snorkelers and fisherman. From there we plan to drive to Corcovado National Park, but what I am most excited to see are the many wild Scarlet Macaws that inhabit the almond trees along the beach. The hotel we picked has pictures on their website of the macaws perched in these trees. I've never seen one outside of a cage. I imagine it must be quite a sight to see them flying freely overhead.

The highway down the coast takes us past many popular beaches: Jaco, Dominical, and Uvita. I would love to stop and show my friends, but we want to make it to Puerto Jiménez before dark. It also doesn't help that the radio is constantly playing Culture Club and Frankie Goes to Hollywood songs. We must have listened to "I'll Tumble 4 Ya" at least a dozen times during this trip, and not just the original. Somehow, Costa Rica has found every seven minute extended version of popular eighties songs, and even the B-side ones that no one would ever want to hear. It's brutal, and Scott reminds us how much he wanted to bring his satellite radio with him. I discouraged him because I wasn't sure if it would work in Costa Rica. I regret that decision as I listen to another mind-numbing extended version of "Karma Chameleon."

The farther we go down the peninsula, the more rural it becomes. The woods grow thicker and the smell of dense foliage fills the air. It is both mysterious and hypnotizing. I know there are things living deep inside, species of animals that have roamed this planet for thousands of years. They survive here through careful efforts of conservation and people willing to fight to keep this area untarnished. We shut off the radio and roll down all the windows. It feels like we're being transported to a place that's revered. We all go quiet, like we've just entered a cathedral during Easter mass.

We drive through the small town of Puerto Jiménez, and it looks like every other small town in Costa Rica. The only difference is that there is an impressive landing strip where small, twin-engine planes take off and land. A few companies offer transportation by air to many tourist areas in Costa Rica. Since it is a long drive, it makes sense for people on a tight schedule to fly. However, I'm not fond of these planes; the last time we were passengers on one was during a trip to Bocas del Toro, Panama. We flew through a storm, and my fingers were gripped so hard into the seat in front of me, one of my fingernails broke off. Thinking I might be overreacting, I looked at Rob for reassurance, but he already had his head in his hands. Costa Rican potholes don't look so bad after an experience like that.

We find our hotel after driving onto a remote dirt road. We search for a lobby or a manager but we see neither. Rob attempts to find someone as the rest of us drop our luggage and put our feet in the pool. Scott and Marie snuggle next to each other, the stress of work beginning to fade away. I love watching how quickly that happens to people while they are here. I can see their posture start to change and the small wrinkles in their faces smooth out. It's as if they get younger right in front of my eyes.

There are no other sounds here beside the birds overhead and the faint hum of a pool pump. I look around and see eight small buildings with two apartments in each. It is more of a condominium complex than an actual hotel. That might explain why it is so hard to find anyone working here.

Eventually Rob walks over with a woman wearing a big smile and she escorts us to our villa. If you want to have a great trip, with excellent accommodations, let Rob take care of the details. His philosophy is if you are traveling a great distance, try to get the best view at the best price. And he usually does not disappoint. The lady takes us to a beachfront villa with two bedrooms and one adjoining bathroom. It has unobstructed views of the ocean and sits steps away from the beach. The wooden terrace has four leather rocking chairs perfect for watching the sunset and later the moonbeams that bounce off the ocean.

Overhead, I notice a flock of Scarlet Macaws cruising across the treetops. We all run to the beach like kids chasing an ice cream truck. We look up and see four macaws performing overhead. The sky is their canvas as they paint it with bold colors like young, avant-garde artists. Their red and blue feathers are so rich in pigment, I've concluded they must have been splashed with rainbows upon creation.

All four of us pause to watch the birds dart back and forth between two almond trees. We are of little consequence to them. They're confident of their own beauty and this narcissism is well deserved. None of us say a word, only briefly looking at each other, nodding in agreement that we might have stepped into the most heavenly place on earth.

Marie was right; she's never going to take that nap.

Good Luck with the Flush

"Is there any excursion you guys have your heart set on?" Rob asks.

"I really want to see a crocodile," Marie tells us, again.

"I don't have any compulsion to see a crocodile," Scott chimes in. "In fact, I want the excursion where you absolutely, positively don't run into one."

Rob holds up a brochure. "This sounds cool—a kayak tour through the mangroves. That will give us the best chance of not only seeing a crocodile but also a lot of birds. Nadine, what do you think?"

"I'm sorry. But I'm with Scott on this. I don't want to be in a little fiberglass boat and run into a crocodile. I'm pretty sure they can bite through a kayak."

"No they can't. We're not talking about the big ones that are in Africa. They are probably just as scared of us as we are of them."

I hate it when people say that. It doesn't even make any sense. I am sure, through the two hundred million years they've been around, a crocodile has lost any fear of encountering a dopey woman in a kayak. I'll go as far to say that he would ring a dinner bell and break out the condiments.

"I'll book the kayak trip for tomorrow, but the day after I want to go to Corcovado Park. Maybe we can drive our car there," Rob says.

"Have you even looked at the map?" I ask. "We can't drive to the park. It's seriously in the middle of a jungle. That's the whole point, it's really out there."

"I saw a sign while driving; it was a turn off down a dirt road. There's got to be the way to get there by car."

"*Frommer's Travel Guide* didn't say that. It said we either get there by plane, boat, or hike for miles. Nowhere did it mention a car."

"Okay, okay. But I might as well ask around. I'm sure we can find the best way. It's the whole reason people come down this far."

"How about seeing some dolphins?" Scott suggests. "We're safe on a boat and dolphins are not prone to biting us in half." I love the way he thinks. Now this is a wise travel companion.

Rob grabs the cell phone and starts making some calls. No matter what he plans, it'll be exciting and Scott and Marie will have a great time. I'm glad they get this opportunity to go on vacation and remember why they are working so hard. I know how they feel; running a business can be stressful on a relationship. And with two small children, Marie often finds herself doing so much for everyone else, she rarely has a quiet moment to herself.

"Look at this," Scott calls from the bathroom. He points to a sign next to the toilet: *Please Put Toilet Paper In Garbage*

"What about it?" I ask.

"They mean like... when I blow my nose?"

"Uh, no."

"They don't mean... come on... not the... not the *dirty* toilet paper right?"

"Yes Scott, the soiled paper," I answer. This is not unusual for Costa Rica; many of the septic systems can't handle—for lack of a better term—the load.

"Am I supposed to drop all my soiled paper in there?" he points to a basket alongside the toilet.

"Either that, or stick it in your pocket. My choice is the former."

"I've never seen this before. I'm not complaining, it just feels weird." Scott is not the first to have this reaction. I've seen this discussed on the internet; people write lengthy diatribes on the post-traumatic stress inflicted on them when having to place poopy toilet paper into a waste basket. "I'll never come back," one suffering tourist wrote. I would have loved to see her face as she stumbled out of the bathroom. *I can't go on*, she probably muttered before collapsing into the arms of her husband.

Marie and I leave Scott in the bathroom and relax in the rocking chairs on the porch. We watch the pelicans catch fish and more Scarlet Macaws dash over our heads. It's our personal *National Geographic* documentary happening right in front of us. I could sit here all day.

"Son of a...," Scott screams from inside. Marie continues rocking in her chair, not breaking her rhythm to find out what's wrong.

"Maybe one of us should go inside and see what's going on?" I ask.

"Don't bother. I'm guessing it has something to do with the toilet paper. You have to see this remote cabin in upstate Pennsylvania Scott takes us to in the middle of winter. Believe me, compared to that place, tossing toilet paper in a basket is a walk in the park." Scott stomps outside flailing his arms around.

"I just want you all to know, you're not going to remember to throw the paper in the basket."

"What are you talking about?" Marie asks.

"It's just a habit. There is no way you will remember. I knew I was supposed to, then not even thinking about it, I dropped the dirty paper into the bowl."

"So?" I giggle.

"I had to fish it out. And another thing you ladies might want to know. The toilet really doesn't flush. You need to hold the handle down, and even while doing that it backs up." Scott pauses, as if he has made a major breakthrough in regards to Central American plumbing. "And now that we are discussing this, I can honestly say, I've never had a good flush in Costa Rica. It always takes more than one flush to get anything down. It's like Costa Rica is a two flush country. Same in your house Nadine, that toilet sucks too…. no offense."

"None taken," I reply.

Scott is right. I'm not sure if it is always the septic system that is creating the problem. I'm starting to believe there might be a faulty toilet bowl conspiracy in Costa Rica. There is a serious lapse in quality control of plumbing here. I have a friend who was building a house and opened up a faucet he bought from the hardware store. It was a famous name brand, top-of-the-line, and he assumed it would be designed similar to the ones in the states. While inspecting the parts, he found they were made of a low grade, flimsy plastic. This might explain why during check-in for your flight at the airport you may see a woman with a kitchen sink under her arm. And don't be surprised when her husband saddles up behind her dragging a toilet on a luggage cart.

Rob returns from the beach with a big smile on his face. "We are booked for a mangrove kayak tour tomorrow. The guide will take us through remote areas where we're going to see a lot of birds and monkeys."

"What about crocodiles?" Marie asks.

"The guy on the phone said you may see them sunning on the muddy banks of the estuary. He even said you can see their heads dive under the water as you are paddling toward them."

"I'm so excited. Honey, wouldn't it be wonderful to tell the girls we saw an actual crocodile in the wild?"

Scott and I both look at each other. Neither of us want to see one, and Rob, well Rob is being Rob. Always open to any adventure, surely thinking that if we did see one, it would pose for a picture before swimming away. I'm not sure why he is so crazy about our security all the time and less concerned about wild animals snacking on us. Brooklyn taught Rob to question strangers but did nothing to shy him away from wildlife.

"We've got the whole day ahead of us. Let's go for a drive into town, pick up some food, and see what other ideas we come up with for the week," Rob says. "But give me a second, I have to use the bathroom."

"Good luck with the flush," Scott remarks.

Two Strikes

We pull our kayaks across the grass and onto the shoreline. Jim, our guide, has been doing this tour for eight years, making a living taking excited tourists like us into the deep mangroves of the Osa Peninsula. He is originally from Seattle and moved here years ago, combining his love of kayaking with his fascination of the jungle. He is the perfect example of someone designing a life to fit around his hobby.

I remember in high school they gave career tests that were supposed to expose your true talents. When the results were tallied, most girls in my class were chosen for nursing, while most boys were picked for police or firefighting. Even the guys who were caught smoking pot were marked for a rewarding profession in law enforcement. It was obvious these tests were useless and didn't accurately predict anything. If these tests had any scientific value, they would have pegged me for what I did best, hiding in the second stall of the girl's bathroom reading *Seventeen Magazine*.

We all jump into our kayaks and follow Jim. I can see why he settled here; the water is clear and the surface so calm I can already see dozens of shapes swimming in the water adjacent to my kayak. This explains all the men we saw in town up so early this morning. They were getting ready to go fishing.

We glide out of the cove and into the gulf. I've already concluded that this area is unique. Looking back at the shoreline is nothing short of spectacular; an undisturbed ecosystem filled with the most incredible birds and animals. We continue paddling parallel to the coast and watch a flock of white herons standing in shallow water. As we approach, they fly off together; their bellies so close to my head I can reach up and touch their tail feathers.

It becomes increasingly quiet as we paddle into the mouth of the estuary. The water materializes into a mirror, reflecting a misshapen copy of the dense canopy overhead. It's darker, and the birds that flew away are now staring down at us. We have ventured into their sanctuary, and I get the feeling that they are standing guard.

At first glance, this waterway looks as empty as a graveyard; however, it's abundantly full of raw and unspoiled life. I can see how people get overconfident here, leading to a bad decision that could put their lives at risk. It's too easy to think no one is watching you in a place where everything is watching you—both above and below. The birds' eyes never look away as we continue into the murky darkness.

We maneuver through tangled branches, pushing through small openings to get to more isolated stretches of mangroves. I briefly acknowledge that we are alone here with Jim, and that I don't know much about him. It's always unnerving to be in a place where you can disappear and there is no chance of anyone finding you. I left Jim's brochure on the nightstand as evidence in case we don't return, a brochure which will have no value once the housekeeper tosses it into the garbage. At least I feel confident it won't be flushed down the toilet. I whisper my fears to Rob as we lag behind.

"I already thought of that," Rob confides. "Think about it, there are four of us against one of him, so I doubt anything will happen. But trust me, it's not far from my mind. Plus, I brought the mace."

Rob recently upgraded his arsenal to include a huge canister of bear mace. "Check this out," he had said while pointing to a video on the internet. The clip was of a man who used mace to chase away a bear. "I'm buying this the next time we are in San Jose. It's the strongest concentration of mace there is and it shoots thirty-five feet. It's going to be great." I agreed with Rob, because it *is* going to be great when he blasts the extra-strength spray into his face at a speed of six hundred miles per hour, almost as great as racing him to an ophthalmologist to save his eyeballs from idiot blindness.

"Do you think we'll see a crocodile?" Marie asks Jim.

"We could. I've seen them before. Check the water for their eyes. Sometimes they watch you for a while before disappearing into the water."

Marie seems excited by this news. Isn't she aware that there is a good possibility the guide is planning to cut our heads off? Or that he might just be innocently reaching for a sandwich when Rob smacks him with a pair of binoculars? Either way, I suspect we are close to some type of violent episode.

"You know, if you jump in I'm sure you'll see a crocodile," I tease.

"You know my dad did that to me once. We were in the Bahamas and saw some fluorescent plankton in the water. We were out there in the dark, and to get them to glow, he threw me overboard. He thought it was funny."

Oh boy, maybe I shouldn't be joking about tossing Marie into the water. I can sympathize with her childhood experience. My father used to play a game called "burglar" when we were kids. He would shut off all the lights in the house and run after us yelling, "I'm going to get you!" Clearly, my dad was not the board game kind of parent; he was more concerned with infusing stranger-danger into our heads at an early age. You have to remember, this is the same guy that considered "family night" an evening gathered together listening to *The Very Best of Winston Churchill* recordings. You can't get those life lessons from playing Candy Land.

We paddle until we see a log blocking our passage. There is no way to continue down the estuary. "The tide is going out so we probably have to wait ten minutes. Then we will have room to squeeze underneath," Jim says. "If you guys are planning on hiking during your trip, make sure you know the tide chart. It's surprising how fast high tide can roll in."

Jim and I get out and sit on the log while the others stay in their kayaks. I look into the forest and hear twigs snapping. The sound starts becoming louder and seems to be getting closer. Jim notices the strained look on my face.

"That's just the white-faced monkeys. In a minute they are going to be all over the trees." I turn toward the forest and watch an army of monkeys racing in our direction. Like a street gang, they surround us, some climb above while others stay close to the ground.

"Are they going to attack?" Rob asks.

The monkeys' lips peel back displaying their sharp teeth. It appears that we have seriously pissed off a bunch of primates. Jim did not mention this in his glossy brochure.

"They're not going to hurt you. They just come out to see what's going on and usually stay far enough away just in case they need to escape. They keep their distance from the bank of the water to avoid lurking crocodiles."

I consider this last piece of information as my right leg dangles over the water. I realize that this is the perfect situation where I should take advice from a monkey. I quickly jump back into my kayak which feels uneasy since I'm now only closer to the water. Scott and Marie don't seem concerned. They're too busy snapping pictures of the monkey posse.

As the water recedes, we push ourselves under the log and continue through the mangroves. The monkeys follow us, hopping up and down in an effort to scare us off. They crash their heads together and roll over each other. It looks like they are wrestling, but are actually trying to give the impression they are fierce warriors. Others run ahead and stand on branches outstretched across the water. One puts his head on top of another monkey like a totem pole.

"When they do that, they are trying to intimidate you. They want to look bigger. Two heads are better than one," Jim explains.

We continue paddling through shadows that cast down across the water like witch's fingers; some so gnarly they look as if they might snatch my kayak and pull me under. The mangroves have a macabre influence on my mood and I cautiously move through the water on alert.

I take the lead while the rest of the crew lags behind to take pictures. I watch as the tiny orange and purple crabs scatter across the roots of the trees, disappearing into deep recesses. Mangroves are exceptional in their design, trees that have somehow adapted to the varying salinity. Only a few species are tough enough to make it, and that fortitude provides an important defense against hurricanes, tsunamis, and erosion. This sophisticated engineering has taken thousands of years to perfect and this passage of time is not dim or eluding in these mangroves. Years are palpable here, brushing over my skin like a fine mist.

I look behind and can't see the group. I've become lost in my thoughts, so I pause, waiting for them to catch up. It's now that I notice a large log in front of me, but this one is not moving with the small ripples of current. I freeze, but the momentum of my kayak pushes me closer to the object. It's becoming clearer that the log is actually a head, with two eyeballs sticking out of the water. It then dawns on me—there are no more monkeys. I am heading straight toward a crocodile.

This is my second encounter with a crocodile, and what races through my mind is dramatically similar to the five stages of grief. At first I'm in denial, *No*, I tell myself. *Impossible, it's just an illusion.* That quickly turns to anger, *Son of a bitch, this should be Marie.* I begin the bargaining process, *Seriously dude, there are some juicy monkeys I can call over.* Only to end in depression, *Let's get it over with. I can't believe my last meal before I croaked was a bag of Skittles—taste the rainbow you bastard.* And as for the fifth stage, acceptance, I never quite make it there because I'm splashing my paddles like an epileptic orangutan, attempting to go in reverse, but since I'm moving each oar in opposite directions, I go nowhere. Remarkably, my hidden ambidextrous skill only emerges when paired with a clenched sphincter.

Once I stop splashing, I see the crocodile has disappeared. In less than one minute, Rob is at my side.

"What the hell did you see?"

"It was a crocodile for sure."

"It was probably a log," he says while aiming the bear mace at the water.

"No, not this time. I saw his eyes…his *eyes* Rob. I was that close." I pause to catch my breath. The crocodiles were probably here all along, watching us during this entire journey.

"Are you okay?"

"Yeah, I'm fine. You know, I bet he was following me since I separated from the group. I distracted him from all those monkeys. If they kept following us, the crocodile would have had a chance to eat one of them. In fact, I just saved a monkey. I'm a monkey saver."

The rest of the group catches up and I share my experience. "It absolutely could have been one," Jim adds. "I've passed some that just stare at you, never sinking into the water. They just watch as you paddle past. Those are the ones that I worry about." Once again, Jim leaves out this fascinating information from his brochure.

Marie is, of course, upset she did not have this near-death experience. She still wants to see a crocodile, and I still want her to drop it.

"Please stop saying it, Marie. You're putting this wish so far out into the universe, and it seems the message somehow got crossed. This is officially strike two for me."

"Listen, I just have to see one. I told my kids I was going to take a picture of it."

There is no talking her out of it. However, we are near the end of our excursion so we paddle out of the mangroves to a nearby beach. Jim slices up a pineapple and hands us a few pieces. It's the kind I like, super sweet and juicy. It's about as refreshing as an icy glass of water. We all rinse off by jumping into the gulf with our clothes on. The cool water feels wonderful against our sunburned shoulders.

"This was a great day guys," Scott says while floating on his back.

We return to our kayaks and head back. I love trips like this. I foresee the next one being even more exciting. And although I paddled straight toward a crocodile, I also got to see monkeys that stacked themselves like totem poles in the jungle. Maybe it's okay that Jim conveniently left these things off his website. The best moments are usually the ones that are unplanned and spontaneous. However, I'm looking forward to something a little less reckless tomorrow. I can't wait to see what Rob has in store.

Two-For-One Excursion

Even though each day is full of adventure, Scott is anxious for more. He even starts obsessively talking about moving here despite the toilet issues. "I can probably open a garage," he says. It's inevitable that this was going to happen. It's hard to imagine leaving this place and going back to life back home in the states. We were the same way when we first visited. For some people, this type of exposure to nature is life-changing and instead of feeling satisfied with your ten day vacation, you become insatiable for more.

Rob calls us out to the front porch to brief us on today's activity. "We are taking a boat around the peninsula to Corcovado National Park. It's going to take a couple hours, so we will fish as we go. It's like a two-for-one excursion, fishing and exploring the park in one package."

"I thought we were driving to the park?" I ask.

"That's not possible. You can only go so far and then you have to hike to get to the camp. Or we can fly in. But I figured we just want to hike for a few hours and come back anyway, so this plan seems perfect."

"So the boat will bring us to the park?"

"Yes, the captain says he'll drop us off right in front."

"Is there a pier or some type of harbor to dock the boat?"

"I didn't ask. He does this for a living, I'm not going to stress over all the tiny details. Anyway, be happy. I saved us a lot of money."

It's hard to believe it's going to be that easy. This is not the San Diego Zoo. It is a nationally protected park in the middle of the wilderness. I've never read anything in my books about getting "dropped off" by a boat. When I press Rob on the issue, he tells me to stop being anxious. However, that's impossible because being anxious about Rob's plans has become a full time job lately. I should be getting paid sick days and given a company car for all the time I've clocked on this job.

"How bad can it be? We hike the park for a couple hours and come back. Pretty simple if you ask me," Rob adds.

"I like the plan," Marie chimes in. "I don't want to camp overnight in the park. I just want to go and see what all the hype is about." Scott nods in agreement and we start gathering our things together.

We drive to the marina and meet our captain, an older man with a face that has weathered years of sunshine. His mate is a young guy with large, muscular arms.

"We will stay close to the coast so you will see how beautiful Costa Rica is," the captain says. "Then, when I see a school of fish, we will cast our lines."

We continue cruising parallel to the shore and get a good view of the area. We travel around the tip of the peninsula, Cabo Matapalo, and watch the brave surfers fight the current. It's not a place for the inexperienced; the swells can be inconsistent and dangerous. However, this group looks competent as they battle the ocean.

Amazingly, we see three young men on the beach goofing around in the strong current. They don't have surfboards, so I can only imagine this is some kind of macho game they are each playing. As each gets dragged out, one of the kids tosses out a red rope to his friend and drags him in. It's a dangerous game and makes me nervous just watching them.

We continue around the bend and are greeted with sparkling views of the Pacific. "It is often calm like this," the captain says, "perfect for fishing." A few minutes later, we spot a large circle of water churning like a giant whirlpool. "Cut the engine!"

As we get closer, we see fins splashing out of the water. Could that be hundreds of fish right in front of us? Is it even possible to have such a large school so close to shore? We toss our lines in and immediately get bites.

"Slowly, reel it in," the captain advises.

I pull mine in; a ten pound black and yellow rooster fish with seven large spines on its dorsal fin. It's the most beautiful fish I've ever seen.

"I got one too!" screams Marie.

"So do I," Scott adds.

"Can we eat these?" I ask.

"No. We will throw them back, but there are more fish out there. I've been fishing these waters for forty years and I always come home with dinner."

We bring our lines in and continue north toward the park. The coast is full of palm trees and forests, but not a soul on any of the beaches. We pass rocky, hollow caves that direct geysers of water exploding up into the air with each rolling tide. It's a rhythmic, thunderous sound that vibrates my breastbone with each passing wave. I wonder if anyone ever gets close enough to explore inside, but the captain says it's too jagged and dangerous. I'm hypnotized by the sight, and continue staring long after we pass.

"Jacks! There are jacks!" the captain yells. Rob grabs his pole and tosses a line; he immediately gets a hit.

"Holy cow, this guy is strong," Rob laughs. The veins in his arms bulge above his skin, his face wrinkling with each pull on the pole. After ten minutes, he hands it off and we each take turns reeling in the fish. It feels gigantic; it must be seventy-five... no one hundred pounds. The front of the boat shifts toward the sun; its rays bounce reflections of light across the surface of the water like skipping stones. *Am I really here?* I think. But the sharp ache in my back snaps me out of my daydream. My shoulders strain with each tug of the pole and I'm almost out of strength.

"Lean in, then lean back," the captain yells.

I struggle with my opponent until I'm exhausted. Scott takes the line and ultimately works the fish to the surface. His body ripples underwater like a silver piece of scrap metal. He's a large jack, approximately forty pounds.

"Reel it in Scott," Marie yells as he arches his back with each pull on the rod. My excitement overwhelms me and I scream, "It's huge! It's huge!" over and over again.

Scott finally brings the fish close enough where the mate reaches down and hauls him into the boat. He doesn't even use a net.

"Now take your pictures," the captain says. "You can't eat this one, but there are plenty here and we will get another."

"Let's cook one over a bonfire," Marie suggests. "We'll pick up some potatoes in town, some aluminum foil, and have dinner right on the beach tonight."

The captain throws the jack back into the water. We quickly catch another.

"This is a Blue Jack," the captain explains as we bring the fish onto the boat. "This one good for eating."

It's remarkable all the things I never knew existed. My first encounter with a farmers market in Costa Rica introduced me to so many new and exciting foods. I couldn't believe how many I had never seen before, and how succulent and delicious the fruit was. Now I'm having the same experience again, but this time out in the ocean.

The captain tosses the Blue Jack into his cooler. We bring in our poles and decide to continue our way to the park, the high from fishing giving us all a second wind. It's not long until the captain cuts the engine once again.

"Jump," he says.

"Come again?" I gasp.

"The entrance to the park is about five hundred meters north. This is as close as I can get the boat to shore. The water is only thigh high, so you can all wade through. But you," he says pointing to me, "you're short, so maybe you swim."

I turn toward Rob who has the same puzzled look on his face as I do. "Is this one of your tiny details you weren't going to stress about?" I ask.

"I'll come back for you in three hours," the captain adds.

Having no other choice, we all jump into the Pacific Ocean.

Corcovado National Park

"I hope he comes back for us," Scott says while pouring water out of his sneakers. The only thing before us is the vast ocean; the only thing behind is the dense jungle. We are officially stranded.

"He didn't get his money yet," Rob replies. "He's definitely coming back."

"I guess there was no pier," I add. "I don't think many people get to the park this way. I'm pretty sure most don't jump into the churning ocean and struggle to shore."

"Which way is the entrance to the park?" Marie asks.

I look around and all I see is forest. "The captain told us to head north. Uh… which way is that?"

"Why don't we start hiking here?" Rob suggests. He points straight into the jungle.

"Rob, that's about the stupidest idea you've ever had. And that's saying a lot. This is a jungle. A *jungle*, Rob. You know: jaguars, tapirs, *big-things-that-can-eat-us* kind of jungle. And how are we going to know how to get out?" I always wondered what kind of person would absent-mindedly walk into a jungle. I just learned I'm married to one.

"There are probably marked trails."

"Yeah… in the *park*. People fly into this place with a guide. They don't take a boat here." I begin to realize just how ridiculous this trip

37

is. To save some money and combine two tours into one, Rob managed to get us dropped off in the most unpopulated part of the country. I immediately start barking orders. "Let's do what the captain said. We need to get to that ranger station. Start rationing your water in case we can't refill our bottles there."

We trek along the beach, our boat already far in the distance. The shore is one solid slab of volcanic rock, with parts of it jutting out of the water like stepping stones. It's as if we are walking on the surface of the moon. And considering we've completely abandoned any civilization, we might as well be in space.

It's still morning but it is already getting uncomfortably hot. Even if we ration our water, it will only last a couple of hours. This environment has stripped the excitement I had from fishing and replaced it with a fierce determination to find that ranger station. The only good thing about this trek is that the sun is already drying our clothes.

After fifteen minutes, we come to a clearing and spy a flattened section of land. It looks like something in the Serengeti: a barren air strip in the middle of nowhere. The dead grass stands straight up, not a puff of wind to bend one blade. It's the perfect hiding place for snakes.

"Let's all stay in the middle away from any tall grass," Rob suggests.

"You think there are snakes in there?" Scott asks.

"Absolutely."

"What kind of snakes?"

"The kind you don't want to run into."

I take my cell phone out of my pocket and look for a signal. Nothing. I then reach my arm straight up and spin around, fully aware of how stupid it looks. I always wondered what kind of absent-minded person would look for cell reception in the jungle. I just learned Rob is married to one.

We finally make it to the ranger station; a wooden building surrounded by pitched tents where groups of people watch our approach. I'm sure it must be an odd sight to see us walking up the landing strip, appearing out of nowhere.

It doesn't help that I'm wearing a large brimmed white hat with a long sleeved shirt tied backward around my neck. I look more like someone invited to a clam bake on Martha's Vineyard than someone who is planning to hike the wilderness.

"Hi," Marie says to a guy leaning over the deck railing. No response. Scott and I walk over to a map on the wall and decide which trail to take. I immediately search for the shortest route, one that will only take a couple of hours.

"Do you know where I can buy batteries?" I hear Rob ask a lady slumped over a chair. Apparently, Rob thinks a battery emporium is lurking around the corner. I'm surprised he doesn't ask for a Pepsi and slice of pizza while he's at it.

"You're kidding right?" the woman replies.

"My batteries just died and I wanted to take some pictures."

"Do me a favor," the woman says as she tries to straighten up. "I drank river water while on an eight hour hike and have had the runs ever since. So if you find those batteries, can you also pick me up some Imodium, asshole."

For all her dehydration and stomach cramping, this lady found the strength to emphasize the syllable "ass" in asshole with such conviction and clarity, for a moment, I wondered if Rob really was an asshole. She even broadcasts the second—but no less diminutive— syllable "hole" so loudly, the rest of the exhausted hikers stare in our direction to witness the impending smack down that is sure to follow. Apparently, Diarrhea Lady has shit herself crazy.

I quickly look back to the map on the wall and move my finger over a trail that will loop back around to the ranger station. It is the shortest one—and by the looks of things—the smartest one to take. I also notice it takes us across a few rivers. I don't remember when high tide rolls in, but Jim said that it was an important piece of information you needed to know before setting out. I want to ask Diarrhea Lady for advice, but I'm convinced she'll machete my limbs off. I'm sure a mass murder of the blockheads who just wandered into town would cheer her up considerably. If nothing else, it would help pass the time while more parasites organize a block party in her colon.

Since Scott and I are the only ones that looked at the map, we start out first. Marie and Rob follow. The trail is not easy to navigate and I wish we would have hired a guide. The occasional red flag calms my fears that we will not get lost, but there are numerous forks in the path that aren't labeled at all. I think back to the map and just keep telling everyone to veer left. I'm hoping that will loop us back to the ranger station.

Last night, while everyone was sleeping, I unpacked a few books about the fascinating wildlife found in the park. I browsed through the section on birds and frogs, but stopped at the part where they mentioned snakes. This park is home to some of the most deadly snakes in Costa Rica: bushmasters, coral snakes, and the feared fer-de-lance. As for the latter, don't let his cute little French name fool you. The fer-de-lance is considered the "ultimate pit viper." A bite from him will guarantee you the ultimate bad day, one filled with an abundance of hematuria, vomiting, spleen tenderness, and hypertension. (Isn't high blood pressure anticipated after twelve hours of bloody urine? I get hypertension from much lesser things, like when reading about snake bites.) Death is a clearly a welcomed event; greeted with confetti and offered a cool soda before shutting your lights out for good. It's all rather daunting.

But not to worry! the author of this article assured me. *They won't attack unless provoked.* This advice felt cozy and logical while I was in an air-conditioned hotel room eating a Twizzler. But out here, I had to question: What does a snake consider a provoked attack? I mean, I'm not going to pick one up and strum it like a ukulele, but what if I step on it accidentally? I'm fairly certain the snake considers that a good enough reason to eject three heaping squirts of neurological poison into my calf.

It was getting late, so I skipped over the rest of the snake chapter and came to one regarding pumas. Now this is a fascinating animal. Their average weight is one hundred and ten pounds and they stalk their prey from either the ground or up in the trees. When it's mating season, they'll copulate up to nine times every hour to ensure conception. I'm tired even thinking about it. The author then goes on to say that if we are *lucky*, we might get the opportunity to be "tumbled" by one. Seriously? What the hell does that mean? He makes it sound as harmless as a girly pillow fight. I don't want to be "tumbled" by my husband, and certainly not by a toothy, wild feline. And since he just discussed their rigorous mating ritual, I make mental notes to avoid all tumbling of any sort during this trip. It was at this point I finished the last of my Twizzlers and decided to call it a night. The only thing scarier about hiking into a jungle is reading about it beforehand.

"Hey guys, look at this," I yell after spotting a large, fallen tree blocking our path. Scott volunteers to jump over first, consequently landing on a crispy snakeskin. "Wow, I'm glad that wasn't an actual snake." That definitely would have been considered a provoked attack, I'm sure of it.

As we get to the other side, Scott points to another snakeskin only a few feet away, and then another one ten feet from that. It's as if we missed a big snakeskin convention. I let out a big sigh. This adventure is becoming more perilous and I begin to feel horribly responsible for bringing our friends out so far into the wilderness. If these are the snakeskins, where are the snakes? I'm already anticipating a bout of bloody urine coming on.

The trail continues to wind around, taking us through empty streams and imposing banks. It's not long before we come to a wide, dry riverbed.

"Does anyone know when high tide comes through?" I ask.

"I have no idea. We should just go for it. What other options do we have?" Rob says.

We all follow him, but I have a queasy feeling in my gut. I hear the rush of water echoing further downstream. It just doesn't feel right.

"I don't remember seeing this on the map. I think we went the wrong way," I tell Marie.

We all cross and continue on the trail. Within five minutes we hear the sounds of water roll through. It is officially high tide and the surf is pouring in. We climb to a high point along the bank and watch this powerful force bring in logs and other debris from the sea and down the waterway.

"That's a lot of water, and it's coming in a lot quicker than I ever expected it would," Scott remarks as we stand there watching. Now I understand why Jim warned us about knowing the tide charts. And I now understand that I want to get the hell out of this park as soon as possible.

"Rob, are you sure we are going in the right direction? What if we have to turn around and go back through that river?" Marie asks.

"Worse comes to worse... we'll have to swim across it." Rob moves closer to the water but pauses and quickly backs up. "Holy shit!"

We all climb next to Rob and observe, what we think are, a bunch of logs float past. "Look Marie, that's not a log," he says while pointing to the river. It's a ten foot crocodile using the force of the water to leisurely carry him into the park. Not only did we miss getting hit with logs and debris, we were almost face to face—or more accurately, face to snout—with a crocodile.

"Wow!" Marie exclaims.

"See honey, you got your crocodile," Scott says.

We all stand there in silence and let the moment wash over us. Once the excitement passes, I acknowledge that we really don't belong here and perhaps Imodium Lady looks that way for a reason.

This is harsh terrain, and at the very least, we should have a guide with us. I look at my watch. A few hours have passed. We only have a little bit of drinking water left and I am eager to find the ranger station and get back to our boat.

I can hear the ocean, which means we can't be too far away. After hiking another half hour, the path spits us out into the sunshine. We are momentarily blinded before realizing we are right in front of the ranger station. The same people are sitting there, staring at us like we just walked off a Carnival Cruise ship.

"Let's get the hell out of here," Rob says. Somehow I successfully guided us through the park. I'm just hoping the captain remembers to pick us up.

We walk back down the air strip and toward the ocean. Once on the beach, we see a small vessel in the distance. Scott screams like he's been a castaway for twenty years. Rob jumps up and down trying to get the captain's attention, fearing Diarrhea Lady and her zombie army is not far behind. I wave my hat eagerly, happy we survived Rob's two-for-one adventure. Even though he left out plenty of little details: jumping into the ocean, hiking up a desolate beach, and searching for a ranger station down an air strip, I have to admit…it really did work out.

The boat navigates around the many rocks and slowly moves closer to shore. We swim out to it and the captain hoists us in. Everyone is exhausted, and as I take a seat in the sun, I notice Marie has a big smile across her face. She saw her crocodile; one not in a zoo but handsomely floating down a river in the wild. It feels good knowing that I took part in giving Marie such a memorable experience. I pat myself on the back feeling confident that the rest of the trip will be equally as memorable.

How to Electrocute Friends & Influence People

"What's that noise?" I ask after hearing a clanking sound coming from our front wheel. We are driving back from the Osa Peninsula in the most remote stretch of the drive. In my mechanically inexperienced mind, it sounds as if the wheel is going to fall off.

"The wheel is going to fall off," Scott says.

"What!" Rob yells.

"It's a ball bearing, and I guarantee the wheel is going to fly off this car."

"But we're in the middle of nowhere," I say as I press my hands against the rear window. I feel a wave of panic. This would be the worst place to breakdown. I scan the car for water bottles, already planning to ration a bottle cap for each of us until we are rescued. As I scramble for supplies, Marie is casually reading her magazine.

"Marie, get with it. Look for water. Didn't you hear what Scott said? The wheel is going to fly off the car."

"I heard him," she says, turning another page.

"We're in the middle of the jungle, Marie! Why aren't you as freaked out as I am?"

"Because Scott always says the wheel is going to fly off the car. So until the wheel is airborne, I'm not going to worry." Marie holds up the magazine and points to a picture of a pool. "Check out the lounge chairs. Aren't they fabulous?"

"Lounge chairs? It's the last thing on my mind right now." I hold my cell phone out the window and try to get a couple reception bars. Nothing. I feel nauseous and hug my water bottle

"You can't drive the car like this," Scott insists. "I'm serious, Rob. We're going to have to walk."

"No way, man. I'm not stopping."

"I'm the mechanic and I'm telling you, you're crazy to drive the car like this."

"Have you noticed where we are? Look around, it's one hundred degrees outside and the nearest gas station is hours away. We're in the middle of nowhere."

Scott tosses his arms in the air and waves them around. Frankly, he looks a lot like I do when I'm upset. "If you keep driving this car we are more screwed than you think. Man, don't you get it? Our ass is to the wind."

"Did you hear him Rob? *Our asses are in the wind!*" I scream.

"Not *in* the wind, *to* the wind," Rob corrects.

"How about this, I'd rather not have any part of me in the wind." I reach in my backpack for the Twizzlers and realize I ate the entire bag the other night. My late night munchies have caused my own demise.

Rob slams his hand on the steering wheel. "I'm not stopping! If we have to drive ten miles an hour, then that's what we are going to do. When I was a teenager, I had a car that didn't have a floor. I used sheets of cardboard to cover the gaping holes. I even drove a car with jammed windows and bullet holes across the doors. Get where I'm coming from? I bet I could probably drive another three thousand miles on this squeaky wheel."

"That's the difference between us," Scott announces. "You're a city mouse and I'm a country mouse. But look around, this isn't a city, this is country mouse territory."

"Well, how about this country mouse. I'm going to throw it in four wheel drive to see if the noise goes away."

"That's the worst thing you can do! I'm telling you this as a mechanic. I do this for a living. It's a ball bearing and you can't keep driving like this."

"I'm still not stopping."

At this speed, we're never getting back home in one day. I grab the map and plan where we will be staying overnight. Once we get on the coastal highway, there will be plenty of great beach towns to stop at. It wasn't what I had planned, but it will give Rob and Scott a chance to find a mechanic.

I often recommend that people rent a car and drive throughout Costa Rica. Although some roads can be a nightmare, the beautiful countryside makes up for it. It's not at all like the congested highways back in the states. And now that we are driving only ten miles per hour, I'm getting to see more than ever before. I'm watching blue-uniformed children walk to school and mothers sweeping their tiled porches. I notice that even though many of these houses are modest, there are thoughtfully manicured gardens out in front. Blooming flowers and lovely palm trees line walkways and small plants are positioned in old milk cartons to root.

We stop in Uvita, a golden beach where a sandbar stretches out into the shape of a whale's tail. It is part of the Costa Ballena National Park, a place named for the Humpback Whales that migrate here every year. We dip our feet into the ocean; however, we don't see any whales in the horizon. A vendor comes by selling pipas frio—cold coconuts. They are a dollar each and we buy four. The man grabs a machete from his belt and hacks off the tops. He's talks rapidly in Spanish, giving us a big smile as he sticks a straw in each coconut. He watches us as we take our first sip; it's refreshing, and once we are done, we scrape off the coconut custard along the sides with our straws. He must watch tourists like us every day take a sip of their first pipa frio; something that is so common to his life, but to us, an experience that makes you want to go home and tell all your friends you drank out of a coconut. It's amazing how full I feel, and for a total of four dollars, this is our lunch for the day.

Often we are too busy traveling from point A to point B to notice what's in-between. If we were going fifty miles per hour, we would never have stopped in Uvita and met this coconut vendor. I would never have noticed the small churches, the roadside hawks, or the soccer games being played in tiny, grassless fields as we drove up the coast. The longer we continue at this speed, the more we talk about the Costa Rican culture and how incredible it is to be in a place so different. This ride is turning into the best part of the trip. Even after seeing Scarlet Macaws and kayaking isolated mangroves, this simple road trip brings me such joy, I'm almost happy our wheel is squeaking.

Playa Dominical is next on our list and we decide to stay overnight. It's a popular surfing town with a beautiful beach. I thumb through my guide and find a listing for an average priced motel right near the water. We get a room and Marie and I collapse on the beds.

"Scott and I are going to see if we can find a garage that is still open. It's Sunday, so it's unlikely. But it's worth a shot. Please, don't wander around alone, just wait for us to get back," Rob says.

I'm too exhausted to consider anything but taking a shower. Marie has the same idea and she goes in first.

"There is no hot water," she yells from the shower.

"Are you sure? Wait for it to run awhile." I didn't get a chance to look inside the shower stall, and consider if I should warn her that it might be a suicide shower, a device that doubles as a showerhead and heats the water. The only problem is this device is then hardwired into an electrical socket a foot away from your head. It's an invention that defies logic; electrical wires running straight into your wet shower. But just as I'm about to ask, the lights flicker. Marie screams then stumbles out of the stall, pulling the shower curtain with her.

"I got electrocuted!"

"Are you sure?" I foolishly ask, as if getting electrocuted can be confused with bad water pressure or mistakenly choosing hair conditioner over shampoo.

"All I did was reach up to adjust the shower nozzle and… and… there was a spark. Oh my Lord. I got electrocuted in the shower."

I'm feeling slightly guilty at this point. Suicide showers were something I meant to talk about, but it had slipped my mind during this trip. I really like Marie, and want to stay friends with her. I'm pretty sure friends don't let friends get electrocuted, so I decide to act just as surprised at the unfolding events.

"I was wearing my flip-flops… and I… I think they saved my life." Marie sits on the bed, the shower curtain still wrapped around her body. Suddenly, Rob and Scott walk through the door.

"There are no garages open," Scott says. "Might as well just hang out and have a good time tonight. Honey, what happened?"

"She got electrocuted," I say, waving my hands around in a dramatic effort to appear flabbergasted. "Her ass was to the wind. To the wind Scott!"

Scott puts his hand on Marie's shoulder. "Are you okay?"

"Yes, I think so. It was just a scary experience…a very scary experience. But I'm fine, except for my fingers. They seem to be numb."

I grab Rob by the arm and pull him over to the other side of the room. "You once told me that suicide showers never hurt anyone," I whisper.

"I might have steered you down the wrong path with that information. But all things considered, she looks pretty good." Marie continues to sit on the bed staring cross-eyed at the wall. "Look on the bright side. I've heard that electroshock therapy is helpful for treating depression."

"Marie doesn't have depression. Or at least she didn't five minutes ago. You *know* I have a hard time making friends. Surely electrocuting them isn't the way to go about keeping one."

48

The next morning, we wake up early and head out to find a hotel at Playa Bejuco. After enjoying the touristy town of Domincal, we want to stay where there are less people. A waitress in Grecia once told me about this quiet area. It's the perfect spot to watch surfers while having most of the beach to yourself.

We get there by nine and have breakfast at a hotel on the beach. We dig into our food and plan out the day.

"I love it here," Scott says. "It's fun to stay in a touristy place, but there is something so incredible about sitting on a beach and not seeing anyone."

"I agree. I think we should just relax and enjoy the sunshine," Marie adds. "I can't imagine a better place to do it than here."

For the rest of the day, we watch surfers and the many pelicans dive in and out of the water looking for fish. I take a short walk along the beach where I notice a dog sitting alone in the sand. He stares out at the water, longing for his owner to return from surfing. I take his picture while standing under a palm tree. For some reason, it brings back memories of me staring into the distance out my office window.

The next morning we continue our ride back to Grecia. What should have taken one day has turned into three.

"I'm happy we did it like this," Marie says. "I love all the places we stopped. I feel like I've seen so much more of this country than I would have if we just drove straight back."

Once back in Grecia, Rob pulls over. "I'm throwing it in four wheel drive just to see what happens." After shifting gears, the squeaking stops. "I told you Scott. We could have driven fifty miles per hour the entire way home."

Scott leans in toward Rob with a weary look a parent might give their teenager. "And like I told you city mouse, the wheel would have fallen off the car."

And Away We Go...

I feel sad dropping our friends off at the airport. They are going back to their home in the states, while I'm uplifting mine to move to the coast. It would be nice to stay in Grecia for a few more years, but Rob is right. We have to do something with this property, and these decisions are too difficult to do so far away. At least I had the trip of a lifetime with my friends, seeing things I used to only dream about.

It turns out Scott was right; the problem with the wheel was a ball bearing. We dropped the car off at our mechanic and he had it fixed by the end of the day. I'm glad I won't have to worry about the wheel flying off the car while we are moving to Tamarindo.

Despite all my budget fears, it turns out living at the beach will only increase our expenses by a couple hundred dollars. There are a lot more fun things to do there, and I predict I'll be spending more on those outdoor activities. I might even learn how to surf. It would be embarrassing to not try while living in the surfing mecca of the world.

I calculate our budget will be between twelve and fourteen thousand dollars a year, the exact amount my friend pays in real estate tax for a nice house in New Jersey. How can I ever move back to the states again? Now I might just have a stroke when I pay thirteen dollars to cross over the Verrazano Bridge. Add the Goethals

Bridge at twelve dollars, and a thirty minute drive from my family's house in New Jersey to Rob's family in Brooklyn will cost us twenty-five dollars in tolls. I rarely see a toll in Costa Rica, and if there is one, it is never more than a couple dollars.

On my last trip back home, I noticed I got a ticket in a parking lot, and I couldn't imagine why. I had plenty of time on the meter, and ended up sitting in the car searching the ticket for some explanation. I finally found it. I got a thirty-five dollar ticket for backing into a space. I couldn't wrap my head around why this action was so problematic. Had there been a wave of people getting maimed by runaway backing cars? If that was the case, if a person pulled in head-on, wouldn't they eventually have to back out anyway? I paid the ticket, hoping my money went to the salary of a police office or teacher. But what bugged me the most was that feeling that everything was monitored. That I couldn't even back into a space without getting fined. It's too stressful living that way.

Planning another move also means planning the logistics of hauling our possessions across the country. Rob hears about an affordable mover from the Kansas couple who used to live next door. They moved out so they can be closer to town, but now they are close to all the traffic and congestion as well. I don't think they are any happier living there than next door to us on the mountaintop. But being closer to town has its advantages; at least you don't have to drive twenty minutes just to pay some bills. I would rather deal with the drive than live around a lot of people again. I'm enjoying having some space between us and the neighbors, and I don't have to worry about anyone seeing Rob watering the plants in his underwear.

When we meet the driver a week before the move, we notice he only has a medium-sized flatbed truck. Rob thinks we can fit all our stuff on it since we don't have any furniture. However, Rob always underestimates how much stuff we own. He also underestimates our credit card bill, always forgetting that he just purchased one hundred dollars in plastic for a greenhouse or fifty dollars' worth of fertilizer for the tomatoes.

My husband's garden—the one that was to make us self-reliant when the end of the world came and marauders roamed the earth— cost us a fortune. The greenhouse that he spent hundreds of dollars building ultimately blew down the mountain in a windstorm while we were away for Christmas. Francisco, the caretaker's son, was paid to watch the house and make sure the greenhouse door was always closed. If it was left open, a gust a wind could certainly set it airborne.

When we came back from the states, the once pleasant drive up our mountain resembled a grizzly plane crash.

"Was there an accident up here?" I asked as we followed a trail of PVC pipe, plastic sheeting, and dead tomato plants.

"Son of a… I swear, I'm going to kill him!" screamed Rob.

For the investment of over five hundred dollars in materials, and dozens of hours in sweaty Italian labor, I figured each one of those tomatoes cost us around four dollars. Not the best rate of return, but at least we have a freezer full of tomato sauce for the zombie apocalypse.

On the day of the move, the driver shows up to our house at five in the morning. Within a half hour, Rob has filled most of the truck with his plants and gardening supplies. Like Steve Martin in *The Jerk*, every time I think he is done, he grabs something else, "I don't need this or this. Just this bougainvillea plant... and this bag of fertilizer. The bougainvillea plant and the bag of fertilizer and that's all I need... and this remote control. The bougainvillea plant, the bag of fertilizer, and the remote control, and that's all I need." Now the truck is full and we look like we're off to landscape the Four Seasons hotel. Most of my stuff gets shoved in the back of our SUV, next to the kitty litter and dog food.

Over the past year, our house became ground zero for Rob's Botanical Gardens masterpiece. He wants to use all the shrubs and flowers that he has grown on the mountain for our property by the beach. I think this is a bit premature. How can you landscape a lot that doesn't have a house on it? Or even building plans that show where the house might go? But he is too excited to listen to any of my recommendations and continues to grow as many things as he can.

Rob can be manic in his enthusiasm for more shrubs, often pulling over to the side of the road to snip a few more clippings of a bush he hasn't found yet. It seems he is replacing his humungous aquarium and coral garden he spent years trying to grow back home with an actual plant garden that can't be confined by the dimensions of a tank. He might end up landscaping clear to Nicaragua if I don't put the brakes on it every so often. And when I say putting the brakes on it, I mean sitting alone in the car while Rob disappears into a field for a half hour scrounging for more plants.

Now, a guy shows up weekly at our house with a trunk full of plant inventory. I have no idea how he found out about Rob, but he shows up like clockwork every week. He pops open his trunk with the same kind of secrecy a guy in Manhattan does when opening his trench coat to reveal the thousand dollar Rolex he'll sell you for twenty bucks. It's fascinating that this salesman already pegged my Brooklyn-born husband for someone willing to buy anything out of the back of a vehicle.

"You've never bought anything out of a trunk before?" Rob asks.

"No Rob, can't say I have."

"You mean to tell me people didn't pull up in front of your house and pop open their trunk?"

"No."

"Okay, so where did you buy your furniture?"

"Somebody had furniture in their trunk?"

"No, they pulled up in a truck, but it was the same idea. You go outside, see what you like, and they drag it up the few flights into your apartment."

"But how do you know it's not stolen?"

"Why do you think everything sold out of the back of a truck is stolen? Sometimes, it's just easier to do business that way. Low overhead." There's no use arguing with Rob; I've been listening to his wacky explanations for years.

A couple months after we met, Rob took me on a date which involved driving down Brooklyn's popular 86th street in the middle of December. He showed me every location where *Saturday Night Fever* was filmed, including the infamous scene where John Travolta swaggered down the street holding a paint can. Rob borrowed his mother's car and drove around Bensonhurst, giving me his Hollywood tour with the windows down. Every time I tried to roll mine up to prevent from freezing to death, he would reach over me and roll it back down. What I didn't know—but found out years later—was the junky car had a deadly exhaust leak and we would have died from carbon monoxide poisoning if there was no ventilation. I can still remember his silly excuses as he reached across me, lowering the window.

"I love the sounds of Brooklyn in the winter. If you keep the windows down, you'll hear the trains going over our heads. Check that corner out. That's were Steven Seagal threw a guy over a fruit stand in *Out For Justice.*"

"That's great Rob, but it's twenty-five degrees out and I'm really getting cold," I'd say raising the window again. "And what's that, a prison?"

"No, it's my high school. Hey, take a look. It's L&B's pizzeria. It's a landmark, you're gonna want to smell that real Italian pizza," he'd suggest while rolling the window back down.

"Could you put the heat on at least?"

"Hmm… that's temporarily not working. All the more reason to snuggle, right?"

Rob was flat broke back then, and if I remember correctly, we had to share a slice of pizza that day. But my husband had a burning desire to get what he wanted no matter what the obstacles were. And carbon monoxide poisoning was not going to keep him from landing the woman who he already knew was going to be his wife. A girl he wanted to make sure remained conscious for the wedding. After all, an asphyxiated wife is no fun on the honeymoon.

I watch Rob squeeze what's left of our things in the moving truck. Amazingly, even with the plants he makes room for the rest of our junk. Everything looks like it is going to topple over, but we have to get a jump-start on the day before morning rush hour hits. The driver is not particularly happy; he thought this was going to be an easy job and has just found out there is a lot more work than expected. There's nothing we can do now but instruct him to follow us. Or at least we try to. I don't know the word "follow" in Spanish so Rob does his typical charades to get the point across.

Unfortunately, the Pan American highway is not a smooth straight road. Our first leg is filled with sharp switchbacks with nowhere to safely pass. A fact our mover ignores by brazenly passing us on a blind curve.

"He doesn't even know where our house is, why is he passing?" I ask.

We watch as the man takes off down the road. We try to pass the car in front but it is too dangerous; it's not worth the risk. We see too many accidents of people trying to pass on these ridges.

I thought there might be a good possibility of this happening. We don't have a clue who this guy is, and for all we know he could be selling *our* stuff out of the back of *his* truck. We go down the laundry list of what was on board: our scooter, guitar, all my clothes, and other assorted items. Luckily, my computer and pets are safe with us. After getting over the shock, I realize it is not the biggest deal. I try to convince myself it is a fresh start, that this will lighten my load once again. But with each curve, Rob has his eyes peeled; he wants his guitar back.

This situation is made worse by the fact that my cat crapped in his pet carrier five minutes into the drive. I don't want to reach around and open the carrier door fearing my cat will leap out. Because of the awful smell, we have all the windows open and can't use the air conditioner. Just like our romantic 86th Street date, we're driving around with the windows down to avoid another cloud of unpleasant fumes. At least these don't have the potential to kill me, however nauseating they are.

After an hour, we spot the truck in the far corner of a restaurant parking lot. The man is leaning on the side eating an apple. He isn't even surprised we found him. I'm still unclear of the man's motives, wanting to give him the benefit of the doubt. Rob doesn't look so forgiving. The rest of the way we spend most of our time watching the truck in the rear-view mirror. Rob won't allow him to pass us again.

"I think we're okay now, Rob. He's not getting around us."

"We just have to stay on top of this guy, I don't trust him. How much longer do we have?"

"At least four more hours." Knowing my husband, he is going to be glancing in his rear-view mirror every ten seconds for the rest of the ride. "You know, once we're all settled in I was thinking about putting my writing together in a book. I'm calling it *Happier Than A Billionaire*, the same name as the blog. Maybe even try to get it published. What do you think?"

"Sure, why not. What's the first step to making it happen?"

"I guess I have to send query letters to literary agents. If they like what I have they can pitch it to publishers. Now I just have to figure out how to write a query letter."

"I'm all for it. As long as you don't make me sound like a giant ape, it could be a lot of fun."

"Of course. You always have final say in editing." I feel fairly confident Rob will not edit any of my stories because I haven't seen him pick up a book since college. He's not the reading kind, so I'm not worried about it. He'll never know what I'll eventually put in the book.

As we continue to our new home, my mind is lost in the possibilities for my future as a writer. I'm already making mental lists of all the things I need to do to make that dream attainable. I begin to get a strange sensation that if I keep an optimistic spirit something incredible might happen. That feeling quickly dissipates, replaced by a whiff of cat poop. But for a moment, I feel like a door has opened for me. I just need to figure out how to walk through it.

Giddy Up

Driving through Guanacaste is remarkably different than the central part of the country. It is the end of the dry season and the brownish landscape is void of any trace of green. It looks and feels like an oven.

"I can actually smell the earth cooking," I groan.

"You know how it is here. Once the rain comes it will explode with color. We are at sea level so of course it's going to be dryer."

We pass fields of cattle grazing on dead grass. This goes on for miles until we come upon twenty-five crossing the road with the help of a rancher. This man could easily be from Texas with his Stetson hat, tan shirt, blue jeans, and cowboy boots. His skin is darkened by the sun, his face a road map of the years working in this harsh environment. While on his horse (one with hair so black it gives off a blue hue in the sun), he guides the herd in the desired direction. The horse earns his keep by blocking five cattle and allowing others to pass. The rancher precisely holds the reins, guiding his horse forward a couple of feet then quickly throws him in reverse to back up six. It's a dance the cowboy has perfected over a lifetime of effort in the fields.

This is difficult work. Some cattle just stand in the middle of the street refusing to move, while others stray away. But the rancher masterfully controls the situation and eventually gets every last one to the other side. We patiently wait until the rancher smiles, giving us the thumbs up. Here I am complaining about the heat and this man is out here all day long doing a difficult job that I surely couldn't perform for even an hour. I watch him gallop off into the adjacent field. He still has a long day ahead of him.

Elizabeth and Henry are waiting for us as we drive in. We instruct the truck driver to back down the driveway closer to the backyard. It will be easier for us to unload there and carry our stuff to the lower level of the house. Also, it makes it a heck of a lot easier for Rob to dump all the plants he hauled into the backyard.

Henry is already helping us and Elizabeth brings us two glasses of cold water. I take my dog, Clementine, into the backyard for a bathroom break before washing my cat in the shower. Pumpkin generously rolled around in his poop and hasn't made the best first impression. I apologize, promising this is not typical for my cat. I scrub him clean while getting the amount of cooperation one would imagine receiving from a cat submerged in water. Elizabeth must think I'm murdering my pet in her bathroom.

Finally, the truck is unloaded and we can take a rest. While drinking my glass of water, I notice the backyard overlooks another house. It is separated from ours by a dirt road. "Who lives there?" I ask Elizabeth.

"That's Sergio. He's the caretaker for the development."

"Is he a nice guy?"

"Sure. If there is a problem, that's the man you need to contact."

Although I miss our old caretaker, Carlos, it seems we don't have to look far for another one. Sergio lives only five hundred feet away. From where I'm standing, I can see his house, four barking dogs, and a flock of chickens running around his front yard. But once the rainy season comes the leaves will fill the trees and there will be a thick barrier between us. I love the privacy one has in Costa Rica.

Elizabeth and Henry disappear upstairs and we are left to sort through our belongings. It's so hot we already have to put on the air conditioner. It's the one big trade off; we didn't need air conditioning up in the mountains. I don't see how anyone can live here without it, especially at the height of the dry season. Even with it going full blast, I collapse on the couch, too uncomfortable to unpack anything.

"So, what do you think?" Rob asks.

"I don't know. The heat stroke is clouding my judgment."

"I think it's kinda nice. This is really different than Grecia. I mean, it's like we are in another country all together. And the ride down, it was beautiful."

"It was flat," I mumble.

"I know, but once we got out of the mountains and closer to sea level, the trees started changing. I noticed different plants and vegetation. It's why I love Costa Rica so much. The environment just keeps transforming the longer you drive."

"We are eight to twelve degrees above the equator. It didn't bother me when we were four thousand feet in the air. Now that we are at sea level, my face feels like it's eight to twelve degrees above a barbecue."

"Nadine, you always feel this way when you are in the heat. We just moved across the country and had no air conditioning in the car. I'm surprised you're still conscious. But you always adjust, so stop complaining, have some water, and you'll cool off in no time."

I sit up while Rob hands me a drink. He is right. I'm overheated and exhausted from the move. This is my new home and I might as well snap out of it. I get up and the first thing I do is pour a bag of litter into Pumpkin's litter box. He promptly goes to the bathroom, kicks the litter all over the living room, and curls up on a chair to sleep. Rob opens a suitcase and dumps all the clothes on the floor so that he can find a T-shirt. His clothes are now mixed in with the cat litter.

Later in the afternoon, Elizabeth invites us upstairs for dinner. Rob and I get ready and try to look as presentable as possible. For Rob, that means his customary black Hanes tank top and black track pants.

"You're wearing that? We're trying to make a good impression."

"But it's my *good* tank top." Rob is the only person I know who rates his tank tops by how long they've been balled up in the back of the closet. "Look, no stains," he rallies. This shouldn't surprise me since my husband "lost" his wedding tuxedo and eventually found it balled up on the back floor of his car.

Rob models the shirt in front of the bathroom mirror with all the confidence of a man who purchased it not from the underwear department at Walmart, but from Armani on Fifth Avenue in New York City. He pairs it with his "good" sneakers, the ones that were never caught in the rain or submerged in mud. It's becoming clear I need to abandon my dream of having a husband who puts any thought into his wardrobe.

Once upstairs, I notice that Henry isn't wearing a shirt. It appears both of these men are at the stage where they are more concerned with comfort than any dress code their wives try to impose on them. Henry does put a shirt on once we sit at the table to eat, but only because Elizabeth urges him to.

My landlords remind me a lot of Darlene and Frankie. Elizabeth and Henry are recently retired and have an incredible zest for life. They fill us in on the best beaches to boogie board and the most scenic places to hike. They have an adventurous spirit that spills over into their future plans. When not spending time at their homes in the states or Costa Rica, they are planning on traveling across country in a motor home, possibly scouting out areas for a future in the RV industry.

"I had a very serious health scare," Elizabeth confesses. "When I was in the operating room, I thought about how great my life was, and I had absolutely no regrets. There was a good possibility I wasn't going to make it. I kissed my husband for what I thought might be the last time. When I woke up, I knew then I wasn't going to waste any time. My life was going to be dedicated to my family, and all those dreams I put on the backburner. So now we are living them. Life is too short to waste one day worrying about things we can't control. If I drop dead, I want to do it while having fun."

They have the same attitude we do. It would have been easy for me to stay put in that office and to continue on the path I worked hard to design. But something was needling me for years, an alter ego occasionally showing up in my brain whispering, "This monotony, this emptiness, will be your life forever if you don't change it."

These voices grew louder and louder, so I tried harder and harder to quiet them. It became obvious I wasn't living the life I knew existed for me and I had to find the courage to alter it. I guess I wanted to exchange my life for something better, as if mine had malfunctioned along the way. It wasn't even clear what that life actually looked like, but spending ten hours a day in the office wasn't it. These running soliloquies in my brain were constant reminders from the person I used to be; the person who always believed I controlled my life's direction. It came to a point where I couldn't ignore the constant chatter in my head anymore.

The next morning we get up early to explore the area. As Rob backs out of the driveway, he hits the main water line where it enters the house, sending a geyser of water over one hundred feet in the air. I run back inside the house but the owners have already left on their daily walk. We scramble to figure out how to shut it off as the front of the house is showered with hundreds of gallons of water. Within ten minutes, we have effectively wasted all the water in the holding tank meant for the entire development.

It's been less than twenty-four hours and Rob is already destroying the place.

Sexy Monkeys

Before Elizabeth and Henry return to the states, they show us around, giving us their advice on the best beaches. Henry is an avid boogie boarder and he and Rob spend hours in the waves playing like a couple of kids. I love seeing Rob so healthy and happy. Before we moved to Costa Rica, he was overweight and dissatisfied with work. We were always in a terrible mood and when we did have some time off, we were too exhausted to do anything. Now he's as muscular as he was in his twenties.

This place is totally geared toward an active lifestyle, and since I will be wearing a bathing suit more often, I need to continue my workout regimen. I've included an hour of yoga and an hour of weight lifting every morning. Cardiovascular exercise is accomplished by spending time playing in these waves. It beats a treadmill any day.

Since starting yoga, I've realized how much my mind used to obsess about past or future events. Yoga makes me concentrate on the moment, and this training has helped me focus more on the things that are important. I never once thought about meditating when I worked. I wish I would have tried it before. Those long days in the office might have not been so draining if I could have found the inner peace that existed all along. And a peaceful mind may be the most important thing of all when trying to stay healthy. No wonder Costa Rica is full of yoga retreats. It's not uncommon to sit up from a stretch to find an iguana staring down at you.

At the same time every morning, I hear small planes fly into Tamarindo bringing excited tourists to their destination. When in town, I watch them get off their shuttle bus with cameras already hanging from their neck. They snap pictures of everything: the hotel lobby, pool, and even the porters that come to unload the luggage. I am living in a place that people come to from all over the world to visit. But unlike visitors, I get to call it my home.

Although the afternoons are hot, the mornings are mild and I wake up early to take advantage of the cool air. A misty fog rises over the trees as the sounds of howler monkeys roar across the canopy. I feel as if I am living in a *National Geographic* documentary. And to think, I was hesitant of moving away from my mountaintop rental fearing I would be moving away from the spectacular wildlife I grew to love. However, that's not the case at all. The same Mot Mots, Squirrel Cuckoos, and parrots fill my backyard with a cacophony of sounds.

This morning I let Clementine out the back door and notice three blue jays flying overhead. They are beautiful, but slightly different than the ones back home in New Jersey. These have a hilarious feather on their head resembling a Napoleonic military hat. It looks ridiculous and I giggle at them as they settle on a branch in front of me. I watch Clementine as she innocently sniffs the grass when suddenly the birds swoop down and charge at her. The attacks are coordinated, each taking turns at soaring inches over my dog's head. I run out and shoo them away before they hurt her.

I search for my bird field chart and identify them as White-throated Magpie-Jays. They are actually the same bird family as the ones from the *Heckle and Jeckle* cartoon. They have neat little high pitched calls that sound similar to a phaser beam from *Star Trek*. But when they attack, they squawk loudly to alert the other birds. They're often found in groups, and several cooperate to raise their babies.

Maybe there is a nest nearby and they went into attack mode to protect it. I'm not sure what I did to stir them up, but two of them return to their post and one lingers, glaring at me through the window.

All this action stirs the monkeys and a few begin howling from the direction of Sergio's house. I grab a pair of binoculars and watch a big family of them in a tree alongside his carport. Two active babies climb to the tippy top of the trees and leap down to another branch. They continue playing as the older monkeys, content to lie in the tree, shove leaves into their mouths, occasionally howling when they feel the urge. They've been hanging around Sergio's house since we moved here and I wonder if they will eventually cross the road and socialize near our place.

Clementine's response to all this action is to curl up in the corner and go to sleep. I turn on the computer and check my email, hoping for good news. I just started sending out query letters to agents, but so far, all that fills my inbox are form rejections. It appears I can't even get the chance to submit my material before getting a denial. It's not like I'm surprised; I already knew this wouldn't be easy. Many times these emails are only opened by assistants, never reaching the intended recipient.

I can't help but feel frustrated. I take a deep breath and plan to send out a few more this morning except once again, I lose my internet connection. This has been happening frequently since moving here. The phone line is also scratchy which usually means the line needs to be replaced. My computer picks up someone else's wireless connection and I spend the next ten minutes trying to hack the security code.

"Do you want anything from the store?" Rob asks.

"Get some water." Yesterday we were without running water for five hours. That, too, is something Henry warned us about. It's a strange thing to walk over to your faucet, turn it on, and see nothing coming out. I can't say that ever happened back in Grecia or the states. Maybe a crew would be working on a pipe turning the water brown, but that only lasted for a couple hours. It is not unheard of to go without water for an entire day here. In fact, the Guanacaste area is the driest part of the country, so there is always an issue with water.

"While you are at the store, also get a bag of coffee, a gallon of milk...," I'm interrupted by the monkey screaming wildly across the street. "Why do you think the monkeys are always at Sergio's house? I haven't seen them once jump over to our side of the street. They're like the literary agents—completely ignoring my existence." I point out the window to the family of monkeys dangling over Sergio's rooftop. "It's like the *Planet of the Apes* over there."

Not only can I not figure out why the monkeys are on Sergio's side of the street, I can't decipher what Sergio actually does here. Carlos used to weed-wack and dig drainage ditches in-between pretending to fix the hydraulic gate. He was a hard worker; the roads were always maintained, and when a tree fell down in a storm you could always count on him to have it cleared up by the next day. As for Sergio, I just don't know what this guy does. The roads are beat up, and when a tree falls Henry tells us the neighbors get together to clear the mess. Supposedly Sergio is in charge of renting out the houses in the development. I wouldn't say he's the dream property manager every homeowner wishes for, but maybe he's not the worst either.

Elizabeth and Henry have a friend a couple miles away that use their house only three months out of the year. They pay the caretaker of the development to manage their house while they are out of the country. Not long after they left, the caretaker rented the house to a man with a horse. Since the house did not come with a barn out back, the new renter did what any sensible person would do with a horse in the rainy season; he moved the animal inside the house. When their friends returned the following year, the entire tile floor was destroyed and a towering pile of crap was shoveled into the corner. Not a pura vida way to start your vacation. I think this story also shook Henry up, making it ever more important to find someone responsible to care for his property. I assured him I would never move a horse into their house or crap in the corner. Rob breaking the water line was enough of a surprise.

Rob returns with the groceries and carries them into the kitchen. "I passed Sergio's place and stopped to talk with him. And just to amuse you, I asked him why the monkeys all congregate over his house."

"What did he say? He gives them food, right? He probably climbs the tree and sticks it in-between the branches."

"He didn't exactly say that."

"So then what's his secret?"

"He said the monkeys congregate near his house because his wife is hot."

"What?"

"That's what he said; he has a smoking hot wife and that's why the monkeys like it over there. Straight faced. Serious as a heart attack."

"And what did you say?"

"What do you mean what did I say? I didn't say anything."

"You didn't stick up for me?"

"Are you out of your mind? What did you want me to say?"

"Well, I don't know. Maybe that your wife is hot too."

"Yeah, right. You wanted me to say that my wife is so sexy she can attract monkeys too? For all I know his wife looks like a monkey. Nadine, aside from picking Giada as my second wife, this is the stupidest conversation we ever had. I'm not telling other men that my wife is so hot she attracts monkeys."

I've only seen Sergio's wife briefly while she works in the yard. Now that I think about it, she does wear short shorts and tight tank tops. Maybe she is sexy. I may not be the best looking gal in town, but if I put on a little mascara I bet I can still turn a few monkey heads. His wife doesn't own the rainforest and I'm not going to let her prevent me from coaxing the monkeys to my side of the street.

Move over hot pants, I'm breaking out the lipstick. Game on.

Why Worry?

Building a house in any country has its degree of difficulty. In Costa Rica, there are a plethora of documents one will need before starting the process. Since we have completely unpacked and settled into our new home, we decide it's time to embark on our next task. We head out on the forty-five minute drive to the municipality building in Santa Cruz. It all starts here.

The municipality is located in the heart of the town across from a park. Every town in Costa Rica has a park where people sit and socialize with one another. Even the smaller villages have a central soccer field that functions as a gathering place, as well as an area for kids to play. This park is particularly intriguing with its many beautiful statues. One is of a man riding a bull, his arm upstretched to balance himself; behind him, a clock tower. It extends three stories into the air, the red paint long faded to a washed-out pink. It's oddly out of place. I rarely see tall buildings in any of these small towns, but even with its chipped facade and inaccurate timepiece, it's charming.

Pigeons peck at the ground as people sit and converse on the benches. A rounded, concrete structure takes up the center of the park. It must provide shelter for performances as a pavilion would in the states. I walk into the shade and notice a carved wooden puma standing in the middle. It has only three legs; I can't tell if the front two are fused together or one is missing entirely. Its face is frozen in a snarled expression, clearly ready to "tumble" the bejesus out of some drunk guy staggering through the park at midnight. It's only a matter of time before Rob gets the same idea and puts one up on our front lawn.

At the front of the municipal building, a helpful security guard directs us to the correct line. The interior is modest and relatively up-to-date. While we are here, we decide to pay our taxes as well. Real estate taxes are one quarter of one percent of the value of your property. It's one of the reasons you'll see people hold onto a piece of land for a long time; there is no rush to sell when your yearly costs are so low.

Rob walks up to a counter and presents our catastro (a legal document for our property). The man in charge of the building permits introduces himself and patiently listens as my husband explains our intentions.

"We are in the beginning stages of building. Where do we start?" Rob asks.

The permit man writes down a number of things we need to do in the following months. A licensed architect must draw up the plans. Soil samples must be taken and preliminary inspections of the lot must be done before any building can occur. So far, so good. These are the same procedures our friends Darlene and Frankie had to do when building their house. But then he pauses, writes down something on the paper, and underlines it three times.

"Necessita una agua papel," he says. We need a water letter.

"What's a water letter?" I ask.

A man taps me on the shoulder and introduces himself. His name is Reynaldo and he's a builder in the area. He first apologizes for his English before attempting to explain the significance of this water letter. I find this so endearing; Costa Rican people apologize for not knowing better English in a Spanish-speaking country. I'm embarrassed in these situations because I am well aware my limited

Spanish is what is causing the problem. And maybe I'm also embarrassed because I remember having limited patience for people in the states who didn't know English. It's one of the best things about moving abroad; the humility alone all but guarantees you become a kinder person. I know this has happened to me.

For years, construction projects were either creating wells without getting permits or digging a well but not getting permission to deliver water to each home within the development. Even though these communities may be miles from each other, they all draw water from the same aquifer. The government had no way of knowing if the water table is providing water to one hundred or one thousand homes. In an effort to monitor the activity and determine how much water is being used, a new law was passed. Today every lot owner has to provide a water letter confirming that they are in a legal water association before they can sell or build on their property.

"So this has nothing to do with the legalities of the well? Because I have papers on that," Rob explains to Reynaldo.

"No. This is about the distribution of the water to the lots."

"I don't understand. I know we have water… it comes right out of the spigot," I add, already getting a sick feeling in my stomach.

"You still need a letter explaining that distribution is legal under Costa Rica law."

"How do I get this?" Rob asks while writing down all this new information.

"The developer," the man answers. This causes a problem. Building has slowed down because of the poor global economy. Many developers have put projects on hold figuring they can start things up again once the economy improves. This leaves many homeowners doing the work of keeping developments functioning. I'm not sure how to find our developer.

"What are we going to do?" I ask Rob. I'm starting to hyperventilate.

"Don't panic just yet," Rob reassures. "We have a water line going straight to our lot, and there is plenty of water in the development, so this just sounds like a little technicality."

I try to remain optimistic as we drive home, but I know a little something about red tape in Costa Rica. It gets handled in "Tico Time."

"So what have we learned?" I ask Rob.

"We learned that we need a water letter. And I think our first stop is Mike's house."

"He's not there," I reply. "I think he comes back to Costa Rica in four months." Mike is one of the first homeowners in the development. He built a small guest house with an incredible lap pool. So far, he hasn't built the main house. It's only him and his wife and, like us, they are finding less is more. They vacation here for a couple months out of the year before returning back home to Portland, Oregon. "What about asking the guy who owns the big house next to our lot? I think he's around."

"We could do that. That last time I checked his house is still for sale. Hopefully he's living there and knows something about the water association. I'm not worried, one of these guys will be able to help."

Maybe Rob is right. Why worry when there is nothing yet to worry about?

Start Worrying

The entrance to our development is a long road lined with trees on either side. Their branches stretch above our heads, entwined into each other like lovers holding hands. They bend and twist in opposing directions casting shadows across the gravel. It reminds me of the olive trees Frances Mayes writes about in *Under the Tuscan Sun*; ones that are over a hundred years old with thick trunks and wrinkled bark. It's a subtle indicator to the passage of time that fills me with a sense of gratitude as I drive underneath them. At night they're foreboding, but in daylight they are cozy and inviting.

Since the economy slowed, there has been little activity. But what first seemed like a problem now feels like an opportunity. During the height of the building boom, the forest's natural sounds had been replaced with jackhammers and cement mixers. One rarely heard a howler monkey or the sweet sound of a Mot Mot. However, those builders have left and nature has returned. Now there is peace, and once again the animals are claiming the area as their own. This has made plenty of people upset; mainly Martin, my old realtor. I heard he took off to another country to sell real estate. As I write this sentence, I am sure he is hiking with optimistic gringos into the forest to sell them a mountain top.

"I can't wait for my parents to see the property," I tell Rob. Rob and I have been sketching and re-sketching designs for the house. There will be no shipping containers or composting toilets. If we are going to build a house, it's going to be a real one. I can't help but let my imagination run wild thinking of all the beautiful things we could do: tiled verandas and curved archways, windows with planters of red geraniums, and wispy palm trees lining our entrance. I'll have friends over for drinks and will always have little sandwiches ready just in case people drop by unannounced.

Oh my, it was a struggle to build, but you know, we wanted our home to reflect the love that Rob and I feel toward each other, I'd say to friends while welcoming them into my living room. I'll return with a glass pitcher of iced tea—sweetened with mangos I picked from a tree in my yard—and place it on a teak table next to the pool. We'll clink our glasses and watch the sailboats in the distance. Yes, that's how it all looks in my head, until we stop the car in front of a boarded-up house with bats flying out a hole in the roof.

"I thought his house was rented. It looks like people haven't lived here in a while," Rob says.

"That is just terrible. What an eyesore... right on the road to our lot. Great."

"But who cares, this is far enough from our property. And we still have that big house next to our lot. That's the one that really counts. Don't worry about it. This one will eventually get sold, they all do."

A large house next to our property was built a couple years ago and is listed for 1.5 million dollars. It's a spectacular five-bedroom, five-bathroom house with an in-ground pool and sweeping views of the ocean. Twenty foot royal king palms shade the front and red bougainvillea surround the yard. It's comforting to have such a nice house in the development. It will help retain the value of the lots and attract buyers. Plus, my parents will love that our house will be built near a mansion. They've already booked a flight and will be here toward the end of the year. My property should convince my dad that all of this is a good idea, that moving to Costa Rica was a smart decision. His daughter will own a house with a pool and an ocean view. He's going to love it. What he is not going to love is all the debris along the road.

"What a mess. Why is all this junk here? This has to get cleaned up before my parents come," I complain before realizing there is a bigger problem, one that I can't shovel into a Hefty bag. The mansion—the house that was going to keep the value of our land intact—the house that was going to convince my father that I made the right choice—the house that was going to prove to all the naysayers that I didn't ruin my life—looks like a bomb went off inside. All the windows are gone, the roof tiles are missing, and the front door has disappeared. The Blitz did less damage.

"Rob… oh my God… what happened to the house?" We pull into the driveway, and see a man standing on the second floor. He waves at us.

"Hola. Que Paso?" Rob yells. The man welcomes us in, which is easy to do since there is no longer a definitive line between the inside or outside of the house. We find out he is a guard hired by the bank. The house has been foreclosed on and everything is gone. There is not one door, wire, switch, toilet, or molding left anywhere in the house. The pool is filled with filthy water; the letters C-H-O-L-E-R-A float on the top like a giant bowl of alphabet soup. I'm in shock and quickly get tunnel vision. I try to sit down but, the guard grabs me by the arm.

"No Señora, vespas. Bees, Africana," he says while pointing to the ceiling.

"What?" I shriek.

"I think he's trying to tell you there are killer African bees buzzing above your head," Rob explains.

I look at the ceiling and see holes in the drywall where a battalion of bees are darting in and out. It's the chandelier of death.

A fascinating thing happens when you realize you've ruined your life. It's a lot like my interaction with the crocodile while kayaking through the mangroves in the Osa Peninsula. Once again I go through the five stages of grief.

Denial: "Poor saps that live in this development. Good thing it's not me."

Anger: "Give me a two by four so I can go ballistic in here. Damn it, there aren't any windows left to break."

Bargaining: "If we do a little gardening, maybe people won't notice."

Depression: "I'm walking the plank straight into the cholera soup. Tell mom there's a 1986 pack of Virginia Slims hidden behind her washing machine."

Once again, acceptance never comes because I am overwhelmed by the aneurysm that is exploding in my head. I can feel the thumping in my temples begin; yes… that's it… lights out. I'm going to be dead by noon. Let's not make this complicated, just wheelbarrow my body into the gaping hole where the king palm used to be. I'll make great fertilizer.

"Honey, you don't look so good. Let me get you back into the air-conditioned car." Rob turns the dashboard vents to blast cool air directly into my face. My blood pressure starts to come back down just to shoot right back up like a puck at a carnival's Strongman game. How am I ever going to show my dad the property after having to drive him past the foreclosed house? *Maybe I'll helicopter them in*, I think. *No, I'll hike them through the forest on the other side.* My mind races but it's inevitable. If my parents are going to see my property, they are going to also see this huge pile of turd. I can imagine how this will play out:

"Look Diane, the kid really screwed up this time. What a mess."

"I always knew her sister was the smart one. Now you understand why I wouldn't buy Nadine an Easy-Bake Oven for her fifth birthday. She could never

handle the responsibility of cooking a cupcake under a light bulb. She'd burn the whole damn house down!"

"Please, honey. Take a breath. It's not as bad as you think," Rob says while trying to comfort me.

"How can you say that?"

"I mean… I didn't see this coming, but what can you do? We just have to move forward."

"Move forward," I shout between exploding capillaries. "My parents are coming!"

"Oh boy. You better calm down. What can we do? Install fifty windows and doors on the house? It is what it is. You are just going to have to tell them that."

"Nope, no way. You're doing it."

"Ah… that's not my thing."

"Well, it's not my thing either. My dad is going to go ballistic when he sees it. And it's not one abandoned house you need to explain. *Two* Rob. Let's not forget the first boarded up house we saw on the way up.

"Nadine, you know I'm the fun guy. I don't give out bad news. That's your department. You're the hammer."

"You mean the bitch."

"Exactly. It's what keeps this relationship running smoothly. You have to be the one who tells them. Once the damage is done, I will run interference."

It's true that I'm the hammer. When we had to collect rent from a tenant, Rob would always come back empty-handed. "She said she needed to buy milk for her kids," Rob would say.

"Buy milk? She just bought a Lexus." And then I'd grab my coat, go to the apartment, and scream at the woman until she forked over the rent. For as tough as my husband is, he never wants to be the bad guy. But those days are over for me. I don't want to be the hammer anymore. I have no energy left for it. I'm hanging up my tool belt.

I recline my head and see that one of the killer bees has made it into the car. It walks along the dashboard before falling into the vent. It's not bad enough that the house foreclosed; did they have to add killer insects to the mix?

"Listen, let's go to our lot and draw in the dirt where we'll put the pool. That'll be fun and it will get your mind off all of this nonsense. Don't blow this out of proportion. Stay focused."

"I just imagined cute little Polish workers building a wall."

"What the hell are you talking about? Oh Christ, are you getting heat stroke?"

"In *Under the Tuscan Sun*, she wrote about the Polish workers who built her stone retaining wall. I thought that we'd have stories like that, adorable little stories I'd write about."

"Well this ain't *Under the Tuscan Sun*. It's *Under the Costa Rica Sun* where my wife is going to have a stroke if she doesn't calm down. If you haven't noticed, we are not in Italy. We live in Central America. This is *our* story, not some Italian broad's story in Europe. So if you really feel the need to write about something, write about how we are going to overcome these obstacles. That's exactly what we are going to do now."

We drive the rest of the way to our property and park the car. I look out at the ocean, at least that hasn't changed. In fact, it seems to only look better. Aside from the Hitchcock house of horrors next door, it is quite pretty up here. The ocean breeze calms my nerves and Rob puts his arm around me.

"I didn't mean to snap at you, I just get annoyed when you don't realize what's right in front of you. Aside from the abandoned and foreclosed house, is it really that bad? Look, we still have our land, our view, each other, and who cares about what's going on next door? For all we know someone will buy it cheap and fix it up. What we need to concentrate on is getting permits and deciding on how much we are willing to spend on the house. Considering that the building boom has ended, it is probably best we cut costs and build a house just big enough for us."

There really is no other choice. I can proceed with this plan in a good state of mind or collapse and cry. I look out at a sailboat in the distance. A group of monkeys howl, setting off others hidden in the forest. All at once the hills erupt with noise. It's beautiful, it's where I want to be, and I'm going to make it work.

"You're right, Rob. I'll try to keep a cool head. Of all the bad things I imagined could happen, I just didn't expect this."

"Of all the things you imagined? Just before moving here you had us kidnapped, murdered, attacked by pumas, bitten by snakes, and infected by every parasite known to man. We have our health and that's what's most important. I'm sure when *you* tell your parents, they will understand."

I want to believe Rob but the fumes of failure are quietly lingering in the air.

Soda-Gas

It took a couple days to recover from the visit to our lot. Apparently, I was not having an aneurysm, just a visceral response to the realization that I've complicated my life in ways I could never have predicted, that and knowing my dad is going to pull me aside and lecture me about ruining my life. I purposely walked away from a life filled with stress and have currently replaced it with one that includes a host of other problems.

The years in Grecia were the best times of my life. I finally understood what life could be like once you scaled back and kept it simple. It's not bad enough I have to figure out how to get a water letter, now I have to pass through swarms of killer bees to get to my lot. However, there is nothing I can do now so I put it out of my mind until our next visit to the municipality. Rob could be right; maybe it will all work out in the end.

Even with the problems we are facing, I enjoy living at the beach. There are plenty of fun things to do and we are surrounded by many happy people. But of course, all the activities cost money and it makes us review our budget once again. I look over my grocery receipt and find that some things are more expensive here than back in Grecia. Even the produce costs five to ten percent more. The cost of trucking everything to this side of the country is definitely reflected in the price.

There is no sugarcoating it; the cost of gas in Costa Rica is outrageous. I don't have to worry about that as much as the fact that the only gas station in town frequently runs out of it. This is compounded by my husband's commitment to drive until the little red indicator dips below empty. Ever since I've known Rob, he has this illogical belief that cars can go miles, even cross country, while the empty tank light blinks.

This has turned me into nothing short of The Gas Tank Kaiser. Considering I don't want to be stuck in ninety degree heat while Rob hitchhikes his way to a gas station, I obsessively monitor the fuel level and alert him on my findings every half hour. A frequency that surely makes my husband look forward to how much less annoying his second wife Giada will be.

"Stop leaning over me," Rob says. "I hate when you do that, it's distracting."

"I just want to check the gas. Look, it's on the empty line." I'm slightly more anxious since we are on the way to a remote beach that I've never seen before.

"I know, but it's not showing the red light yet."

"The red light just went on, Rob."

"Hmm… well… we don't have to be concerned until it starts to blink."

"It's blinking."

"Can't be. I usually have at least fifteen minutes before it blinks. It's probably just a glitch. Maybe it's because we are going downhill. Yeah, that's why it's blinking, the gas must have shifted."

"I'm not sure where we are, Rob. Oh Lord, we are going to run out of gas in the middle of nowhere."

"Stop being dramatic. We have at least thirty more miles before we are in trouble." I think about those thirty miles, how scenic and wonderful they would have been as the car putters and finally stops in the middle of the road. It appears Rob's theory on gas mileage is a bust. Rob starts the car, but it drives only a couple feet before stalling. We only have enough gas to go a couple more blocks before we are stuck for good. To make matters worse, we are along a dirt road with no prospects of finding a gas station within a ten mile radius. Luckily, a woman sees what is happening and approaches the car. She says a gentleman in the corner house will sell us some gas.

"It's the house with all the chickens in the yard," she tells us. "Just drive around the back, he is usually there working on his car." We find the man who gives us a big smile. He's got a good gig. I'm sure we are not the first gringos who have run out of gas and wandered into his backyard. The savvy entrepreneur pours some mucky stuff out of a Coca-Cola bottle into our tank, which in retrospect, might have actually been Coca-Cola. It was the most expensive five gallons of soda-gas I have ever bought, but it did ultimately get us to a gas station.

In an effort to save money and avoid getting stuck without gas again, we are using our scooter more and saving the SUV for longer trips. It's just too expensive to fill up the tank. But even with the scooter, we try to get everything done in one trip. This is common in Costa Rica; you will rarely meet an expat who has one errand on their agenda. Just take a look at the list in their hand, it's a mile long. For example, if you see Mrs. Cunningham at the bank, just say hello and don't chat for too long. You will most likely be running into her again at the supermarket, the pharmacy, and the gas station. Furthermore, if you get picked up by your friend at the airport expect to hang out a while as she stops at the mechanic for a quick oil change.

Even though the scooter costs us very little in gas, Rob still insists on doing everything in one trip. If we forget something while out shopping, he'll just say I'm out of luck until next week. No toothpaste? No problem. There's a box of Arm and Hammer baking soda in the refrigerator, suitable for removing unpleasant odors from your produce drawer, as well as, your dirty mouth. Apparently, having our breath smell like the refrigerator in order to save a couple bucks on gas is a worthy sacrifice.

Like Rob's logic defying theory about gas gauges, he's crafted another one concerning how much stuff can actually fit on the scooter. He's does this by squeezing food in every crevice, no matter how precarious the position is. He assures me it can handle the load.

"There is more than enough room," he says while pushing me further back onto the luggage rack. Although there may be room for groceries, MaGilla Gorilla leaves little room for his wife. It turns out the most precarious position is not the loaf of bread dangling off the back, but his wife who is one butt cheek away from eating asphalt.

"I have a system. It's foolproof," he brags. A foolproof system, I quickly discover, of losing things we just bought. These are but a few of the items that never made it home: a bottle of Windex, bag of tortillas, three cans of creamed corn, and a gallon of 2% milk that had the unfortunate mishap of exploding all over a confused Chihuahua.

This is not all altogether surprising since my husband is the type of guy who has fifteen assorted bolts left over after assembling a barbecue. "There are always extra pieces," he says with confidence as the grill leans thirty degrees to the right. And If you ask Rob to assemble an IKEA bookcase, for safety reasons I would suggest you never actually use it for books, but to store something like paperclips, bobby pins, or air.

Since losing our groceries down a hill and making enemies with the neighborhood Chihuahua association, Rob has perfected his skills and now uses a variety of bungee cords, rope, and a complicated plastic bag locking system. And I have to admit, we get a suitcase full of produce from the farmers market, a sack of kitty litter, and a week's worth of groceries piled onto our tiny scooter. We can even fit three cartons of eggs with a minimum amount of casualties.

Rob's not the only one with this idea. We constantly see people carrying unconventional items on their scooter. Rebar is one of my favorites, as is three generations of family members. We recently passed a man carrying a six drawer dresser on his shoulder while his friend drove.

The scooter is a great way for us to save money. Even if Rob gets a little overzealous in his approach, I'm happy with the purchase and actually look forward to the ride. It's still the best way to explore the area, and it's fun searching for new beaches while wrapping my arms around my husband. We can usually get down roads that are normally impassible, but unfortunately one of the worst roads is the one leading to our house. It seems to deteriorate more every week. It's incredibly steep, and is beyond challenging to drive the scooter up the bumpy terrain. Sergio must have skipped a year grading it; the potholes and ditches now stretch across the entire road. There are parts where our tiny scooter simply can't carry both of us. Of course, I'm the one who has to get off and walk to the next smooth patch.

This morning after a jarring ride up the mountain with a months' worth of groceries, I notice Rob holding his right side as we walk into the house.

"What's the matter?" I ask.

"Nothing."

"I know there is something wrong so tell me."

"The scooter's been irritating my hernia."

"How do you even know it's a hernia? Maybe something else is wrong?"

"I've had this for years; I know what it feels like. It's not a big deal, sometimes it acts up. There is nothing to worry about."

"Maybe you should stop lifting weights for a little while," I suggest. It's not like Rob to complain about anything so I know he must be in pain.

"No way. I'm in the best shape of my life and if I quit I'm going to get soft. Anyway, I can't get all sloppy again because I need to protect you."

"You will not get fat again if you take a break. And will you stop worrying about protecting me? Take some time off."

"I know myself, and if I stop working out I'll get lazy and put on weight. I'll be fat by the end of a month. The road just rattled it, I'll be fine."

Rob goes inside, lies down, and asks for a couple Ibuprofens. This is disconcerting. I wouldn't even know where to take him if something were to happen. Thankfully we are residents now and are included in the national health care system. We're eligible for medical care but I wasn't planning on needing it so soon. I'll just hope for the best. I'm praying Rob will be okay.

"I'm already feeling better," he says after gulping down the pills. "Let's talk about something else. How's the book coming? Any responses from agents?"

"They were all rejections. It could be years before I make any progress. It's a shame because I believe other people would love to do the same thing we did. Anyway, it depresses me just talking about it. Let's change the subject. Did you talk to Sergio about the internet line? It's making it difficult to send things out when the connection goes off and on all day."

"Yes, I saw him yesterday and asked him to fix it."

"What did he say?"

"He said what he usually says, he'll do it mañana."

"But that was yesterday. Can't you ask him again?" I plead.

"I will if I see him, but let's give him the benefit of the doubt and see if he gets it done by the end of the week. Forget about that for now. As for the book, do you really need an agent? Isn't there a way you can just do it yourself? Can't you sell it on your website?"

"You mean self-publish?"

"Sure, why not? Everything we've accomplished we did ourselves. I would go that route if you can figure out how to do it." Rob struggles to sit up but he can't hide the pain on his face. "I think I'm going to sit in a hot bath for a while."

Rob brings up a good point that I never previously considered. I go online and Google "self-publishing." I quickly find out there is a way to upload your book as both an electronic file and paperback to Amazon and other book sellers. This is completely different from the model I heard about years ago. Back then, you would need to lay out thousands of dollars to have your book printed, and then be responsible for distributing and mailing it on your own. It appears that technology has made it possible for one to self-publish with a minimal investment.

If I go this route I have a lot of work ahead of me. I'll need to find out how to make an e-file and design a cover. If no one is going to give me a shot, perhaps I need to grab control of this project and make it happen on my own. There's really nothing stopping me. The question now is: What am I waiting for?

Minutes later, Rob steps out of the bathroom gripping his abdomen and says something I had prayed I would never hear while living in a third world country: "I think I need a doctor."

Part II

Health Care in Costa Rica

Since moving to Costa Rica, I have frolicked through a crocodile-infested bat cave, have come face to face with a kinkajou, and even watched my husband mace himself in the face. But few things prepare you for when your husband walks up and says, "I think I need a doctor."

He removes his hand from his abdomen and unveils a bulging protrusion across the lower part of his stomach that goes all the way to his pubic bone. Either my husband is going to give birth or he finally blew out his hernia.

After the initial shock, I really wasn't surprised this happened. He's been nursing a hernia for the past twenty-two years. It started after a stint in the high school gym where Rob was going head to head with his stronger friend Ralphie Zamboni. If Ralphie benched two hundred pounds, my husband did two hundred and twenty-five. If Ralphie did five squats with a heavy barbell on his shoulders, Rob would do six. After one of the exercises, Rob felt a sharp pain in his groin area. Although he walked away the champion of the stupidest competition ever performed at Lafayette High School, he also walked away with a hernia. It's amazing any teenage boy makes it past puberty.

Rob would feel it tear over the years, but he refused to see a doctor. "We have a ten thousand deductible," he complained, "and I would rather spend that on a vacation than having surgery." This procrastination had brought us to this moment—him standing naked in front of me holding in his guts.

"You have to see someone immediately. How did it get so bad? You must have felt something going on for a while."

"I guess you were right. All those heavy weights must have done it. I felt some pain so I started wrapping things around my stomach to give it some extra support."

"Is that why that rainbow belt is on the table? It's meant for wrapping around our suitcase so it doesn't explode from all the weights you insist on packing. It's not a medical device. What the hell is wrong with you? You used it as a weight belt?" I am beyond angry. When is he going to realize he is not twenty-five anymore? I want to kill him, but I'll wait until he gets better first.

I'm not even sure where to go for medical care in this rustic beach town. At times it feels like the Wild Wild West out here. Grecia certainly had many more amenities. The hospitals—some of the biggest in the country—were less than an hour away and there were plenty of doctors to choose from. It is as if comparing the medical facilities of New York City to the rural outskirts of Kentucky. I feel like the coal miner's daughter, ready to honky-tonk my way to the nearest outpost that can stitch up my husband's belly.

"We should go through the CAJA system," Rob suggests. "We pay for health care every month, why not use it. How bad could it be?" He makes a good point; however, I always imagined our first introduction to the government-run healthcare system would be for something as minor as an antibiotic. It never occurred to me that one of us would require surgery. Needless to say, I am hesitant about Rob going under the knife in Central America. But he must be in a lot of pain, and if I don't do something quick, Doogie Howser will start wrapping himself up with duct tape—his usual remedy for ailments of this sort.

"I don't know, maybe we should just drive to San Jose and pay cash at one of the better hospitals. The ones all the gringos use."

"It's an option, but why do that when they use the same doctors as the CAJA?" Rob adds. "If we are going to get the same doctors, and pay more, let's get it done under our insurance and pay nothing. Before we drive the six hours to San Jose, let's see what we can get accomplished around here. Plus, don't you think I should know what you'll be in for if you ever get hurt?"

"Why are you dragging me into this? You're the one with your intestines falling out. Rob, you're not making a lick of sense."

"I know you are worried about me, but I think I should go through the national healthcare system. That way I'll know the kind of care you'll receive if you ever get hurt. I'll take one for the team."

Somehow, Rob has got it in his head that he needs to protect his wife—who, by the way, has absolutely nothing wrong with her—by getting surgery in a hospital we know nothing about. Perhaps not wrapping a suitcase belt around his waist would have been a better way of displaying his affection.

While considering Rob's suggestion, I go online and search the cost of a hernia operation in the states. If we were to return for this surgery, we will have to pay the full expense. After reading a few articles, I find the cost fluctuates between fifteen thousand to twenty thousand dollars depending on whether you are in New York or Alabama. The decision is made for us; I am going to ship my husband off to a Costa Rica clinic. The budget demands it.

We make a couple phone calls and find the closest clinic. It's only ten minutes away in Brasilito. We have to go there first so that Rob can get the referral he needs for a surgeon. So far, it doesn't seem much different than what my sister would do in New Jersey.

The clinic turns out to be a small, run-down building surrounded by a chain-link fence with barbed wire on top. Aesthetically, it is about as appealing as a North Korean work camp. Rob is optimistic as usual; I in turn say a prayer under my breath. With our limited Spanish, we explain Rob's condition to the receptionist, and she directs us to a back room to speak with the doctor. I am immediately impressed.

"Wow, Rob. That's fast service. I was under the impression that we would have to wait all day." We find the doctor behind her desk with approximately fifty patient folders piled in front of her. For a moment, I am back in my office sitting in front of my own tower of patient files, all of which need chiropractic treatment plans that will take me hours to write. I know how she feels. I've been there. I give her a big smile, and just when I start to open my mouth, she shoos us both out of the room and tells us to return on Friday morning. Before we walk out the door, she suggests we show up before five AM if we want a spot in line.

Two days later, we wake up super early and make sure we are at the clinic before dawn. There are already six people sitting along the side of the road in front of the gate. I have no choice but to join my amigos and sit down next to them.

"When do they open?" I ask. The crowd shrugs; it could be seven or eight. It all depends when the staff decides to show up.

It has been a long time since I sat on the street for any length of time. But it does give you a fascinating perspective from which to observe what is going on around you. All in all, it is not the worst place to be on a Friday morning—sitting under a palm tree only two hundred feet from the beach. In fact, my sister might just consider this a vacation. I can already hear her voice in my head:

You want to know what I did this morning? I wrestled your niece for twenty minutes so she'd brush her teeth. Do you have any idea how strong a four year old is? She could rip a phonebook in half. And I did it without the sound of the ocean or one palm tree in sight.

I watch as people walk and bike to work at a leisurely pace. The guides gather their horses for the day's beach tour while ATVs offer rides to pretty girls dressed up for work. Scrappy stray dogs pause in front of the crowd and entertain us with their antics. It is a complete one hundred and eighty degree shift from my old life.

While I was working back in the states, I stopped every morning at a gas station to get a cup of coffee. We were a sorry looking lot, stumbling around like a scene from *Night of the Living Dead*. I could practically hear my fellow zombies moaning in the Krispy Kreme aisle. It was just a matter of time before we all turned and ate each other's faces off.

Mornings don't feel the same here. Everyone looks happy. Not jump-up-and-down-hysterical happy, just a calmness that radiates as they stop to talk with others waiting for the bus. I thought Grecia had a slow pace, but beach towns in Costa Rica practically turn back time.

Overall, this is an interesting way to watch the morning unfold—sitting on the side of the road with two stray dogs at my feet, even if it is to see a doctor about surgery.

Turn & Cough

After a couple hours of waiting, a woman dressed in white scrubs opens the gate and we all file in. We start forming a line directly in front of the reception window. I glance at a piece of paper taped to the wall which says the doctor will only see six people today. Our lack of Spanish makes it difficult to understand why there are thirty-five people sitting here totally unfazed by this news.

"That can't be right," I tell Rob. "What doctor treats six people a day?" I point to the sign and ask the person in front of me if this is true. The woman nods her head in agreement. "That sucks, there are already six people in front of us."

"I don't care, I'm not going anywhere. We've been through stuff like this a dozen times. You can't give up right away." Rob is right. It's amazing how often I want to wave the white flag. But people immediately seem to like my husband, and hopefully the doctor remembers she told him to come back today.

We wait in line for another hour until the receptionist props open the window and takes everyone's name. The doctor is nowhere in sight so we all sit on long wooden benches under the aluminum covered patio. I can already feel the cool morning air lift and the heat of the day taking its place. It's going to be a scorcher.

One hour passes… then two… then four. I try sitting on the bench, but after a while I begin to get sore. With no other choice, I stand for the next couple hours. Sitting along the side of the road was actually the most comfortable place, and I would return there if it wasn't in the hot sun. As we are all waiting, a delightful older man entertains the crowd with a stand-up routine. I don't get the jokes, but judging by the audience reaction, he is the Costa Rican Chris Rock. Everyone erupts with laughter as he does impressions of someone. I hope it's not the doctor. I'm not in the "top six" so I don't want the doctor to show up thinking I'm laughing at her expense.

After five hours, Rob talks to the receptionist to remind her we are still waiting. She smiles and nods her head. Meanwhile, a man rides up on his scooter with a large, padlocked container secured to the back. He reaches into it, grabs multiple boxes, and walks into the clinic. I watch as a window on the other side of the building opens. A bunch of people walk up and form a line.

"Should we be on that line too?" I question. It turns out he is the pharmacist and most of the people waiting are here for their monthly supply of medications.

As each person approaches the window, small talk ensues with the pharmacist. Everything in Costa Rica is centered around community interaction. The pharmacist spends time with each client before giving out their medication. All the pills come in sealed strips; he never has to count individual tablets into a bottle.

This continues until a pretty girl is next in line. My friendly pharmacist quickly transforms into Antonio Banderas, taking on the seductive voice and mannerisms of the actor. I've seen this before, how fast the Latino men slide their hands through their thick, black hair while laughing at something an attractive woman says. The girl blushes, takes her bag, and throws a kiss back to the man. I tell Rob he better turn on the charm for the doctor. Antonio might be out of his reach, but he can do a pretty good Vinnie Barbarino from *Welcome Back Carter*. Unfortunately, I think that makes me Horshack.

Finally, after six hours, Rob reminds the receptionist once again that we are still waiting. He leans in and chats it up with the lady, making funny faces, and tries to do a John Travolta imitation that ends up sounding more like Joe Pesci in *My Cousin Vinny*. "Work it, Rob, work it," I say to myself. The lady giggles and waves us through to see the doctor.

While in her office, Rob describes his injury, using his uniquely patented combination of Spanish and charades. He goes into what looks like a professional bodybuilder's routine, flexing his muscles, doing squats, before reaching his groin and making a face that looks less like a man who ripped open a hernia but more like one who's significantly constipated. The doctor leans back in her chair and watches as he repeats his performance; alternating between lunges and shoulder presses before dramatically concluding by grabbing his gut and wrinkling his face.

The doctor writes some notes (probably a grocery list), and tells Rob to take down his shorts. One would assume Rob would have prepared himself for this but his eyes bolt out of his head much like Marie's did after her unfortunate shower electrocution.

"What... okay... but..."

"For heaven's sake, Rob, drop your shorts," I snap. All I keep thinking is we are number seven. The rug can be pulled out from under us at any time.

Rob yanks his shorts down as the doctor gives him the cough and squeeze test. Dodgeball comes to mind while I watch her aggressively fondle my husband. She nods her head. We were right; apparently, my husband's nuts are broken and he needs to have hernia surgery. She writes a script for us to see a specialist at Nicoya Hospital, but we have to go there in person to make an appointment. The hospital is over an hour away. It has been a long day but we head out, knowing the system takes a long time and we want to try to get the ball—no pun intended—rolling.

It's a beautiful day and I try to stay upbeat as we drive to the hospital. "You looked a little nervous in her office. If you had any idea the embarrassment women go through when they have to see a doctor. What's the big deal?"

"It was weird. She was all over me, digging in there, I didn't expect that."

"What did you expect, a Hallmark card?"

"No. It's just… do you think it looked okay?"

"What looked okay?"

"My stuff. It was really cold in there."

"You can't be serious? What did you want, time for hair and makeup? You're unbelievable." I'm trying to have sympathy for my injured husband, but all I want to do now is pull over and push him out of the car. "And she wasn't all over you, she did an *exam,* Rob. She's a doctor, not a blind date. And they looked fine if that's what you need to hear."

"Just making sure."

We make it to the hospital, which initially looks beautiful. Palm trees planted outside sway in the breeze and a large awning shades us as we walk inside. The room is completely empty except for one woman behind a computer. There is no air conditioning and it has that open-air feeling you get everywhere you go in Costa Rica. However, as nice as it looks on the outside, the inside appears worn and dark. The walls are covered in chipped paint, and I start getting a pit in my stomach. We show the receptionist our script and she scribbles down an appointment to see the surgeon in two weeks.

"Not so bad," Rob says. "I thought we would have to wait months for an appointment. And look around, there is no one here. I bet we will be in and out of here when we meet the doctor. Finally, a place without a line."

However, when we return two weeks later it is standing room only. At least seventy-five people are waiting to see the doctor. There is a mix of women with babies and seniors in wheelchairs. It reminds me of a busy emergency room in New York City. I imagine there must be some reason why we are all packed in here, a place with no air conditioning and blistering hot.

We hand the receptionist our appointment card but she is busy putting on two layers of black mascara. After putting her make-up away, and a few minutes to gossip with the other girl behind the desk, she instructs us to go to another office to get our file made. Her careful application of cosmetics suggests she has a considerable amount of time on her hands, and perhaps she could make the file herself. But, like always, there is no suggestion box.

When we return with our manila file, we find two open seats. There are five doors in front of us for different categories of care. One door looks like it leads to an OB-GYN doctor, whereas another door leads toward geriatric care. The door we are watching is for surgical consults. I stare at it nervously, hoping not to miss the moment when they call my husband's name.

It always amazes me how calm and patient Costa Ricans are. In this hot and inhospitable environment, we all wait our turn. There is no television to watch or any magazines to read. We just sit here. The only diversions are the numerous vendors selling candy and popcorn that are balanced on their heads. It is as if we are all waiting for a matinee to start.

After three hours, we hear a nurse shout *ROBERTO*. I jump up and race to the door, relieved they did not forget about us. We enter the room and meet a short roly-poly shaped doctor. He asks Rob numerous health-related questions, some in Spanish, others in English. He gives him the cough and grab test, much more gently than the previous female doctor. He is almost romantic in his approach. I want to dim the lights and give them time to cuddle. I am happy for Rob; finally, a doctor who is sympathetic to his plight.

"Si, you need an operation," he says as he opens the desk drawer and whips out a Winnie the Pooh notebook. He opens it up and schedules Rob's surgery.

In the… Winnie the Pooh… Notebook.

I try not to be judgmental. I've lived here long enough to keep an open mind, but having a major surgery scheduled in a notebook with Piglet and Eeyore on the cover did nothing to ease my fear of Rob getting cut open in a foreign hospital. However, I look on the bright side: at least he didn't write down the appointment with a glitter pen.

"I can't believe we have a date set in just three weeks. I was under the impression I'd have to wait at least six months. It's all going to work out," Rob insists as we leave the hospital.

I, in turn, make a mental note to buy the doctor an appointment book that is not adorned with Disney characters.

Catheters, Blood Work & Burger King

We return to the hospital three weeks later where we check in with the receptionist. However, instead of preparing a hospital bed, she reprimands us for not showing up to the La Chala. Clearly, something has been lost in translation.

"What the heck is a La Chala?" I ask. Although I do not understand her response, I can tell she is not happy with us. All I do know is we now have another appointment to come back in a week. We are told we have to attend a "La Chala" or we cannot get the surgery.

"Maybe it's blood work and stuff like that," Rob says.

"I think we should go to San Jose. I don't feel good about this whole thing. I just can't figure any of it out. And come on, the surgeon scheduled the surgery in a Winnie the Pooh notebook. Maybe that's a sign we should go someplace else."

"I don't care what he wrote it in. What do you need to see, a complicated computer scheduling program? They don't have the money for that here, and that doesn't mean he's a bad surgeon. Stay the course. We will come back and do whatever they want us to."

When we return for the La Chala, we are told to go into another room where metal chairs are lined up and a long wooden bench is against a far wall. There are over eighty people either sitting or standing around staring at the front of the room. We find two places at the end of the wooden bench and stare ahead like everyone else. I can't even begin to imagine why we are here.

A man comes in and sets up a laptop and projector. It appears we are going to have a PowerPoint presentation. When he turns on the computer, the projector displays his screensaver on the wall. It's a wintery Alaskan scene with snow-tipped mountains and frozen lakes. It's amusing how most people in the states have a beachy, palm tree scene on their work computers, a picture that helps them daydream of hammocks and piña coladas. Here, this guy has skiing and ice skating on his mind.

A nurse stands in front of the crowd and starts talking to the group. She holds up antiseptic, bandages, and catheter bags. She takes the catheter bag and handles it like a model on *Let's Make A Deal*. Oh boy. I think she's telling me I have to remove Rob's catheter bag myself. If my husband thought he had it rough with the female doctor, he's really in for it now.

"What is she doing with that?" Rob asks.

"I think you are getting a catheter." Instantaneously, all the blood rushes out of his face. Rob looks back at the nurse, then at me, and proceeds to stutter. "No way... I'm not... no... sorry... I'm not getting a catheter. Absolutely not going to happen."

"You don't have a choice. When you are in surgery, they stick one in." It's only now that I see fear splash across my husband's face. Not from getting his abdomen cut open, the threat of infection, or staying for three days in a Central American hospital. He's freaking out about the catheter procedure. "And to make it worse," I say as I lean in for dramatic purposes, "I think they want me to take it out."

"Are you out of your mind? Why would they want you to do that? I'll take it out before I let you do it. Oh God, is it getting hot in here?"

My husband is one minute shy of passing out on this hospital floor.

I hear someone speaking English in the hall and run out to ask what this meeting is all about; specifically, if I will be yanking a catheter out of my husband.

"Oh my," the nurse laughs. "No. This is just to explain how things work, let everyone know how to care for a wound, reminding them to always wash their hands, and the warning signs that require you to alert a doctor immediately. She is showing everyone the catheter because most of the time one is inserted into a patient when surgery is performed." Now I understand. The doctors don't have the time to explain procedures and all the care that is involved to each individual patient. Instead, they make everyone show up at the same time to get this lecture. It makes perfect sense. This is a health care system for the entire population, and money needs to be reserved for actual care. By getting everyone in the same room, it saves the doctor valuable time that can be used to see other patients. I explain this all to Rob before he crashes to the floor and Mascara Lady gives him mouth-to-mouth.

"Did you ask her if I need a catheter?"

"All good news. You won't need one. Too bad, I was so looking forward to pulling it out." I can't help but lie. Rob will obsess about this and I'm afraid he'll call off the surgery just because of the catheter. Slowly the color returns to his face as he leans back against the wall. We continue to watch as the nurse shows everyone how to wash their hands and replace a bandage. She then grabs the catheter bag and makes a joke about sex which has the entire room laughing. The men all look at their wives and smile. I laugh too, even though I don't get it. I'm in Central America watching a catheter stand-up routine. Priceless.

After the presentation, Rob gets in line to get his blood work drawn. For as tough as my husband thinks he is, he can't stand needles. The thought of getting stuck is already giving him anxiety.

"It'll be okay," I reassure him as people are quickly going in and out of the little rooms.

"They are going so fast, I hope I don't pass out. It'll be so embarrassing if I pass out."

Not long ago we had to get blood work done so we could renew our Costa Rican driver's licenses. All motor vehicle needed was our blood type, but the lab required us to provide a whole tube of blood. Rob got so pale that the young girls circled him, trying to make him feel better. One even went so far as to get him a glass of orange Tang. As he was valiantly sipping his drink, no one appeared overly concerned on how I was faring. Rob relaxed for the next ten minutes with a cold compress on his head while I was escorted to the waiting room. No beverages were offered.

Today, the hospital is quickly going through dozens of people. When it is Rob's turn, he walks in the room and returns less than a minute later. "That was the best phlebotomist. He was so fast, I didn't even feel the prick."

I'm glad this day is over and we are one step closer to getting the hernia surgery.

"Are you hungry? I could go for a Whopper," Rob suggests. With lightning speed, he forgets about catheters and blood work and pulls into a Burger King on the way home. I've never seen a man so easily distracted by onion rings.

Surgery & Tommy Walnuts

After enduring a day of sitting on the side of the road, watching Rob get fondled, missing the La Chala, and then attending the La Chala, it is finally the day of the surgery. We report to the admissions office and take ten minutes to fill out the remaining paperwork. This step may have been accelerated by the fact that we could not understand a word of it. We are directed to the emergency ward where Rob is instructed to go into a utility closet and change into a pair of scrubs.

"In there?" Rob asks.

"Si." The man opens the door for Rob and he disappears inside what appears to be a broom closet. Perhaps we will be doing some janitorial work to pay for this operation. Rob then walks out wearing an ill-fitting green, scrub ensemble with numbers stamped across his chest. The pants are too short and the top doesn't even cover his navel. My husband looks less like a surgical patient and more like a gay prison inmate.

"What do you think?" Rob asks.

"I'm thinking I want to erase this image from my memory."

Rob returns to the closet and walks out again. He's wearing a different pair but they barely cover his abdomen. The orderly says it's their biggest size and he will have to make do. Rob then sits in a wheelchair and is taken to the hospital ward, a large room with about twenty beds and no dividing curtains. The screenless windows at the top of the room are all open. This allows the breeze—and later the heat—to creep through. Little lizards jump around the ceiling darting in and out. It reminds me of the television series *MASH*, and I am all but ready to see Hawkeye and Hot Lips Houlihan saunter on through.

Rob gets a bed next to a young guy who had a motorcycle accident. His entire leg is bandaged and propped up on a few pillows. He has a woman by his side holding his hand and wiping sweat off his forehead. I leave to use the communal bathroom where I find no toilet seats or toilet paper, a predicament far more unappealing than having to pull a catheter out of Rob's wiener.

An hour later, our roly-poly doctor walks in, his Winnie the Pooh appointment book under his arm. He introduces us to another doctor who is a dead ringer for a Spanish Groucho Marx. He is wearing jeans and a collared shirt. It must be casual Friday.

"This is your surgeon. He is from Mexico and very good," he says.

Rob is quick to respond, "The best doctor I'm sure. Nice to meet you."

"Rob, how do I know this guy even has a medical license?" I whisper after Groucho walks away. "I want to find his office and look at his diplomas."

"Don't you dare," he threatens. "You're going to tick him off. Whether we like it or not, this guy is doing the surgery, I don't want him to have a grudge against me while he's working near my junk."

"Then I'll be nonchalant, just look like I'm lost, and take a peek to see if his credentials are hanging in his office."

"No."

"I'll knock on his door and ask a question."

"No!"

I am sick to my stomach. I'm beginning to have buyer's remorse, even before Rob gets the surgery. I can't imagine a good outcome. So many bad images come to my mind that I start to hyperventilate. I think I'm having a panic attack.

"Please, I'm going to be fine, stop worrying. Listen, it's all going to be over in a few days. What's the worst that can happen?" Rob's ability to be optimistic in the face of great odds is incredible. He is calmer now than at the La Chala.

"I love you," I say before leaving. His surgery will be the next morning and I plan to be there as early as possible.

"I'm more worried about you, it's raining outside. Just get home safe. Don't speed. Don't pull over for anything. Go straight home. Make sure you lock all the doors. I'm going to see if I can find a phone so I can call you. Please, please go slow and take your time."

"I know how to drive Rob. Just rest. I'll be fine." I give him one last kiss and leave. The rain really begins to pour so I drive extra slow all the way home. I feel numb and pray that tomorrow will go well. The minute I walk through the door, I hear the phone ring. Rob borrowed a cell phone and is already checking in on me.

The morning of the operation, I sneak into the hospital early and go straight to the surgery ward. I glance over at Rob's bed but he is not there. I turn to the motorcycle guy, who curiously has a different woman at his side holding his hand. I am trying to speak Spanish, but the right words won't come out. He doesn't understand me so I get even more anxious. I panic and blurt out "Is Roberto dead?"—the perfect amount of optimism for a situation such as this.

106

"Que? No… Nooooooo," he says. He mimics getting his side cut open. It's at this time I hear moaning in the hall. A few seconds later, Rob is wheeled back into the room.

"Does it hurt?" I lean over him as one would a wounded soldier in battle.

"Holy shit… yes… shit…. shit… wow…"

This is one of the few times I've ever witnessed Rob so vulnerable. He is in a tremendous amount of pain and needs me more than ever. With these factors in mind, I do what any wife would do in this situation…. I start bawling all over him. Not the pretty cry, which I am prone to do at the end of a sappy movie. *Women, you know the one I am talking about.* The ugly cry. The snotty, double shoulder pump cry; the one where your face looks like Ernest Borgnine while your shoulders spastically bounce up and down.

A nurse wearing a cute white cap, the kind of hat nurses wore in those old *Ben Casey* episodes, tries to console me and tell me all the things I need to do to help. I notice she is carrying a Dora the Explorer file folder, which in turn causes me to collapse once again over Rob in a display that can only be compared to someone draping a corpse before the coffin is closed. It is quite a scene.

"Honey, calm down, I'm okay. But you really need to get the hell off me, you're lying across my stitches."

"I'm sorry… you look like you're in pain. I just want to help."

"Start by calming down and asking if I can have some pain medication." I try to pull myself together but I am overcome. I was terrified of him dying, and now I am terrified that he may never recover. Moreover, I can't understand one thing anyone is saying. For the little Spanish I've learned, none of it includes medical terms. The nurse talks so fast I can only understand every fourth or fifth word. Eventually, she gets frustrated and walks away. I don't blame the nurse; she has plenty of other patients to tend to who have no problems understanding her.

Finally, I pull myself together and ask for pain medication at the front desk. "No," she says. "He had a shot already and he'll get another one later." I calmly inform Rob he will not be getting another shot until eight o'clock that night.

"Are you kidding me? Shouldn't I be on a morphine drip? It feels like they're just giving me a shot of Tylenol."

"I don't know what to do. If you want me to go demand that you get something stronger, I'll go back there and start yelling at someone."

"No. Maybe it's for the best. I'm just going to stay perfectly still. I can't even imagine how this is an out-patient procedure in the states. How do people get out of the bed to go home?"

"Apparently, they get more than a shot."

"Well, I guess I'm not going anywhere anytime soon. I'll probably be here for the full three days. Man, it hurts like hell. Before the surgery, the anesthesiologist told me I must stay calm when I wake up on the gurney. I told the doctor *no problema*. I flexed my bicep and said *muy tranquillo*. I don't know what they did to me in that operating room, but when I woke up I was screaming *DRUGA DRUGA DRUGA* and trying to pull out my breathing tube. I guess I'm not as tough as I thought."

I am glad to see my husband still has his sense of humor.

"Thankfully, I didn't eat anything," Rob continues. "I couldn't even imagine having a bowel movement right now. Not a chance."

A lack of food for two days is not the only thing keeping Rob from going to the men's room. It has come to my attention that men have a prevailing fear of performing a bowel movement in a public bathroom. Since they get the luxury of standing to urinate, they rarely have to go through the many indignities that women do. Women have to deal with unseemly toilet seats all the time... men do not. So now that Rob is confined to a hospital ward and sharing a bathroom with other patients, he has devised a plan. And like many of his schemes, he consulted his friend Tommy Walnuts from Brooklyn, a man who had the misfortune of landing in Central Booking on a four day weekend for outstanding traffic tickets.

"Man, trust me. Don't eat anything," Tommy Walnuts advised. "Do you know what Central Booking is like? A cell full of the craziest guys from the neighborhood with only one toilet in the middle of the room. You don't want to crap around these maniacs. Whatever you do bro, don't get caught with your pants around your ankles." Rob takes his advice and tries to figure out how to not go to the bathroom for four days. You can always count on Tommy to provide guidance on such pressing matters.

Rob also took Tommy's advice when they were seventeen and picked up two girls on 86th street in Brooklyn. They were supposed to drop them off at Fort Hamilton, but in-between flirting with them, Rob missed the exit and wound up on the Verrazano Bridge. No one had any money for the toll, so Tommy Walnuts convinced Rob to pull a U-Turn… on the bridge.

"I don't know Tommy. It's rush hour."

"Come on, everybody does it. Look, there's a break in the median." Rob pulled in, and waited for traffic to ease up.

"You got it," Tommy said.

"Are you sure?"

"Yes, go, you got it."

Rob put the pedal all the way to the floor but the car stalled. However, his Nova had just enough momentum to get into the far right lane. A second later, a brand new Lincoln Continental Limousine rear ended them, shooting radiator fluid into the air and all over the road. The only damage to the Nova was that the bumper dropped about half an inch. The limousine was completely totaled.

"Go, go, go!" Tommy and the girls screamed.

"Uh, but I just got my license. I think I'm supposed to stay."

"No way, you don't want to stay here, just go," Tommy yelled. Rob pulled away only to be chased by a car full of blue-haired, old ladies who witnessed the accident. With NASCAR-like maneuvers, they ran him off the road at the following exit.

While waiting for the police, Tommy noticed the girls giggling, whispering, and scheming. A few moments later, one of them blurted out "Do you have good car insurance? My neck hurts." The second girl was quick to chime in, "Mine too. It's killing me. I need a lawyer."

"You need a lawyer?" Tommy said. "Don't you mean a doctor?" He then leaned in and whispered something to the girls. Suddenly, they no longer had neck pain and decided to leave before the police arrived. It was the quickest whiplash recovery ever recorded on the side of a highway.

Once at the scene, an officer called Rob the dumbest kid in Brooklyn for making a U-Turn on the Verrazano Bridge. To confirm that distinction, he wrote Rob over a thousand dollars in tickets, causing his insurance to double that year. Now, when we are stopped at a stop sign and I say, "You got it," I get to hear this Tommy Walnuts story again and again. It's the gift that keeps on giving.

Taking Tommy's Central Booking story into consideration, Rob only consumed a few glasses of a chocolate protein shake the night before the surgery. He has vowed not to have a bowel movement for the full three days he is in the hospital.

"Did you bring the protein powder?" he asks.

"Yes. And I brought a whole goody bag full of stuff: soap, toilet paper, anti-germ gel, a fan, and your mp3 player." I was responsible for all of these things and made sure not to forget any of them. Especially the fan; it gets really hot in the afternoon. I feel so bad for Rob I want to do whatever it takes to get him through these next few days.

I stick around and watch some dramatic soap operas with the nurses. The girls swoon as the leading man kisses his wife while she lies in a coma. It looks like she's not going to make it; the husband is holding her hand and crying. One nurse takes a tissue and dabs her eye. I too get a little weepy and I lean over to give Rob a kiss on the forehead. I couldn't imagine my life without him. He, in turn, hands me a jug of urine, the size of which one might use to irrigate an entire corn field.

"Please don't tell me that whole thing is filled with pee."

"Yup."

"I suppose I have to get rid of it?"

"Yup."

"But there isn't a lid."

"I know."

I gingerly empty the contents in the bathroom and when I return I notice motorcycle guy has a different woman at his bedside. Rob informs me he is married but appears to have an admirable amount of female friends. And when I'm not there, this harem of women helps Rob by getting a nurse or helping him out of bed.

Throughout the day, I watch as people come in and out cleaning the floor and disinfecting the beds. For all that this hospital lacks, it turns out to be an incredibly clean place. The janitor even gets on his knees and washes not only the plastic-lined mattress, but the metal frame beneath it as well. He takes his time and hits every crevice of the bed. I am impressed by his dedication to his job. It becomes apparent where the allocated budget is spent. It is not on newly painted walls or private rooms, but on things that actually matter. I am always surprised how much I am willing to leave behind, but at the same time, expect things to be just like the United States. But if this was the United States, we would be paying twenty thousand dollars for the surgery. We pay nothing in Costa Rica.

The next morning I return to find Rob in better spirits. He still can't move around much, but the color in his face is coming back. It probably helps that he is no longer dealing with a hysterical wife.

"It was crazy last night, the male nurses came in and played dominos for three hours. And throughout the night, female nurses kept coming in and pulling up my gown to look at the scar."

"That doesn't sound unreasonable. They have to look at it."

"No, I mean a group of ten, young female nurses. They come in and check out my stuff. They leave giggling. It's like bad hospital porn."

"They are probably in training. I doubt they are giggling. You're just imaging it." Five minutes later a group of nurses march into the room and walk over to Rob. The obvious boss out of the bunch tells the girls about the hernia surgery, grabs Rob's gown, and lifts it while the trainees take a gander. And it is an impressive gander. The head nurse points to Rob's crotch, telling the girls to get closer for a better look. The girls look wide-eyed, nod professionally, but as they walk away I can see the nurses in the back giggle. Wow... this *is* bad hospital porn.

"It's all so weird. Last night I'm listening to "Parris Island" by Billy Joel on my headphones and looking at the lizards running in and out through the windows. The words were about going through a terrible experience together. I felt like I was in Vietnam." Rob has grown fond of his motorcycle friend so the lyrics really hit home. I also think he is getting a little nutty from being confined to a hospital bed for days. "Hey, since you're here, go get my buddy and I a grape soda." I look over at motorcycle guy and yet another woman is helping him. She props up his broken leg and begins to stroke his face.

Between young interns looking at his crotch, me running around for him, and the motorcycle guy's many girlfriends helping him out of bed, this whole hospital stay isn't so bad for Rob. No wonder he is in pleasant spirits this morning. He's got it pretty good here. If only there was a toilet seat, he might never leave.

On his last day, Rob is finally handed discharge papers. They include a slip to return so Rob can get his stitches removed. We are given a bunch of antibiotics, Tylenol, and told to go to the discharge office. There a nice older man asks us how our visit went. He is happy that things turned out well and dismisses us with nothing more than a handshake. I am all but tempted to give the hospital a Tripadvisor.com review.

"Great all-inclusive. Staff was friendly and helpful. Although no swim up bar, they do have an active night life. Ask for the four day/ three night special. You can't beat the price."

What have I learned from this experience? My initial first impressions were wrong. All the things that I thought were bad actually turned out to be good. The open windows that allowed little lizards to come in also allowed a constant breeze of fresh air and the soothing sounds of rain. Unlike in the states, where infectious air continuously recirculates throughout the ventilation system, this breeze stifles unwanted bacteria and keeps the place free from unpleasant odors.

Without curtains you had little privacy. However, it was easier for other visitors to see if you needed assistance. Everyone helped everyone. This built a sense of community and freed up the staff to care for other patients.

The many interruptions while Rob tried to sleep also kept the nurses on top of their patients. Rob noticed no one sat in a dirty diaper or went for a long time without someone checking on them. They had a high level of care even though there were limited resources.

There was less pain medication, but they did give enough to get by. It made Rob aware of what he could and could not do. Maybe the trend of out-patient surgeries has gone too far. Drugging someone to the point where they can't feel their limitations and then sending them home may not always the best solution.

In addition, although you had to bring your our own soap and toilet paper, the surgery didn't cost anything. I am sure many people in the states would be happy to bring their own supplies if they could just get the surgery they needed. It wouldn't take much for people to volunteer these items to those who couldn't afford them.

In the end, I am grateful for many things: to the Costa Rican government for allowing us into their health care system, the other Ticos who helped care for my husband along with their own ailing relative, the nurses who giggled at Rob's crotch, and for Groucho Marx, our skilled surgeon. The process taught me not to judge a book by its cover… even if the surgery is scheduled in a Winnie the Pooh notebook.

I turn to Rob and give him a big smile. "You know what? You were right about this whole thing. It all worked out." I help him out to the parking lot and open the car door for him. As I walk around the front of our car, I notice someone stole my license plate.

It *almost* all worked out.

Removing Stitches & YouTube Videos

While Rob is healing from the surgery, I spend the next couple weeks working on the book. I'm stuck on trying to figure out how to format it into an electronic version. Every time I think I've got it down, it spits back chapters that resemble Egyptian hieroglyphics.

I also need to come up with the most important thing in this venture: a book cover. It will make or break the success of the book and I know nothing about designing one. All I have is a basic Photoshop program and I barely know how to use it. Eventually, I come up with a cover that I believe is presentable and I email it over to my sister for her advice.

"It stinks," she says.

"Really? Did you look at it carefully? I thought it was pretty good."

"I would never buy this book. Why is there a big flower on the cover? At first glance, it looks like a poetry book."

"But I worked on it for weeks."

"I don't care if you worked on it for a year. Do you want me to lie to you? If something stinks, you need to know. And if you can't take any criticism now, how are you going to handle it when the book comes out?"

"I don't have any other cover ideas. I'm lost. I'm not even sure I remember how I made this crappy cover."

"You have a lot of good pictures. Why don't you use the shot of the dog sitting on the beach watching the surfers? It's one of my favorites."

"It was taken at Playa Bejuco when Marie and Scott came to visit. It never occurred to me to use it."

"I like how he's looking out at the surfers, waiting for his owner to come back. And with the palm trees framing it, I think it's perfect for a book cover. Now I have to run. Do you know your niece told me ten minutes ago that I have to make one hundred cupcakes by tomorrow?" I have not had a conversation with my sister in ten years that has not ended with her rushing off to pull an upside down child out of couch cushions, run a bath that is never for herself, or prepare a meal that at least one child refuses to eat, and more often than not, these things all occur simultaneously.

Now that I take a closer look at this cover, my sister is right. It stinks. I can't believe I spent so long on it and it still looks terrible. I feel like tossing the whole project. As many times I feel inspired to continue, there are an equal number of times I want to quit. It's in these moments my mind conjures up all the reasons I should. Why complicate my life when I came to Costa Rica to simplify it? Why do I think I could be successful at this when so many others have failed? My mind races until I'm ready to throw in the towel. I'm close to taking my manuscript and burying it at the bottom of my sock drawer.

I erase the book cover from my computer, but before I close the Photoshop program I open up the picture of the dog on the beach. I can remember taking this shot. It was an incredibly sweet moment; a surfer and his faithful dog.

Maybe this dog simply sitting on the beach is what really describes the book; a small thing that represents my move and search for a happier life. This dog was living for the moment. Happy to be enjoying what's on the beach and ready for his owner to ride a wave back to shore. He is happier than most humans I know. I decide to use that as my cover but I can't work on it now. I have to drive Rob to the hospital to get his stitches removed. So far everything has gone as planned with his recovery. There have been no signs of infection and Rob is able to walk around with little pain. However, he still is under doctor's orders not to lift weights for five months. I can see Rob is already getting antsy.

We walk into the busy hospital room and are greeted by Mascara Lady once again. Today she is busy putting on lip liner. I hand her our slip from the doctor and she tells us we need to come back in three months.

"Well, that sounds wonderful, but my husband has stitches that need to come out this week." She shrugs her shoulders and finishes drawing the line around her mouth. Rob disappears to find someone who can translate for us. Perhaps Miss Maybelline doesn't understand the situation. A nurse walks over and explains our predicament to the receptionist.

"She says to come back in three months, you missed your appointment this morning," the nurse replies.

"I'm just going to take them out myself," Rob states.

"No, I wouldn't do that," the nurse says. "Have you thought about going back to the local clinic?"

"Last time I was there I waited six hours to see the doctor. I'm not going to waste time when I can just take them out myself." We thank the nurse and head back to our car.

"You don't really mean that?" I ask.

"I sure do."

"Seriously? You're going to take out your own stitches?"

"No, *you're* taking out my stitches."

"Oh no. No way Rob. Those are abdominal stitches. It's not like one or two in your finger. I'm not doing it. Nope. Forget about it."

"Okay, then I will. I can barely see them, but I'll do it anyway."

I can't believe this. I just want to go back to the local clinic and have the doctor remove them, but Rob doesn't want to wait. I give him all the reasons we why I shouldn't do it, listing the things I have broken over the past six months, how I trip and fall almost daily, and even reminding him how bad my eyesight is. "You see how close I have to sit in front of the television. And night driving? Forget it. I almost drove into a mango tree the other day. I'm just about legally blind. I can't even thread a needle. In fact, I think my eyesight is fading as we speak." Rob nods his head, agrees to everything I'm saying, and pulls into the first parking space in front of a pharmacy.

Rob speaks with the pharmacist and discusses Operation Stitch Removal. As always, our Spanish stinks so Rob resorts to pulling down his pants and showing the woman his scar. He pretends to hold a pair of scissors as he cuts out his stitches. It's clear there is no end to the number of women who will get a glimpse of my husband's nether regions.

She gathers supplies and piles them on the counter: surgical gloves, bandages, antiseptic, and a pair of cuticle scissors. She appears generally concerned about what we are attempting to do and even hands us a pamphlet on washing our hands to prevent the spread of germs. I appreciate her attention. Before we are about to pay, she adds a large bottle of Ibuprofen. I'm touched by the gesture.

Once home, I lay the equipment out on our kitchen table like a heart surgeon. And like any professional would do when preparing for such an important procedure, I watch a sixty second YouTube video on how to remove stitches. It gives me the marginal amount of confidence I was hoping for.

"I swear Rob, never, ever, ask me to do this for you again."

"Just do it."

"Okay, I'm looking at them. Wow, they are thick."

"Don't talk, just cut."

"You know, there are a heck of a lot of them."

"Why are you still talking? Can't you see I'm holding my breath? Get in there and take them out."

I think back to the one minute instructional video I watched and locate the area on the stitch right below the knot. I snip it and pull it out with my sterilized tweezers.

"Wow, I did it. I got one. Did it hurt?"

"No, but it felt really weird. Just cut the rest and don't stop. I don't need a play-by-play."

I go in and repeat the procedure. Things are going well until I snip one and before I can pull it out, it gets sucked back into his scar and disappears.

"Hmm…"

"What is it? What happened?"

"We just had a casualty, Rob."

"A casualty?"

"Uh… I lost one. I cut it but it kinda disappeared into your scar. What do you think will happen?"

"How the hell do I know? Just be more careful when you take out the rest." But the last few do the same thing. Somewhere in Rob's body, three stitches are floating around. They didn't discuss this scenario in YouTube nursing school.

"I've got good and bad news. We lost a few but the rest are out. I wouldn't worry about it, eventually they will come to the surface. Right? I mean, where can they go?" I put ointment on the wound and re-bandage the area.

Overall, I think I did a good job. I kept the wound clean, the equipment was sterilized, and Rob suffered little discomfort. In the end, no one needed the big jar of Ibuprofen and for the first time in Rob's medical history, absolutely no duct tape was used.

Can I Get a Water Letter?

Rob's scar is healing and he feels well enough to return to the municipality and continue our quest for permits. There has got to be a way to get this water letter.

It's not crowded at the municipality and we are the first at the counter. Rob greets the man and asks for a "vestido."

"Que? I'm sorry sir. I don't understand."

"Necessito una vestido," Rob repeats. I look at the man's face and understand his confusion. My husband just asked the guy for a dress. This exchange immediately puts me in a jolly mood.

"I need a vestido to build a house. I was told I can get a vestido here," Rob explains.

"I don't think you mean vestido…maybe you mean *visado*?"

"I pretty sure my architect said *vestido*."

"If that was the case, then you are asking for a dress. Do you want a dress, sir?"

Rob squints his eyes and turns to me. "Did you know I was asking for a dress?"

"Of course not." Since I've already been reprimanded for screwing up the words "punch" and "pay," I keep quiet and enjoy the sweet sound of Rob asking for women's clothing—twice. It's almost as good as him asking for directions to a Radio Shack in the jungle.

The clerk takes Rob's catastro and disappears. He comes back with a copy of it stamped with an official looking blue circle.

"This is a *visado*. This paper starts the permit process. Now you need to get soil samples and surveys done on the property. You also have to provide us a water letter."

"That's the problem. Where can we get one if we can't get it from the developer? Shouldn't there be someone in town to help us?"

The clerk looks over our catastro. "If you can show us an inspection of the well by the proper authorities, perhaps we can waive the water letter. The man in charge of the well inspections in your area should also be able to help you. I would speak with him first." He disappears for a few minutes and then comes back with an address. "Stop by and see what he says."

We follow the man's directions which takes us down an unpaved road. Our SUV kicks up a wicked dirt storm. Even though riding these roads can be fun on our scooter, the mouthful of dirt can be awfully unpleasant. I won't have to worry about that for a while; we're not driving the scooter until Rob fully recovers from his surgery.

The road winds around a small marina where a neighborhood of fishing boats and catamarans are secured offshore. A large, stuffed sailfish is anchored onto the building tempting you to try your luck at sport fishing. Typically, the waters in the Tropical Pacific are low in oxygen and are not suitable for sailfish. But something unique occurs a couple times a year. A current coming north from Chile collides with one coming south from California. These currents bring with it waters that are hospitable for sailfish. Along with powerful winds, the area outside Central America creates a unique pocket of water where sailfish congregate. There is no better chance at catching one then when these two conditions line up perfectly.

I would love to watch a sailfish jump out of the water, its purple-silver fins capturing the sunlight. They are the fastest fish in the ocean, leaping at speeds reaching sixty miles per hour. It must be a sight when the spear of its upper jaw shoots in the air like a harpoon.

Whenever I pass this stuffed fish it reminds me of Ernest Hemingway's *The Old Man and the Sea*; a story of luck, perseverance, and pride. The protagonist, Santiago, struggles for three days to capture a marlin, only to have it torn away and eaten by sharks in the end. When I look out across this tiny harbor, I imagine how many times that story has played out in this fishing village, how a tale of losing that great fish grows to become as big a part of the man as his own beating heart.

My memories of the Osa Peninsula flood back and I wish Marie and Scott were here. I can picture us as a group out on the water, taking turns reeling in the fish. I'm sure Rob could even negotiate another two-for-one excursion.

We drive through a small village of houses shaded by mango trees and towering palms. An ATV tour passes with the riders wearing handkerchiefs wrapped around their faces. I can see why these tours are popular. The bumpy roads must make it a thrilling adventure at first, but they all return with a crusty layer of dirt stuck to their sunburnt faces.

"Can these directions be right?" I ask as we pull up in front of a house. For some reason I thought it might be an office.

"I'm not sure, maybe he works from his home."

We walk up the pathway and the door is open. A man with no shirt is sleeping on the couch. Apparently, Rob is right; this *is* his home office.

"Señor... pardon," Rob shouts into the room, but the man keeps snoring while tucking one of his hands into his shorts.

"Maybe we should come back?" I interrupt.

"It's the middle of the afternoon and I'm not coming back just because this guy is taking a nap. Señor!"

The man finally opens his eyes and stares at us. He gives us a quick look, then rolls over to his side and goes back to sleep.

"Hey buddy. I'm not leaving so can you please get up?" Finally, an older woman comes into the room and yells at the man. He rubs his face and stumbles toward the door. It's clear this guy had a late night; he looks like someone stuffed peppermint candies into his eye sockets. Rob explains what we are here for and the man shakes his head. Before he goes into a long explanation, we call our lawyer and have him speak with him. The guy eventually gives us the phone back to Rob and lies back down on the couch. He sticks his other hand down his pants and goes back to sleep.

"The man told me he is not in charge of that development," our lawyer says.

"But this is the guy the municipality told us to meet with."

"He won't inspect the well since it is not technically part of his territory. I'm sorry."

"What do I do now?" Rob asks.

"You should go meet with the official Costa Rica water agency, AYA. They have an office in Liberia. In the meantime, get the survey of your property and soil samples. At least you can do that while you wait to hear about the water situation."

I feel like we are spinning in circles. No one knows what we should do, not even the municipality. But like always, Rob feels confident we will somehow find the right person who can help us.

On our way back, we pass the marina again. There is no breeze today and the catamarans remain motionless, barely bobbing along the current. The palm trees on the shore cast their reflections in the water, their images so still, at first glance you might believe they are tiny bridges connecting you to the boats in the distance.

Building this house will be as big a struggle as reeling in a sailfish. And like Santiago, I fear it will be eaten by sharks in the end.

"It won't be easy, that is why I have always failed where others have succeeded."

-Inspector Clouseau

I spend the next month designing the book cover and working on the final stages of formatting the book. It's the perfect time since Rob is finally getting back on his feet. He still can't lift weights, but otherwise he's doing really well. He's now back to his old self, staying busy and securing the house with four thousand motion sensors. He carefully places them to ensure an impenetrable barrier around the perimeter of our house. In order to make sure that every square inch of the property is secure, he sneaks around the house surprising me like Cato from *The Pink Panther*. This morning I'm sitting near a window when all of a sudden his head pops into the frame.

"Aha! We have a breach in security," he says.

"Will you stop doing that to me? I'm going to have a heart attack."

"But you see what just happened? I walked along the side of the house, crawled under this window, and tried to get in. The alarm never went off. You could have been victimized if it wasn't for my due diligence."

Rob's going to be victimized in a couple minutes if he doesn't leave me alone.

This is repeated a half-dozen times during the week. Sometimes he surprises me when I'm standing near the sliding glass doors, and other times when I walk outside to get something out of the car.

"Aha! You see how I snuck up behind you. If we had more motion sensors that would never have happened. Now I have to make sure this front area is secured."

"You're crazy Rob."

"I'm crazy like a fox. Remember, I'm doing this all because I love you." Rob apparently does a lot of things because he loves me: backs into water pipes, lifts weights with a bulging hernia, and demands that I yank out abdominal stitches. I fear what my life would look like if he didn't love me.

I'm trying to enjoy our new home but I'm on guard all the time; not due to an intruder but because of my nutty husband. I call Tommy Walnuts and complain that security is turning into Rob's fulltime job.

"Tommy, he's completely obsessed."

"Finally, a hobby that blends perfectly with his paranoia," Tommy laughs. "Nadine, he's been like this since he was seventeen years old. There is nothing you can do to change him."

"I just wish he would relax and stop worrying about it for a while. I know he was robbed while driving car service, but why does everything have to be about security all the time?"

"Rob was like this long before car service. He started getting twisted after someone threw a refrigerator off the roof of a building at him."

"What?"

"Yeah, when we were teenagers he used to clean boilers in the projects. He would wear these denim overalls and come home completely covered in black soot. But he made a lot of money doing it. On one call, he and his partner drove up to a building and all these guys that were standing in the lobby disappeared. Rob didn't want to get out of the van but his partner said they had to get the job done.

As they walked up to the complex someone from the rooftop twelve stories up yelled, "Go home Mario Brothers," and tossed a full-size refrigerator off the roof. Rob stepped back just in time and it crashed right in front of him. The door whizzed right past Rob's head. Ever since then, Rob's been a little screwy."

"Did he quit after that?"

"Quit? No, he went into the building and cleaned the boiler."

Rob is constantly on the defense. He's not waiting for something to happen first, he's going to secure the house as much as he can. "You're the most valuable thing," he always says. "You wouldn't understand, it's a guy thing. We are the protectors. It's our job to keep the family safe."

"Listen, just let him have his fun," Tommy insists before hanging up. For the first time, I'm actually going to take Tommy Walnuts' advice. I'll do my best to ignore all the crazy things Rob is doing. I glance out over the terrace and watch as he digs dozens of holes in the backyard. There is no use fighting it. Our house is turning into the Thunderdome.

To get my mind off Rob's booby-traps, I go back to work on my book. Surprisingly, all the files look correct and I realize everything is finished. The only thing left to do is to upload the project to Amazon and the other bookselling websites.

Rob walks in from the backyard, dragging mud all over the floor. He sits next to me and unscrews one of the sensors, surely jerry-rigging it to shoot poisonous darts out the back.

"I'm going to do it," I tell Rob.

"Do what?"

"I'm all done with the book. I'm finally letting go of my fear and putting my work out there."

"Good. I'm happy for you. I hope it works out, but don't get discouraged if it doesn't. A lot of this has to do with luck. I know the writing is great. Be proud of yourself that you did it."

"It just feels good to finish the project. Now, I'm not saying to people I'm writing a book. I actually wrote one. And it's not sitting in a drawer; it's up for sale where people can buy it. That's pretty cool."

"I'm glad, honey. And you never know, maybe we will make a couple extra bucks. Wouldn't it be nice to have a little spending money to go out to dinner? It could really loosen up the budget. I could even buy more motion sensors."

I glance back at the computer and move my mouse to the "upload" button. It hovers there for a few seconds. As usual, my mind plays a loop of negative thoughts. The voice is louder and deeper than ever before. Evidently, James Earl Jones is holding a press conference in my head:

"Do you really want to do this, Nadine?"

"I do. Now, get out of my head."

"Do you want to put my work out there to be critiqued by everyone? It's not a particularly kind world and you tend to cry a lot. I'm just saying."

"Leave me alone! Why do you always have to show up when something good can happen?"

I've listened to this voice before, but this time, Darth Vader is not going to discourage me. I'm at a fork in the road. Am I going to follow Darth Vader's advice as I have in the past and toss my dream out the window? Or do I dig as deep as the hole Rob is making in the backyard to find the confidence buried inside of me?

I would be easy to embrace my fear and walk away from this project. A majority of people do, whether they have talent or not. Maybe talent has little to do with success. Plenty of people succeed because they try harder than everyone else. They step into the ring knowing they'll be knocked down. But like Rocky, they know it's getting back up that's important.

Successful people seem to have inexhaustible amounts of self-esteem. Their belief in themselves appears unshakeable. But maybe that's not quite the case. Perhaps it's not a tidal wave of faith that keeps them going but just a tiny sliver as small as a grain of sand. It's this last particle that eventually tilts the scale in their favor. If I can find that one grain of sand within me, I may have the courage to put my book out there.

I stare at the upload button. A minute passes. I procrastinate and walk away. *I'm not sure if I can…* Before any more negative thoughts take over, I rush back and tap the mouse.

It's done. I'm an author.

Neighbors & Shrimp Dinners

Our neighbors from Pennsylvania, Matt and Julie, are coming to visit. We've had many good times together, even on the few occasions when my husband broke something in their house. That's not unusual; Rob breaks something in everyone's house. If you ever ask him to visit, I urge you to put away grandma's valuable dinnerware. It'll be in a million pieces by the time soup is served. And be aware it's not just the delicate things Rob destroys... he can even sabotage your driveway.

One rainy night, Rob drove down into Matt's steep, newly top-coated driveway with our old 1980 Mustang. It was my grandmother's car, built during the gas crisis for fuel efficiency. For some crazy reason, the all-knowing car executives imagined a stampede of people rushing to dealerships to purchase a Mustang that had a horsepower of a Schwinn ten-speed bicycle. And that mob did come, in the form of little seventy-year-old ladies. Executives (but no one else) were surprised to find people didn't buy Mustangs for fuel efficiency but to go fast and look cool. They quickly got rid of that model and went back to making muscle cars that had big, shiny engines. In my grandmother's defense, she may not have gone fast, but she did look cool behind the wheel, even if she never burned rubber in the ShopRite parking lot.

When Rob was leaving Matt's house, he was unable to back out of the driveway since our tires were too bald to get any traction. Rob gunned the engine and skidded out with the confidence of someone driving the dumbest Mustang ever designed. This resulted in two long skid marks on the asphalt. We were never invited to park in our neighbor's driveway again.

Matt's an incredibly neat guy, and it's important to him that things remain orderly. Considering he has an important job working with computer systems in a bank, that trait appears to work for him. But he takes that binary mind home. I've seen Matt close kitchen drawers while his wife was still looking in them, shine things that already look shiny, and keep his pool so clean I hated to swim in it.

On the other hand, Rob is a mess. His clothes pile on the floor, dishes stack up in the sink, and his sneakers are abandoned in places—usually at the top of the stairs—where I inevitably trip over them. I often picture *The Odd Couple* when Matt and Rob are together. Julie and I both end up staring at our crazy husbands; it's obvious we are the only sensible pair out of this bunch.

With all this in mind, I question how much Matt will enjoy Costa Rica. "He will want to be in control during a lot of uncontrollable situations. He also has a bad back, and that never goes over well here."

"Oh, come on. Matt's a tough guy," Rob says. And to prove Matt's a tough guy, Rob drives up our bumpy mountain with Julie and Matt in the car going eighty miles per hour.

"Whoa, I think we left the ground a few times. Let's not do that again," Matt groans. "There aren't going to be a lot of roads like that, right?" I try to reassure Matt that everything will be fine. Italy has the Roman Forum, Paris has the Eiffel Tower, and this country has crappy roads. For some tourists, it's their favorite Costa Rican attraction, for others it's a kick in the sciatic nerve.

Once in the house, Matt unpacks his tablet and asks to sync it to my Wi-Fi connection. Like many people, he reads all of his books and newspapers on an electronic device. It's amazing how now you can download publications in a matter of seconds. Technology has changed so much this past year it gives me hope that my book can find a place in this industry.

After Matt synchronizes his device to my Wi-Fi, Rob and I try to use our computers at the same time. The connection becomes weak and makes it difficult for us to surf the web.

"My speed at home is about ten times this. Why would it matter how many are on it at once?"

"It's usually okay when two people are on, I guess three is too much," I answer.

"That's interesting, Costa Rica must be a two-person internet." I am grateful Matt did not need to use my internet while I was living in Grecia. The service I have here is ten times better than when I lived in the mountains. I am certain the problem is caused by a rickety telephone line.

"Rob, did you ask Sergio to fix the line again? It's been a week."

"Yes, I did. He'll have it done mañana."

"That's great," Matt says. Rob and I know when Sergio says "mañana" it may mean next mañana or the mañana after that. Maybe it's best that we let Matt keep the faith. Somebody has to.

Everyone said when I moved to the beach a good internet connection could be an issue. However, even with a glitchy phone line, it's not too bad. When it's working, I get a decent enough signal to email and stream video. Although it's nothing like the internet in the states, I've adapted to living with less. It's an ongoing lesson that continues to pop up while living here. When I only utilize the resources I truly need, I feel more grateful for what I actually have. It makes me feel connected to my environment instead of being in competition with it.

Even though Matt and Julie are exhausted from their flight, they are eager to take us out to dinner. We know a place where they treat us great and the price point has always been just right. It's the perfect restaurant to bring our friends. I'll also take some pictures and post them on my blog. I've been adding to it weekly, and what was once a small hobby is now picking up steam. I've been tracking visitors and they are coming from all over the world. Many leave comments or questions about what I did, how I did it, and if I think they can do it too. They are like Rob and I before we moved to Costa Rica, staring out their office window wondering if a great adventure still awaits them. It's fun to share my experiences with them and tonight I'll make sure to take a picture of this restaurant.

It is only a fifteen minute drive and our friends are already impressed. It seems much busier than before; more tables are occupied than the last time we were here and even more people are pulling into the parking lot. It seems everyone wants to enjoy the fading sunset while having dinner.

After sitting down, I notice a couple cuddling in the water out in front of us. They are wrapped in a heated embrace, passionately entwined, oblivious to anyone around them. The last time we were here a different couple was doing the same thing. I guess this spot brings out the romance in people. Or perhaps it is the magic of Costa Rican sunsets, up lighting the clouds with a lavender hue one might see in a movie. But this is not a theater, it's real, and it makes you want to kiss someone. I lean over and give Rob a big smooch. It's wonderful having our friends here to share this with us and it helps curb the occasional feeling of homesickness.

The waiter returns with our tropical drinks and places them on the table. "Wow, this tastes great," Julie raves. "I ordered a citrus Mojito. I'm not even sure what's in it, but it's awesome." She takes a long sip of her drink until half of it is gone. "I can totally see why you guys moved here. This might be the prettiest place I've ever visited."

"Is the water always so blue? I would go swimming everyday if I lived here." Matt stirs his drink and lets out a big sigh. It's one of those healthy sighs—the ones that release pent-up stress. I did this hundreds of times when I first moved here. It was as if a pile of cement blocks had lifted off my ribcage. I am no longer exhaling stress as much as I'm inhaling the energy surrounding me. It inflates my lungs and makes them as buoyant as water lilies. There are moments I feel so light I could fly.

I watch Matt as he runs his finger along the rim of his glass. I'm sure he's not thinking about deadlines, quotas, or computers right now. He's absorbing the lazy, sea air and releasing his worries into a passing breeze. You can almost see them unraveling toward the horizon like a bolt of fabric.

Rob suggests our friends order two coconut shrimp appetizers and a lobster dinner. "It's your first night here, let's enjoy ourselves," he says. Everything has always been reasonably priced at this restaurant so Rob doesn't ask the waiter how much the specials cost.

A woman approaches the table carrying a beautiful wooden bowl filled with ice water and flowers. We each dip our hands in and the woman wipes them dry with a soft towel.

Matt sniffs his hands. "This smells awesome." He asks the lady what's in the water but she will not disclose the ingredient.

"No, that's our secret," she says before drying his hands.

"I asked the exact same thing when I was here before, and she gave the same answer," I remark. "It would be great to find soap that smelled like that."

"I would buy it in a heartbeat. But you know what? Everything smells good here. While we were driving, I caught a whiff of some kind of flower circulated through the car. It's awesome how a simple smell can make you feel so good."

The waiter brings over our appetizers: two orders of six perfectly fried coconut shrimp presented on half of a pineapple. They are delicious and we all take turns dipping them into the accompanied mango sauce. He soon returns with Julie's lobster. She tears into it, pulling out the tender meat and dipping it in the melted butter.

"I love it here," Matt says. "The moment we flew over the country, I looked down, and everything was green. All different shades of green, it was amazing. Even the smell at the airport. I loved that too."

"That was probably airplane fuel," Rob laughs.

"Really? Even jet fuel smells better here. I felt my stress disappear the minute I walked off the plane."

We watch the colorful afterglow of the sunset while dogs dash across the beach. As darkness approaches, the restaurant turns on little, white lights that hang from the awning like stars. This unassuming restaurant is a gem; a twinkling constellation in the sand.

The evening is picture perfect until the bill arrives. Those small appetizers Rob suggested cost twenty dollars each. The lobster that he urged Julie to order was forty dollars. Prices are significantly higher now that it is the peak of the tourist season. But our friends hardly bat an eye; they are already falling in love with Costa Rica and one expensive dinner doesn't appear to be shifting their attitude.

"What are we doing tomorrow?" Matt asks after paying the bill.

"I've got something great planned," Rob replies. "And you guys are going to love it."

Rincon de la Vieja

When people discuss Rincon de la Vieja National Park, they often do it with a smile. "Have you been there yet?" they ask. "You're going to love it. Once you go Rincon-ing, you'll be back for sure."

An hour and a half north of Tamarindo, Rincon del la Vieja National Park is 35,000 acres of pristine forest, rivers, and streams. The area has an abundance of wildlife; it's not uncommon to see owls, tanagers, eagles, and the secretive quetzal. I often run into groups of birdwatchers, most of whom ask me if I've ever seen a quetzal while living in Costa Rica. People love this creature, and will travel around the world for the opportunity to catch one brief glance at it. It must be one heck of a bird.

But what I'm most interested in is its volcanic activity. There are boiling mud pots, steaming fumaroles, and hot sulfur springs. It provides just the right mix of adrenaline and adventure.

"What will we be doing?" Matt asks while we all pile into the car.

"We're going to hike then do some zip-lining. It'll be fun," Rob says.

Julie looks concerned. "Do you think your back will hold up?"

Matt twists to the right and stretches his low back. "I think I'll be okay. The zip-lining thing, is that really strenuous? And how safe is it?"

"Dude, it's a tourist thing. You are strapped in a harness and go from one platform to the next. I promise it won't be rough on your back."

The roads to the park aren't too bad until we veer off the Pan American Highway. Now it's full of potholes. Matt shifts in his seat with each bounce, but I assure him the discomfort will be worth it. I've said it before and it rings true each time I explore Costa Rica; the best places are at the end of a dirt road. And sometimes that road will jostle every joint and tendon in your body. It was true for this one, so I know there is something fabulous at the end.

As we climb the mountain, the air becomes cooler. We watch as Rincon de la Vieja rises in the distance with its dormant sister cone, Santa Maria, resting alongside it. Rincon de la Vieja means 'Old Woman's Nook'. The name comes from a legend in which an angry father launches his young daughter's lover into the volcano. My dad would love this story; it's a combination of *Guess Who's Coming to Dinner* with a bit of *The Shining* thrown in. And because every box-office smash has to end on a happy note, the tale has the daughter growing old with miraculous healing powers. Maybe these healing powers can help Matt's back. I hope I don't have to toss him into the volcano to get them.

We stop by an outfit selling tours and sign up for a four excursion combo: nature walk, horseback ride to waterfalls, zip-line, followed by a relaxing soak in a mud bath and thermal springs. We skip the river tubing for the sake of Matt's back but I will surely come back one day to try it out.

Our nature walk takes us along a path into the forest. Our guide, Tito, cheerfully describes the many plants we pass. Some have medicinal properties, while others have more interesting uses.

"You cut the trunk, then cover the top and capture the juices. The liquids will get you drunk. But what is unique is that the next day, you will be fine... until you walk in the sunlight. You will then be inebriated all over again."

Wow, sunlight activated alcohol. Perfect for those cash-strapped college students.

"Look at this," our guide says after pulling off what looks like the bud from a marijuana plant. "Smell it." One man in our group practically tramples over me to get a whiff.

"This is not marijuana. If you smoke it, it will get you intoxicated, but it's a powerful hallucinogenic as well. Some who've tried it ended up with brain damage, so I would not recommend it."

Tito then walks over to a number of glass tanks. In each are frogs so colorful they could pass for Christmas ornaments. One is the blue-jean poisonous dart frog. He's the cutest thing with an orange body and dark, blue legs.

"Don't lick him," Tito says sternly while looking in my direction. "He emits a toxic secretion that can make you sick."

I'm unclear why Tito feels the need to stare at me while delivering his heartfelt frog licking speech. I may not be a Playboy Playmate, but surely I don't give off the amphibian slobbering vibe. I mean…the guy who's still sniffing the pot plant is a more likely suspect.

So far I've learned that the forest produces quite the rave party. There is sunlight-activated alcohol to my left, a brain-damaging hallucinogenic to my right, and according to Tito, I'm fighting an irresistible urge to tongue lash blue-jean frogs. Luckily, our next stop is a butterfly garden where I hope things are a little calmer.

Once inside the netted structure, we get the chance to see a Calico butterfly. The males smack their wings together, making a snapping sound to attract a female. He's like the Fonzie of the forest. This explains the snapping sound I hear back at the house. I always thought someone was sneaking up on me. Who knew that it was just a butterfly? I'm surprised Rob hasn't tasered it yet.

After the butterfly garden, we continue on to the snake gallery. The tone becomes less festive as Tito teaches us about all the snakes that can kill us within a few hours (there are a lot). At least these are enclosed in glass and not like the ones lurking around Corcovado National Park.

We walk past harmless green tree snakes, as well as venomous jumping pit vipers. Now that's a snake that can really make an entrance. He's like Superman, flying through the air before sinking his jaws into the enemy. Unlike other snakes, he doesn't let go, but holds on and chews. It's a disturbing image, and not one I care to experience. I would rather get tumbled by a puma if I had the choice.

However, the most worrisome of all snakes is the coral pit viper. I know for a fact they live near our house; a neighbor's dog was bitten by one and died soon after. It can be confused with the harmless milk variety so our guide tells us a nifty rhyme to remember how to identify their markings: *Red next to black is a friend of jack. Red next to yellow is a dangerous fellow.* I look in one of the cages and see a snake curled on top of a rock with a red band adjacent to a yellow band. "Don't pick this one up," he warns. I assure him that will never happen. If I ever have the misfortune of stumbling across one, my discharging bladder would keep me, and others around me, too distracted from making a proper identification.

Toward the end of the tour, Tito reaches into a cage and takes out an eight foot albino boa constrictor. He wraps it around my shoulders like a mink stole. The snake is heavy, but surprisingly cool. A boa will strike his prey, quickly wrapping himself around it, and depriving the animal from taking a breath. Just what I want to hear while one is curled around my neck. The guide then points out that after copulation, a female can hold the sperm inside her for up to a year. I'm the only one who giggles. It's a lot to ask of a girl... is all I'm saying.

"I just love the woods. I grew up on eighteen acres," Matt explains as we walk through the forest back to the tour desk. With each passing day he's revealing more of his childhood. "There was a time I could never have imagined working in an office."

We continue the rest of the way back in silence. The more that I'm out doing these wilderness excursions, the more I learn what kind of dangers lurk off the beaten path. And I haven't even seen a steaming fumarole or mud pit yet.

"You know, my back doesn't even hurt anymore," Matt smiles. That's until he sees our new guide walk over to us with four horses. It looks like Matt will be getting back in the saddle again.

Waterfalls & Canyon Walls

"Do you think you'll be okay on a horse?" I ask.

"I hope so," Matt replies. "But I haven't been on one in twenty years. I stopped riding after my back surgery."

"I doubt she'll bounce you around, tourists ride them every day," Rob says as Matt strokes the horse's face. The man holding the reins nods his head in agreement, but I can tell he doesn't understand English. I recognize his befuddled expression because I pretty much look like that all the time. I was recently at the post office where a clerk was trying to explain my package hadn't arrived yet. Instead of moving out of the way for the next person in line, I just stood there nodding like a big, dopey bobblehead. I remained there for a good five minutes before a nice person in line told me I had to come back the next day.

Matt examines the saddle and looks over the stirrups. "She looks like a nice girl, so why not? I'm already here, right? I didn't come all this way not to participate."

We each get on our horse, but before we start the tour the guide hands out helmets. I notice these helmets are not the flimsy plastic ones most tourists get; gratefully, these are heavy duty. Once in Panama, Rob and I had rented a scooter and were given hard hats instead of helmets. They didn't even buckle under our chins. I loved the easy, breezy feeling of flying down the street knowing that my protective head gear would become airborne long before my skull would smack the asphalt. It reminded me of the time I was riding my banana seat bicycle in 1978 and flew head first into my garage door. My mother gave me a cold compress, turned on *Bugs Bunny*, and went back to doing laundry. In those days, most mothers treated a concussion, mild blood spillage, or anything that didn't involve a splintering bone emanating out from one's body with minimal medical attention. I'm all but certain my friend Donny fractured his skull while jumping ramps and all he got from his mom was a pack of Fruit Stripe Gum. (He is now a city councilman.)

We follow our guide into a grassy meadow. Orange butterflies skip across purple flowers while thousands of blue dragonflies hover in the air. If a male fancies a female, the dragonfly will lift her up and fly her around during the mating process. This is about as romantic as you get in the insect world and makes me love these little guys even more. If this was three hundred million years ago, their wing span would be two and a half feet long. I have no doubt that if any of these humongous dragonflies are still on this earth, they are living somewhere in Costa Rica.

As we continue along the trail, we approach five calves sitting in the middle of the path. They look up with eyes as big as hubcaps and ears that look humorously disproportioned to their heads. After a couple shouts from our guide, they eventually get up and lazily move a few feet out of our way. It would seem no one is in a rush in Costa Rica—except for Matt's horse. She's getting antsy and tries to get to the front of the line. Matt gently pulls back on the reins but it only makes her agitated. Matt winces with each sharp movement.

The trail twists around a bend and narrows onto a thin ledge. One side is a dirt wall, while the other is a ten-foot drop. We continue single file, my horse's hooves barely missing the edge. There's no reason to get nervous since these animals have done this dozens of times. However, it's always unsettling when you are totally relying on an animal to guide you to safety.

A man wearing a cowboy hat steps out from behind a tree and tells us to stop. He helps us off, secures the horses, and points down a path. We follow the sounds of water and find ourselves at a rocky bluff. We all gasp in unison.

The La Chorrera waterfalls rumble below us forming a circular swimming hole. The lagoon sparkles like a queen's crown, the color an incandescent turquoise from the high sulfur concentration. It looks magical. No wonder this mountain is believed to have healing properties.

We climb down and take off our shoes. The water is icy cold, but Rob immediately jumps in and swims toward the waterfall. The current keeps pushing him back like a treadmill, but he fights his way stoke by stroke, until he is under the cascading water.

"This is one of the most beautiful places I've ever seen," Julie remarks. "It couldn't be more perfect."

I climb a metal staircase to the top of the falls and step out onto the edge. There is not one souvenir shop, fast food restaurant, or sound of a passing car. It's completely silent except for the thunder of the falls and the laughter echoing from Rob and my friends. I believe this is one of the best gifts Costa Rica can offer; tiny corners of serenity.

"Vamos," a voice calls from above. Playtime is over.

"It's hard to explain what that was like. How can I possibly tell people what I just saw?" Julie says on the trail ride back. It's always difficult to get the adjectives right. Sometimes a place creates such an emotional connection just saying "it was pretty" doesn't do it justice. Maybe this is for the best; people have to come here and experience it for themselves.

On the way back to the stables, Rob gently nudges his horse to take the lead. Always worrying about me, he wants to be in front to keep my horse at a slow pace. However, his horse has other plans. He gets to the front of the line but then suddenly takes off in a gallop that sends Rob bouncing down the trail and out of sight.

"That's not going to be good for his hernia," Matt remarks.

"Nadine, where did he go?" Julie asks.

"I have no idea." I can't believe another horse has taken off on Rob. I can only hope they are on their way back to the stables. I'm anxious to get there but all three of our horses continue their slow pace, oblivious to the one that disappeared. Fifteen minutes later, I can see the stables and Rob sitting on the side of the path.

"Why did you take off like that?" I shout. "I was so worried, at every bend I'm looking over the edge terrified you were down there with a broken back."

"Why are you yelling at me? You know that fifteen minute trail ride you just had? I did it in thirty seconds. The horse barely stayed on that narrow ledge before careening me into the stables. Every time I'm on a horse, all he can think about is kicking me off."

"Why are there red blotches all over your face?" I ask.

"I smacked into a hundred dragonflies going fifty miles per hour, that's why."

A stable boy helps us off our horses and Matt walks over to Rob. "How are your balls?" he asks.

"Don't even ask, man. Don't even ask."

We are escorted to a neighboring hotel which provides us lunch as part of the paid tour. There is a large buffet of chicken, beans, rice, and assorted fruits. While in line I ask Matt how he is feeling.

"You know, not too bad. Between the road and the horse, my back is surprisingly okay. Better than expected."

"So, what's next?" Julie asks.

"We are going to zip-line through the jungle," Rob says while finishing the last of his plantains. "It's going to be easy. I've done a dozen of them."

Matt looks down at the brochure and slides it over to Rob. "It says right here that it's nothing like any other zip-line in Costa Rica."

"Trust me. This is going to be a breeze," Rob says.

It's exactly these words that ring in my ear as we are soon standing:

On a five foot wide ledge.

Along a canyon wall.

Over a roaring river five stories below.

I am terrified, but there is no other choice but to scale the rock horizontally to the next platform. With the amount of concentration one could only muster when faced with the possibility of a very uncomfortable and disheartening fall, I briskly latch onto a handle and steer my legs blindly to an adjacent peg. I repeat the process until I am safely on the next rocky ledge.

"A breeze, heh?" Matt mumbles under his breath while following me. I can see his hands are shaking. Once he joins me on the ledge, we both watch Julie and Rob work their way across. "I thought Rob said I would be zipping from platform to platform. This isn't at all what he described."

Like many things Rob suggests, he didn't quite research this excursion thoroughly. It's not just zip-lining, but a vigorous workout that includes rappelling, rock climbing, and the occasional Tarzan swing just in case you're looking to increase your odds of smashing your face on a stone wall.

Julie slowly makes her way across. "I don't know if I can do this," she says repeatedly under her breath. Even though she is questioning herself, she never stops or hesitates. It's amazing how the adrenaline kicks in, forcing you to keep moving.

"Did you know we would be doing all this?" I whisper to Rob once he finally reaches the platform.

"No way. Nadine, I swear, I would have told them. But this is really something. They're not kidding, this really is the best zip-line tour in Costa Rica."

There is no time to explain all that to my friends since the guide is urging us to rappel down the canyon and climb our way out. Rob and I decide we will go while Matt and Julie take pictures from above.

Doing these crazy excursions makes me realize not to think too much; I can easily talk myself out of doing something and later regret that I never tried. When the guide gives me the green light, I disappear over the edge.

I feel like a dragonfly as I float over the Rio Blanco River before being lowered onto a platform. The river tears through this narrow passage, stealing with it little grains of minerals. One day it will be as wide as the Grand Canyon. I glance up and see Matt and Julie staring back down at me.

My brain tries to stitch together this new point of view. The images—like snapshots—slowly piece together to form one glorious, panoramic picture. A rush of exhilaration runs from my toes to my head; I am completely present in this moment. I grab a rope and Tarzan swing to another platform. Here is where I start my intrepid ascent.

As I climb, I feel the safety of the rope attached to my harness. When I begin to slip, the trusted guide pulls on the slack and gives me the confidence that I will not fall. I push myself harder than I've done in years. I dig deep, grabbing each handle and occasionally pressing my face into the rock. I'm so close I can taste the dirt. I finally make it to the top, drag myself over the edge, and receive a round of applause. Rob is quick to follow and we all continue on with the rest of the tour. It finishes with an Indiana Jones hanging bridge, with a sign that reads: *Only Two People at a Time.*

"I love it... only two people at a time. It's like your internet at home. It looks like Costa Rica is a two person country," Matt laughs. We both hold onto the railing and try to balance ourselves. It feels like I'm on a sailboat in a storm; each step I take bounces me in the air. As I make my way across, I think about what Matt just said. Maybe Costa Rica is a two person country. It's definitely a two flush country according to Scott.

We're all exhausted and happily look forward to covering ourselves in mud and soaking in the thermal springs.

"You know, if I had known too much about that tour, I might not have done it," Matt confesses.

I nod my head in agreement. "Maybe it's best not to know. Sometimes anxiety can keep you from participating in a life changing event."

Matt and Julie sink into the hot water. This was a great day; a unique combination of nature, adventure, and relaxation. They got to enjoy some of the best things about Costa Rica and will leave with great memories. Once again, I got to share a piece of our life with friends.

I can't imagine my life getting any better than this.

It Ain't Spam

It was fun showing our friends around. They had a great time and it gave them a much needed break from work. Matt will return to his corporate life; one that includes high pressure meetings, rushed lunches, and late nights in the office. But for a short time, his mind wandered back to the days of growing up on his parents' farm. He recalled baling hay with his brother and riding horses across grassy meadows. He reminisced in great detail; his mother's voice, young and clear, calling him inside for dinner.

Nature has a powerful way of extracting joyful childhood memories. When I'm mindful of this, the happiest moments of my life bubble to the surface and burst open like trapped gas in a soda bottle. It could be remembering the smell of my grandmother's rose garden or the cracked laugh of my Aunt Louise. They come in small doses, never lasting more than a minute. But when they appear, I pause to drink in the seconds and revisit a place that had long disappeared.

Even though Matt and Julie had a great time, I think a week in Costa Rica was long enough. I'm not sure how many more spine splitting pot holes Matt's back could have handled. Rob's driving didn't help the situation. He's so used to these roads he forgets how scary it is for someone in the passenger seat.

"You could have slowed down when we drove up the mountain ridge," I mention on the ride back from the airport. "I saw Matt gasp when he looked down over the cliff."

"I think my driving was fine," Rob defends moments before he turns into a parking lot and clips the side of a two foot wall. Our front tire explodes, and soon a crowd forms to laugh at the ding-dongs who have just plowed into a slab of concrete.

"Holy cow... I didn't even see that wall," Rob confesses. "Oh well, I'll put the spare on. We needed new tires anyway. All four of them are bald so it's actually a good thing this happened."

While Rob changes the tire, it strikes me how the timing of Matt and Julie's trip was perfect. It stopped me from obsessing about my book and made me realize why I'm in Costa Rica in the first place. It's easy to get sucked back into the rat race and I don't want to recreate the physically and emotionally exhausting lifestyle I lived before.

There is a figure in Buddhism called The Hungry Ghost; a person with a bloated stomach, thin neck, and tiny mouth. The person tries to satisfy his hunger by continuously cramming food into his mouth. However, it's an impossible feat. No matter how hard he tries, or how painful it becomes, he can't get enough to satisfy his cravings. It's an insightful metaphor that demonstrates how many of us live our lives. Sometimes our desires become obstacles that prevent us from enjoying the achievements we have already made. In spite of our many blessings we continue to experience pain, unhappiness, and longing for more. It's easy to get caught up in this whirlwind. Clutter, material and emotional, takes up a lot of space in your head.

Since leaving the trappings of my former life, I have found that my creative side has room to grow. I'm thankful that my book is a small project; the last thing I want to do is complicate my life. I don't want to end up like the Hungry Ghost.

One spare tire and bumpy ride later, we're back at the house. I turn on my computer while Rob calls a garage to inquire whether or not they sell Firestone tires. His eyebrows shoot up three inches before hanging up the receiver; the price certainly must be making him reconsider the merits of driving into that wall. I log onto the website that tracks the sale of my book and I am surprised to find that it's selling close to five copies a day. I'm ecstatic.

"Rob, come over here. I'm selling five books a day!"

"That's great sweetie, it looks like we can afford those extra motion sensors now. And four new tires."

"I can't believe it. This means we can go out to eat a little more often, and even do some fun stuff at the beach, like rent a kayak or paddleboard. But the first thing I'm going to do is buy some dishwasher detergent. Absolutely, that's how I'm going to celebrate." Dishwasher detergent is over twelve dollars a box here; a real budget blaster but a necessity. My husband is the type of guy who will use every single glass before washing the dirty ones. It is—and will continue to be—our biggest marital squabble.

When I complain that I'm the one always stuck doing the dishes, Rob swiftly suggests that I volunteer to do some of *his* chores: like clean out the gutters, wasp-nest removal, or suffer the weekly raccoon ambush when he tosses the garbage in our development's collective trash bin. Frankly, I don't like any of those options, so the argument usually ends with me washing the dishes and Rob plunging a toilet. Having a dishwasher is as good as marriage counseling, and now that I have some extra cash coming in, I'm going straight to the expensive grocery store in Tamarindo and hoarding every box of Cascade that I can find. If you see a crazy lady with a cart full of dishwashing detergent this week, that's me.

I check my email and begin deleting all the spam. I'm about to delete a message when I pause. It must be a joke, probably a virus, but my curiosity leads me open it anyway. This email is not spam. In fact, it's the polar opposite. It is a reporter from CNN.com.

Hello, I am a writer for CNN.com and I would be interested in receiving a copy of your book, "Happier Than A Billionaire." Would you be able to send one to my attention at the following address:

One CNN Center
Atrium Newsroom
Atlanta, GA 30303

"Rob," I yell. No answer.

"ROB," I scream. No answer.

"R... O... O... O... B."

"What's going on?" he asks, but I can't speak—half of my brain has turned to applesauce. All I can do is point to the screen.

"Is this some kind of a joke? Could it be spam? Identity theft?"

"No... I think... I think it's for real," I stutter. "That's the actual address for CNN. She wants a copy of my book, Rob."

"You have to get one to her ASAP. Call your mom and have her ship one. What are you waiting for? Go, go, go!" I run to the phone faster than Gordon Liddy feeds a paper shredder.

My head spins. This email—this exciting news—is not something that happens to someone like me. I barely had the courage to self-publish my book, and now I have a reporter from CNN.com asking for a copy. Just moments ago, I was doing a happy dance about splurging on dishwasher detergent. I *should* be jumping up and down, but all I feel is uncomfortably numb.

At this time in the morning, my parents are probably sitting in Burger King having a cup of coffee. They are now entitled to a senior citizen discount, which is the only reason my father is willing to pay for something that costs five cents to make at home. I once bought him a four dollar Starbucks drink; a big, whipped cream concoction. After seeing the price, my father drank it in silence only to tell my mother later how careless I am with money. "That kid is never going to make it," he said, wiping whipped cream off his face. "She's living a Starbucks lifestyle on a Folgers budget." He fears my occasional Starbucks splurge will have me moving back into his house with my old hamster cage under my arm.

I nervously dial my mom's cell phone number. It takes her a while to pick up because she can never remember which button to press.

"Hello… are you still there? Hello?" my mother screams into the receiver from two feet away.

"Mom, where are you?"

"I'm at Burger King. Your father is reading the newspaper. He refuses to hand over the obituary section. Every morning he does this to me."

"Ma, pay attention. I need a favor. CNN just contacted me and asked for a copy of my book."

"CNN?"

"Yes, Ma."

"Are you sure this is not a joke?"

"I just went through this with Rob. Seriously, I got an email from CNN and I need you to mail a book ASAP."

The next thing I hear is crumpled newspapers, screeching tires, and people running for cover (clearly adding another poor soul to tomorrow's obituary section). My parents left Burger King like they were driving a getaway car. Ten minutes later I get a phone call from my mother.

"Your father wants to talk with you."

"Nadine, this is your father speaking. You might consider this email a casual thing, something that happens frequently in the literary world. But I can assure you, this must be taken seriously and you must act in a prudent manner. I know you are in la la land over there watching monkeys all day, and taking pictures of every godforsaken sunset. But this deserves your attention. Handle this business at your discretion, but all I can say is you are missing out on a great opportunity."

I'm missing out already? I just got the email about a half hour ago. I go from numb to feeling a massive parent-induced migraine.

"Now talk with your mother on how we should proceed." He hands the phone back to her before shouting, "Diane, tell the kid to get on top of this!"

"Don't listen to your father. You know how he gets. Where do you want me to send it?"

"I'll email dad the address. I want you to ship it UPS. They'll even box it for you."

"I can't go to the post office? It's right around the corner."

"No, please go to the UPS store."

"I don't like that parking lot. Your father hit a pole the last time he backed out of there."

"For the love of everything holy. Please mom, the package needs to be traced. I want it to go through UPS."

"Fine, but I can tell you this is not going to be easy for me. Can I do it tomorrow? I'm going to the beauty parlor and then I won't have to make another trip."

"Yes, mom, that's perfect. I will tell CNN you are getting your hair done and they will get the book this week."

I get off the phone and review current events. Could this be my big break? Will I actually get on CNN and what would that mean? Surely many people will read the article and perhaps they will visit my blog. But that's only if the reporter likes the book and decides to do a story on me. I suddenly feel like I've been smacked in the back of the head as I recall my opening line; a fart joke. My dream is over before it ever began.

This reporter will never get past the first page.

CNN Advice

On Thursday morning, I'll receive "the call." The CNN reporter will be interviewing me over the phone. If it makes it into the CNN.com travel section, my book will potentially be exposed to thousands of people, and I'm already tallying the thousands of ways my family thinks I will screw it up.

"For heaven's sake, don't say anything stupid," my mother insists. From past experience, that will be impossible for me. "And whatever you do, don't mention your father or how cheap he is. He hates that you wrote about him in the book."

I call my sister hoping she can calm my nerves. "Don't curse," she says. "And don't try to use any words you can't pronounce correctly. You'll make a fool out of yourself." The unshakeable confidence my family has in my professional endeavors is heartwarming.

My father remains stern with his suggestions. "I don't think you are taking this seriously, Nadine. This is CNN. Crash and burn baby. You should be preparing sample questions, index cards, and reviewing your book. You don't know what she is going to throw at you. And if she asks if your father is really that cheap, tell her yes. I'm a cheap SOB. I love that you wrote that in the book. Got it?"

So far I've learned not to say something stupid, avoid using vulgarities of any kind, and to make a list of sample questions. Oh, and to confirm that my father is a cheap SOB. "Wow, my family was pretty hard on me," I tell Rob. "They make me sound completely incapable of handling this interview. Couldn't they just tell me I'll do a good job?"

"They are just trying to help, but I would like to add one more."

"Oh Lord, now what?"

"Don't toss your arms around during the interview."

"You can't be serious. I don't do that."

"When you talk fast your hands go to the side and start to wave."

"It's a phone interview. Even if I did that, she can't see me."

"I know, but when it happens your voice gets really high and squeaky—like Lucille Ball. I'm just saying, don't do it."

Wow, uncontrollable arms accompanied by a squeaky voice. *Do I really sound like Lucille Ball?* That would explain why people end their conversations so quickly with me. And it also might explain why I was recently reprimanded on a plane by a woman so disturbed by my voice she stood up and yelled, "You have no idea how far your voice travels through this fuselage!" accentuating the word *far* as if my voice might crash through the cockpit and plunge our aircraft into the Atlantic Ocean. She sat back down and I shut up for the remainder of the flight.

I consider everyone's advice and take my dad's suggestion by preparing for the interview. Rob decides to give me an impromptu pop quiz at the kitchen table. He wants me to answer quickly; no pauses. He hands me the phone thinking that the tactile sense of a sweaty receiver against my head will provide a more realistic rehearsal. I hold it with both of my unruly hands, ensuring that they will remain safely on the receiver and not flailing dangerously around.

"Okay, you ready? Let's go. Why did you quit your job and move to a country where you didn't even know the language?"

"That's a good question. Hmm... I didn't like my job anymore. I was stressed out and ... hmm... Costa Rica has monkeys."

"Costa Rica has monkeys? That's your answer? Oh brother, we have a lot of work to do. And you have to stop saying "hmm;" it sounds like amateur hour. What is this, your first interview?"

"This *is* my first interview. What did you expect, the "I Have a Dream" speech? When I wrote this book, I never planned for this to happen. How could I have known anybody would read it, let alone a reporter from CNN? If I thought that could happen, I would have never finished writing it. I can't handle the pressure."

"Calm down, everyone is on your side. Your family is as nervous as you and they just want you to do well, but you need to be more confident. The book is great Nadine, and now someone who has the power to put it front and center is taking an interest in it. Any other author would be grateful to have this opportunity, but the only one who can make this work is you. I can help you with sample questions but during the interview you're on your own. There is something special about your story. It's not just about moving to Costa Rica, it's about understanding it's never too late to pursue a happier life. Isn't that what we always say? Tell her that."

"I understand. I just get a sinking feeling that I'm going to blow it."

"Blow it? We never blow it. We're fighters. Get it together and take your dad's advice. Let's make a list of twenty-five questions she may ask and have a good response to each. It will give you confidence and guarantee that you won't be caught off-guard without a great answer for each."

Wow, Winston Churchill couldn't have said it better—this *is* my finest hour. If England could orchestrate the Miracle of Dunkirk, I have to believe I can do a simple interview. My dad was right for making me listen to all those Churchill speeches. I can't be afraid of failure—and even more important—be frightened of success. Perhaps that is where this fear is coming from. Maybe the idea of what this interview can do for my book is why I'm so nauseous. And if that's the case, were all my past fears a symptom of the potential for success?

It's easy to sabotage oneself, believing people just get lucky. They somehow met the right person or got a huge break in their career. We learn about people at the height of their fame, but rarely while they are busy climbing the ladder. Eddie Cantor once said, "It takes twenty years to be an overnight success." No one sees the struggle behind the scenes, the daily work that one puts into their vision. It often separates the people who eventually find self-fulfillment from the people who give up. I have terrific admiration for those who have overcome great obstacles in order to make it to the top.

At the beginning of this process, I ignored the rejections (if you call ignoring sobbing into my pillow and planning Armageddon on the New York publishing world) and uploaded this book myself. Wasn't that a step toward creating my own destiny? This is partially a lucky break, and partially due to what I always do: ignore what others think and do what I believe is best for me. When someone said I couldn't do something, I either stepped around or jumped over them. (Okay, maybe I tripped over them. But either way I never gave up.) When people told me changing my entire life in mid-swing and moving to Costa Rica was a mistake, I listened to their thoughts but followed my heart. If I had waited for someone to give me the green light, I would still be stuck in that office, and I would always be thinking of what could have happened if I took a chance.

"Okay Rob. Let's do it!" I rev myself up like it's halftime at the Super Bowl. "Start making a list because I'm going to nail this interview. Get your boxing gloves on. Nothing but one hundred percent from me."

"Now you're talking. Okay, here's a question for you: How do you think the Central American Free Trade Agreement will affect the Costa Rican economy?"

Crickets

Oh boy… this is going to be a long night.

License Plates & Robbing Houses

Doing just about anything in Costa Rica can turn into an ordeal. A couple of weeks ago we stopped at the municipality in Santa Cruz and inquired about how to replace the license plate that was unceremoniously stolen off of our car while it was parked outside the hospital. The clerk looked at us, then his watch, and swiftly directed us to a different building six hundred meters down the street. Rob tried to ask about our water letter problem, but the man disappeared, undoubtedly enjoying his mid-day siesta at the Pizza Casa across the road.

At the next building, a nice gentleman took our documents and made a few important sounding phone calls. I'm pretty sure one of them was to the guy at the last building. After getting off the phone, the man informed us that this was the wrong office and to return to the municipality building. Luckily, someone behind us just went through the same situation and filled us in on what we had to do: go to Liberia's National Registry office above the Bank of Costa Rica with a letter from an attorney stating we lost our license plate. The man behind that guy began chiming in as well, explaining we didn't need that letter, just our registration.

If this story makes you want to shove something sharp into your ear canal, then we would get along great. It is impossible to get a straight answer on anything here. I guess I'm getting used to the nuances of Costa Rica since this time my blood pressure only elevates slightly. It stinks that we now have to pay a lawyer to fix something that wasn't our fault in the first place.

We stop by an attorney's office that was recommended to us by our landlords. Ricardo eagerly welcomes us inside and we explain our predicament with the license plate and water letter. He prepares a document that states our license plate was stolen and notarizes it. In regards to our water dilemma, he suggests we go to AYA in Liberia to talk with a heavy set man. He doesn't remember his name, only that he is a big guy.

"How big?" Rob asks. "Like Mr. Muscularo big or just big-big?" Ricardo then stretches out his arms and raises his eyebrows. I can only conclude this man is of generous proportions. Supposedly, he has the authority to help us with our water problem.

Liberia is a small city filled with fast food, clothing stores, and lots of people bustling around town. We easily find the bank and the National Registry located above it. It's the same place you would go for the papers to take your car across the border, certifications of documents, and practically everything else you would like stamped with dozens of nifty, swirly ink stains. I am sure that during the process of getting our building permits, we'll be here often. It seems to be our lucky day and we find a parking space right outside the building.

We make our way up the stairs and get in line. Once it's our turn, a nice woman takes our papers and informs us we will need to pay a fee of twenty dollars at the bank downstairs before she can process our documents. She also needs photocopies of our passports.

If I could change one thing about this country, it would be its shortage of Xerox machines. I have never seen one at a bank, motor vehicle department, municipality, or any other building where you think you might find one. Every time we need to get something done, we are instructed to go make copies. Sometimes it is across town, but fortunately there is one across the street. We go downstairs, pay the twenty dollars at the bank, and continue to a small internet café and copy center. With papers in hand, we head back to the National Registry where the lady processes our request. We have to return the following week to pick up our plates. She has been incredibly patient with us so I tell her how much I love this country and its people. This has been my closing farewell ever since moving here and always seems to end the conversation on a good note.

As we walk back to the car, I get a call on my cell phone. It's a recorded message in Spanish that keeps repeating itself. It's too fast for me to understand so I hand the phone to Rob.

"Holy crap. That's ADT." ADT is the alarm monitoring system we have on our house. If anyone tries to break in, they first call the house, and if they cannot reach anyone there, they call our cell phone. Unlike the United States, police rarely show up when called, sometimes arriving on the scene two hours or even two days later. It's going to be up to us to take care of this situation. It doesn't appear to be our lucky day after all.

While Rob sits in the car, he calls the ADT headquarters. The representative on the phone tells us that the alarm was tripped in the upstairs bedroom—the only bedroom in the house that does not have security bars protecting it. "Señor, from my computer I can also see that the alarm was tripped for only five seconds. Perhaps a lizard ran across the sensor," he assures my husband.

"Yeah, right. For all I know some bastard is breaking into my house and I am an hour away." Rob is anxious to start the car but he first has to remove the two Clubs he clamped onto the steering wheel. Then he must flip the four kill switches he has hidden all over the car. This surely gives the burglar time to do a load of laundry, make a few international phone calls, and invite his bowling team over for a barbecue. Rob finally gets the car started and speeds out of Liberia.

"Slow down, Rob, we're going to get a ticket. It's got to be a lizard, right?" I look at Rob as he squeezes the steering wheel. Are we really getting robbed right now? I get sick just thinking about some creepy guy walking around my house. I can't believe it's happening now while we are so far away.

"I'm gonna strangle this guy," Rob mumbles under his breath.

"We can't be getting robbed. I'm going to be on CNN. I'm *Happier Than A Billionaire* Rob, I'm supposed to be *happier* for Pete's sake. How am I supposed to write about this?"

"Write about it? That's what you're worried about? You're not going to be writing anything on your blog because José just ran out the back door with your computer."

"Who's José?"

"I don't know but he's got your computer and he's about to get his ass kicked."

I think about all of the hard work, the pictures, my book, and blog material in the hands of some sweaty guy. I've lost everything. Maybe I'll never make another post or answer anyone's emails. I'll just disappear like Amelia Earhart and vanish into thin air.

Rob flies past cars, tractors, and herds of cattle. I swear we are on two wheels during some of the turns; I can practically feel us lift off of the ground. As we drive up the road in our development, Rob explains his guy-breaking-into-our-house protocol. I didn't know we had one, so I'm interested to hear exactly what my role will be.

"You're going to stay in the car. I'll circle the perimeter first and then I'll come back around to the front door. Don't say a word. If you see anyone come toward you, duck behind the wheel and run the bastard over with the car."

After circling the house, I see my husband walk up to the front door and sneak inside. I remain in the car and get ready to run José over as he attempts to sneak away. I'm glad we have new tires on the car; it will make for a much better grip when I back over him a dozen times. After five minutes of waiting, and no one sneaking out of any windows, I decide to see what's happening inside. There I find Rob kicking in each door like James Bond. He hides behind corners before jumping out with his gun in hand (you know, the one with the melted handle from trying to hide it in the fireplace).

"I told you to stay in the car. Here, take this machete."

"No. I don't want the machete because I don't think anyone broke in. Everything looks like it's locked up. If someone had burglarized the house, they wouldn't have taken the time to close up all the doors and lock the windows again." But 007 isn't listening to a word I'm saying. He is all but climbing into the ventilation system and rappelling from the ceiling.

"There's no one here," he finally confesses. I check out the bedroom where the alarm was tripped. A gecko is lingering an inch from the sensor.

"I think we found our intruder," I tell Rob. "Do you want the machete back? Or would you rather finish him off with a spray of bullets?"

"Very funny. Wait until something really happens. Then you'll be glad I go a little crazy. Don't write about this either, this is one embarrassing moment of my life I'd rather not be on your blog."

Don't worry Rob. I won't share it with anyone.

Release the Kraken

I take a deep breath between questions as Rob gives me a thumbs up from across the room. This helps me stay calm and concentrate on my answers.

"How long did you plan for the move?" the reporter asks. I respond with confidence, or at least the veneer of confidence after hours of practice with Rob. I talk as slow as I can—which is still way too fast. She has a friendly voice, making it feel more like talking with a girlfriend than someone who works for a major news organization.

Her questions are mostly travel related and we discuss several destinations such as Tamarindo, Arenal, and Manuel Antonio. But my favorite question is, "Why do you compare Costa Rica to the movie *Avatar* in your book?"

James Cameron hired some of the most talented artists to create the science fiction world, Pandora. It was their imagination that made the extra-terrestrial beings, wildlife, and vibrant landscape. While watching I couldn't help but notice that much of the film looked like Costa Rica, and that the underlying story of taking more than we need paralleled my own life. Or perhaps the movie was just about blue people, and if that is the case, maybe I am overanalyzing the story. Nevertheless, I think often about the night we watched it with Darlene and Frankie, and how much fun we had together. It wasn't that long ago that I landed in Costa Rica with four suitcases, a dog, and a stinky cat. Everything was so foreign that the entire country might as well have been Pandora.

After we finish the interview, the reporter says the story will be out by the end of next week. She'll need me to email her a few pictures and sign a photograph release form. My big interview is over; I can finally breathe again.

"She was really nice and many of the questions were about Costa Rica."

Rob walks over and gives me a hug. "I'm proud of you, you didn't squeak once. You spoke a little fast, but not like you usually do when you get nervous."

"I just hope it gets on the website. If it happens, I'm going to howl like a monkey off the terrace."

"Of course it will," Rob insists. "Why would she bother with the interview if she wasn't going to submit it? Let's not waste time worrying about it and get those pictures out to her."

Rob and I go through our photos and find a few great shots. The one with the ocelot on Rob's back is a given; a snapshot of one of those magical moments that no one would believe unless there was evidence. I find a picture of both of us on the beach, but we can't agree on one for the top of the story. The problem is we can rarely find a picture with both of us in it, and even worse, one where we are not blinded by the sun and actually have our eyes open.

In most pictures I look like I am melting. I either just took off my scooter helmet and/or I'm suffering from some varying degree of heat exhaustion. I have about fifty pictures where I'm a dead ringer for Edvard Munch's *The Scream*.

I discard most but find one where I look pretty. I show Rob. "I want this one."

"No, absolutely not."

"Why? I think you look fine."

"That's right after surgery, I look pretty soft—like I need a bra."

My husband started working out a lot since moving to Costa Rica. We don't go to a gym, but we have free weights and a pull-up bar. I like to practice yoga while Rob perfects his MMA moves throughout the day. Training has made Rob quite muscular; his chest has grown huge, projecting out like Arnold Schwarzenegger's in his prime. Before his operation, Rob was in the best shape of his life, but since he's stopped bodybuilding, he feels like he's started to get flabby.

"Rob, you are worse than me. Don't be so critical. You look great. See, your arms look huge in the picture."

"No. We are not using that one. But I like this picture of us in Darlene's yard. My head is shaved nice and I have my black tank top on. I look less like Uncle Fester and more like Vin Diesel. We should use this." I agree. Rob looks great in the shot, but I look hot and sweaty.

"I hate it Rob, why can't we use another one."

"I don't want to look like one of those tourists wearing a Hawaiian shirt walking around with a two thousand dollar camera around his neck. Besides, you are always adorable, so what are you worried about? When it comes to looks I am obviously the weak link."

I consider Rob's feeling as I glance again at the photo. I hid away for hours while writing this book, even when Rob wanted to watch a movie or have dinner with me. He was very supportive when I received those rejection letters from literary agents and kept insisting I keep at it. Maybe I should give him this one, and let him pick the picture where he looks like an action movie star.

"Okay, you win. Let's use it. But if there is a next time I choose the picture." I look over the snapshot and notice the outfit he is wearing; a black tank top and black track pants. He looks like he stepped off the set of *Goodfellas*. He might as well be leaning against a Cadillac with a couple of goons standing alongside. He should really reconsider the Hawaiian shirts.

"Okay, now there is nothing left to do but wait for the article to come out. I'm going out back to do some gardening. Do you know the iguanas ate all of my plants on the side of the house? I can't figure it out."

In my attempt to lure Sergio's monkeys over to my side of the street, I've been dumping fruit rinds and rotten vegetables outside. There have been no monkey sightings just an endless battalion of iguanas. "Sorry honey. I don't have a clue where they are all coming from." No need to disclose my strategy just yet. I need a little more time for the monkeys to find the compost pile. As for Rob's plants, they've become an unfortunate casualty.

"Have you seen my mp3 player?" he calls out. "I might as well listen to some crazy rap music while I try to scare these lizards away." I tell Rob to check my purse downstairs while I pour myself a glass of iced tea.

It isn't long before Rob returns with a big red mark on his arm. He looks slightly dazed. "Oh no, what happened?" I ask.

"I reached into your purse and got bit by something."

"You reached into the black one on the dresser?"

"No, you had a purse hanging on the doorknob inside the closet. When I started feeling around in there, something stung me." I'm trying to remember the last time I used that bag; it must have been over six months ago. Practically anything could be living in there.

"It's starting to burn," Rob complains. While he's busy looking at his arm, I see something crawl from behind his back and creep up his shirt. "Nadine…why are you looking at me funny?"

I can't speak but the expression on my face gives it away. Ironically, it's the same *The Scream* expression I have in most of my photos. It is—by far—the largest scorpion that has ever roamed the planet. It's clearly a monster straight out of *Clash of the Titans* and I do… precisely nothing… to warn my husband. There's no need, he's a goner for sure.

I have never seen Rob get flustered by a bug. He never gets hysterical or spins in circles like I do. However, Rob makes up for lost time by pounding on his chest with such intensity I'm positive he's going to knock the wind out of himself. The scorpion flies into the air and lands a few feet away. But get this—the scorpion charges back toward Rob. It's a fight to the death.

In my mind, the scorpion has just grown over six feet tall. His stinger is raised so high it casts a shadow on Rob; his pincers outstretched ready to apply the ultimate death grip. He runs toward Rob at full speed. My husband holds his ground, raises his foot, and...

Splat!

Yellowish gook spreads across the floor underneath Rob's sneaker. "The next time you see a scorpion crawl across my chest, would you mind giving me a head's up? You just stood there staring. How does that help me?" He wipes off his shoe while I get the broom. In a way, I feel bad for the scorpion, but you have to admit—the little shitter had it coming.

After working in the garden, Rob returns and gets a glass of water. He takes a sip but makes a funny face. "That's strange. My tongue is getting numb." I Google his symptom and find out it's a serious side effect to a scorpion sting.

"When you say serious, how serious are we talking about here?" Rob asks.

"Well, they lump it in with blurred vision, roving eye movements, seizures, and salivations. Hmm... they mention death, but it's the last symptom listed. I wonder if it's similar to reading the ingredients on a label. The first is the most prevalent while the last ingredient is negligible. So maybe death fits in the negligible category. You want me to call a doctor?"

"Nah... just get me some Ibuprofen. And can you make me a pork chop too? I'm starving."

This is so Rob. Not even a mouth full of neurotoxin can make him miss dinner.

Blame It on the Moon

When Rob wakes up the next morning, the numbness in his tongue is almost gone. It swelled slightly after the scorpion sting rendering him unable to pronounce certain words. Mrs. Cohen would have loved this and numerous phrases involving Sally's ability to ride red roller coasters would have been prescribed immediately.

It appears he will recover from the scorpion sting, but I notice he is holding his side where he had hernia surgery. It's been months since the operation, and for the most part, Rob is doing well. He's back to his usual routine with the exception of his weightlifting. He feels the area of the surgery is still swollen and fears re-injury.

"It's like I know something has been done down there. I get an ache near the scar every month."

"You're not eighteen anymore," I say. "You have to expect that after surgery you may never be one hundred percent again. Face it. You and I are getting older."

"I refuse to accept that. Professional bodybuilders come back from stuff like this all the time. I need to speak to the doctor."

"What are you going to say—you want to start benching three hundred pounds again? Sooner or later you have to start accepting your limitations or you'll end up needing another hernia surgery. I don't want to go through that again, and I know you don't want to either."

"I have that follow-up appointment scheduled. I was going to cancel, but it's probably best that we go and speak with the doctor." The surgeon had previously explained this type of surgery takes time to heal, but apparently Rob feels his superior Italian genetics should allow him to recover faster than the average mortal.

We take a ride back to the hospital and sit in the crowded waiting room again. Today I come prepared with a few things to keep me busy: Sudoku puzzle, WWII history book, and a roll of toilet paper. I learned on our last visit that all three of these things are invaluable when visiting this Costa Rican hospital.

This doesn't bring back pleasant memories, especially since the last time we were here they wouldn't even take out his stitches. We have since learned that this hospital is one of the most underfunded in the country, and when we tell Ticos that Rob had his surgery there, they raise their eyebrows and make the sign of the cross (not the reaction you are looking for when evaluating a medical center). But somehow Rob still believes he will get some miraculous answer from the doctor that will turn back time and make him as strong as he was before the surgery.

After waiting five hours, the receptionist waves us into a room. The doctor on staff today is the roly-poly surgeon we saw at our first appointment. Rob tries to explain the discomfort that he feels near his groin.

"It seems to hit me every month. I get achiness in the incision area." Rob lifts his shirt, touches the area, and makes pained expression. He then gives the doctor a double bicep pose, and tries to explain that he wants to work out again.

"Este Lunes," the doctor says.

"Uh… what does that mean?" Rob asks.

"I don't know, Rob. Lunes means Monday. Maybe he asking us when you had the surgery?" Rob and I continue whispering this lengthy side conversation in front of the doctor like we are deciding whether to buy an extended warranty for a refrigerator.

"Lunes," the doctor impatiently repeats.

"No, Julio. I had the surgery in July, Señor."

"No, no, no. Lunes dolor!" The surgeon grabs a calendar off of the wall and points to a little picture of a full moon. "This week... full moon," he says in English. Now I remember; Lunes also means moon.

"Rob, I think you have moon pain." It appears that this celestial body is responsible for residual hernia discomfort.

"That's just perfect. I'm a crippled werewolf."

The doctor promptly takes out his Winnie the Pooh notebook, checks off Rob's name, and gets up from behind his desk. Since the two nitwits in his office don't appear to be leaving, he walks over to the door and escorts us out. But before we leave, he hands Rob a prescription for Ibuprofen. Not intergalactic Ibuprofen, but actual earthly drugs that will help with inflammation.

"You know, I think that it's a pretty good diagnosis," I say as we drive home.

"Oh really? I come all this way to find out I'm being molested by the moon."

"Let's think about this: you have some discomfort in your incision area, nothing major. It hits every month for a few days, then goes away. If we were in the states you would most likely be getting an MRI and about a dozen other tests to find out there is nothing seriously wrong. You might even get a little exploratory surgery to boot, when all the while the moon is using your nuts as a speed bag."

There are things I love about Costa Rica: the friendliness, the incredible wildlife, and the laid back lifestyle. But a moon pain diagnosis is about the most delightful thing I have experienced so far. The next full moon can't come around fast enough as far as I'm concerned.

Once back at the house, Rob collapses on the couch and asks for a cup of coffee. When I suggest he do it himself, he explains he can't—moon pain requires him to relax for the rest of the day. It turns out this uncommon diagnosis suits him just fine.

Buried Treasure

"Let's go somewhere new today," Rob proposes. "I heard of a place called Pirate's Bay."

"Where is it?"

"It's only twenty minutes from here. There is a small cave in a huge rock a few hundred yards off shore. There's an old legend that Captain Morgan hid his treasure and rum there."

"Sounds like a pretty cool day out. How do we get out to this rock?"

"Just walk, I guess."

I love how we keep finding fun things to do since living here. There are so many coves and beaches; it will take years to explore them all. We gather up some towels and suntan lotion. It looks like we're hunting for booty today.

We drive toward Playa Grande, a popular beach for surfers, before veering down a dusty, dirt road. Our path darkens as sunrays struggle to pierce the thick vegetation overhead. We stop the car and let an iguana cross the road when I notice two Calico butterflies on the side of my window. The male is snapping his wings, but the female ignores him and flies away.

"Are you sure we're going in the right direction? I don't see anyone around." Rob asks.

"I think so. We passed a sign five minutes ago that said it was only a few more miles. Turn left here. That's west, so we will eventually hit a beach. I don't know which one, but we'll hit something."

A moment later, we turn a bend and are welcomed with a startling view. A monstrous rock rises from the ocean as if pushed from below. It reminds me of Neptune, the Roman God of the sea. It's an indomitable presence in an otherwise ordinary seascape. If I were a pirate, this is exactly the place where I would hide my treasure.

Waves smash against the rock spraying sea foam into the air. Pelicans circle the top and land on the narrow ledges. They fluff their feathers and stare at us with measured interest. Trees have somehow rooted into the stone and cover the top half like a thick layer of moss. Tall cacti are scattered along the lower half, and from a distance their stems resemble the arms of waving giants.

"Fantastic!" Rob exclaims as we park the car and walk toward the beach. "Who would have thought before turning that corner we would see this. I think the only way to get there is to swim."

"No way. It's high tide and too far." While we consider our options, a dog runs toward us and playfully sniffs our feet. A man and a woman follow close behind.

"I'm sorry. My dog is so friendly she runs up to everyone. Hi, I'm Sandy." The woman reaches out and shakes my hand. "This is Ian."

"Do you guys live around here?" I ask.

"Yup, just ten minutes away," Ian says. "I bet you're thinking about going out to that rock."

"You read my mind. Do you know how to get out there?"

"I sure do. You have to wait for the lowest tide of the month. The channel opens up and you can actually walk there. I've done it before and it's pretty cool. Do you want to do it with us the next time we go?"

"That sounds great. When do you think that will be?" Rob asks.

"This Friday. Just give me a call and we can all go out there together."

We talk a little longer and learn that they are not a couple but neighbors who live across the street from each other. Sandy is in the process of building her home, while Ian already bought his and is living the perfect retired life. We make plans to get together on Friday and hike out to Captain Morgan's rock.

On the day of the outing, we wake up early and drive over to Ian's house. It's a beautiful, newly remodeled two-story with an in-ground pool and a yard full of fruit trees.

"I'm enjoying every bit of my retirement," Ian remarks as we all head out to Pirate's Bay. "I love living here. I'm off the beaten path so it's always quiet. The howler monkeys wake me up every morning. There are lots of birds in my trees. Life couldn't get any better. I even pick my own bananas."

"Where else can you live like this?" Sandy adds.

I learn Sandy has lived all around the world but has decided to make Costa Rica her home. She spent a considerable amount of time in Paris, and I can't wait to drill her with questions. It's a dream of mine to travel there one day and I hope to finally do it within the next couple years. I flood her with questions about museums, cafes, and what she misses most about the "City of Light."

"I miss the bowling," she replies. I must have heard her wrong.

"You miss *bowling*?"

"I sure do. A bunch of us girls would get together and bowl every week. It was a blast and they were so much fun to hang around with. It's my fondest memory of living there." This is probably the most pragmatic answer I've ever heard. It seems no matter where you have lived, it's the people you meet along the way you miss the most. I think about Darlene and Frankie and realize just how true this is. When I reminisce about Grecia, I think of them and all the good times we had. I miss them terribly. Dolores the Dog Lady... not so much.

Pirate's Bay looks completely different today. Low tide has opened up a sandy path from the beach all the way out to Captain Morgan's rock. It's as if Moses parted the sea once more just for us.

Ian steps out first and we all follow close behind. "The rocks are slippery so be careful. I should have told you to wear an old pair of sneakers."

Unfortunately, I'm wearing my only pair so I take them off. Ian skillfully walks across while Rob, Sandy, and I lag behind. At any moment a wave can sneak up and push us all over. Once again, knowing the tide chart is crucial when exploring Costa Rica.

We finally make it to the rock, but I can't find any cave. "Where is it Ian? I don't see anything."

"You don't see it," Ian smiles and points toward two pelicans watching us from a ledge, "because it's up there." I follow his finger and realize the only way to the cave is a vertical climb straight up. It's like I'm back at Rincon de la Vieja but without the safety rope and brain cushioning helmet.

"Rob, I'm not sure I can do this," I whisper.

"I wasn't expecting this either. But it's only twenty feet, that's not too bad."

"Watch me first," Ian says. "Make sure you pay attention where I put my hands and feet, and whatever you do, don't look down as you climb." He swiftly scales up the wall. It seems as natural to him as his retirement. Sandy follows, taking her time and placing each foot with care. She eventually makes it and stares down at us.

"You can do it, Nadine. It wasn't that hard."

"I'm going to be behind you, so if you were to fall, I'll soften your landing," Rob says.

I reach for a rock and immediately feel Rob's hand on my foot. "Stop touching me, Rob. It's distracting and making me nervous."

"I don't like where you placed your foot. I don't want it to slip off."

"Seriously, stop it. I just started and you are already making it harder for me." I place my other foot on a small ridge and Rob once again puts his hand on it.

"I'm just guiding you." I climb quickly, mostly to get away from Rob. He is only making me anxious and is going to end up causing precisely what he is trying to prevent.

I think back to my last rock climbing adventure and dig my hands deep into the small rocky, ledges. Once near the cave's edge, Ian hoists me inside with the strength of a linebacker. Within seconds, Rob is inside as well.

It's completely dark; the only light coming from the entrance of the cave. Sandy takes a picture and the flash startles hundreds of bats. Like a scene from *The Birds,* they fly straight toward our heads. Everyone leans back against the wall but I don't want to rest against any bat guano. I just stand there while dozens dart over me, brushing their tiny wings across the tips of my ears. I'm not sure how many bat caves a person typically explores in their lifetime, but I'm pretty sure I'm bordering on above average.

"This is sweet, let's look around and see if there's anything in here," Rob says after all the bats are gone. Unfortunately, there is no treasure; not even one bottle of rum. I turn around and glance out through the entrance of the cave. It's a remarkable view. As I walk to the ledge, I'm startled by a passing pelican. He is so close I could reach out and touch his feathers. He continues riding the breeze before disappearing around the rock.

After making sure we did not miss any cannon balls or gold coins, we decide to head back. Exiting is equally, if not more treacherous, and I pray that I don't miss a step and lose my grip. The minute I get far enough down Rob reaches out, grabs my waist, and lowers me into his arms. He holds me for a moment against his chest. I reach around his neck, bury my face in his shoulder, and know his love for me is as mighty as this rock.

And just like Neptune, Rob safely places me on the ground and we walk hand in hand back across the sandy channel.

Free Falling

We seldom had problems with car repairs in Grecia. Pedro, our favorite mechanic and good friend, had the best prices and would quickly have our car back on the road. When he couldn't get the part you needed, he learned to make do with what he could find. Things always seemed to work out. However, since moving to this small beach town, even something as simple as replacing the belts on your car can lead to a number of problems.

"Oh brother, this isn't good." Rob says while trying to start the car.

"What?"

"This keeps happening. The engine is taking longer and longer to turn over. Damn it, I shouldn't have let our new mechanic replace those belts."

"Why did you have them changed in the first place?"

"Because I was trying to keep up proper maintenance. Now look at it. Soon the car isn't going to start at all. Serves me right."

"So what do you think went wrong?"

"I know that meatball put the wrong belts on the car. Either they are slipping or we may need a new alternator."

"Now what?"

"I guess I have no other choice than to bring it back in."

The next morning, as Rob predicted, the car won't start. He calls the mechanic and asks if he can get a tow to the garage.

"No, we don't do that. Just ask a friend to pull you with a rope," the mechanic suggests. This is pretty much the method used in all of Costa Rica and fits perfectly with Rob's do-it-yourself philosophy. As long as I've known my husband, he has never paid for a tow. Once he broke down in New Jersey and called his friend Mike for help. Mike showed up in his Mercury Cougar and pushed Rob over both the Goethals and Verrazano Bridge back to Brooklyn. As far as I know, no illegal U-turns on either bridge were made (probably because this story does not involve Tommy Walnuts).

"Maybe we can pay someone to help us," I suggest.

"Why would I do that? You don't even get in trouble here for pulling a car with a rope, and the shop is right down the road. I'm calling Ian for help."

"Really? We just met him, and his car isn't all that great either. It's too big of an imposition," I say, but Rob is already dialing Ian's number. He seems like a really nice guy and I hate that in the first week of our friendship we are asking for roadside assistance. However, we don't have anyone else to ask and Ian agrees to come over in an hour.

Two hours pass but there is still no sign of Ian. It's not surprising since no one is ever on time in Costa Rica. It is a challenge for me to get used to this since I'm an on-time kind of gal. I'm a punctual person living in a country designed for tardiness. On the other hand, this suits Rob's laid back personality just fine. That and pulling a car with a rope is paradise according to my husband.

Eventually, Ian calls. "You're never going to believe this. While coming to help you, I drove right into a ditch full of mud. I'm not only stuck, but it's swallowing my car like quicksand. Sandy is with me and we need someone to pull us out." I am all but positive Ian may never volunteer to help us again. We are turning out to be those friends who invite you over for a dinner party only to upsell you Amway products.

"Sorry buddy. My car is shot and my scooter has two flat tires. Not that I can pull you out with that, but I could have shown up with my winches."

"No sweat, we'll find help. I'll get there. Hang tight."

"I hate having no transportation," Rob complains after hanging up the phone. "If the scooter was working, I could at least get over there. What if something happened to you right now? How am I going to get you help?"

"I don't know Rob. Call a taxi like everyone else?"

"What if you fell and were bleeding?"

"Why do you have me bleeding already? Where did I fall anyway? Did I get caught in one of your booby traps out back? Or did I get startled and crack my head on the dresser after you jumped out of the closet? Now that I think about it, there really are so many scenarios to choose from."

"I'm not joking, Nadine. Bad things happen all the time and there is no way to get you out of here."

"You mean like when you lift weights with a suitcase belt and your guts fall out of your abdomen? Something bad like that?"

"Laugh all you want, but I'm looking out for you." While we wait for Ian, Rob decides to bring the scooter to the mechanic as well. He's anxious to get the flat tires fixed but doesn't own the tool to get the wheels off the bike. Rob explains how we will both lift the scooter into the back of the SUV through the hatchback.

"Both of us?" I repeat.

"Yes. I can lift it; I just need you to guide me."

"The last time we shoved the scooter in the back, it hung out over the bumper and both mirrors broke off. Can't we find a different way to get it there?"

"No."

"This is ridiculous and a really dumb thing to do after hernia surgery."

"We have to get it to the mechanic. If I had the tools to get the tires off I would do it myself. Trust me, I'm doing all this for you. Now when I say three, I will lift and you push toward me. One… Two… Three."

Rob lifts the scooter with all his might while I try shoving it through the opening; however, it hits something and slips out of Rob's hands. It narrowly misses my foot. It's certain that if we keep this up I might actually end up bleeding out all over the driveway.

"This is crazy. And look how red your face is. Your hernia is probably about to bust open."

"Okay, I see the problem," Rob says as he inspects the back of the SUV. "We need to tilt it to the right. You see, it got caught on this hinge."

"Are you listening to me?"

"On three."

"I'm not going to do it."

"Okay. One…"

"No."

"Two,"

"Wait!"

"Three." Rob struggles with the back wheel and I have no choice but to help him push from the front. Our scooter is now precariously hanging out the back of our SUV.

Eventually, Ian and Sandy show up completely covered in mud. "A guy in a truck down the road pulled me out for a couple bucks. He probably parks there because so many vehicles get stuck. He's got a pretty good thing going," Ian laughs while rinsing off with the hose.

Rob brings out the jumper cables and attaches them to Ian's battery. Our car starts and Ian decides to follow Rob to the mechanic. Unfortunately, the car dies again just a few feet outside our driveway. He suggests that Ian pull the car with a rope but our friend does not look too enthusiastic about the idea.

"If you don't want to pull the car, why don't you push it?" Rob asks.

"But you have a scooter hanging out the back."

"Oh, crap. That's right. But there is plenty of room. Don't worry, I secured it with a rope."

"Are you sure?"

"Absolutely."

"Okay, I hope that scooter is tied tightly in there. I don't want it rolling out the back." Ian lines his car up with our back bumper and guns his motor. He pushes the car and they both disappear down the road. Rob calls twenty minutes later; he has to leave the car at the garage for a few days but he can pick up the scooter in a couple hours. Ian and Rob decide to hang out in Tamarindo until it's ready and promises to bring dinner back for Sandy and me.

I hand Sandy a glass of wine as she tells me stories about her life in Europe. "I love learning about new cultures. You get used to living a certain way, only to learn an entire country does everything differently. At first it's jarring, but then you adjust and start to make friends."

It's fun to listen to someone who is so upbeat. I'm even more impressed because she moved all around the world as a single woman. I have Rob to lean on, but Sandy is on her own. She proves that being single shouldn't prevent you from traveling. She could easily do seminars on this topic or run a travel agency specifically for women. In the short time she has been here, she has already started participating in many expat groups and charity functions. She reminds me a lot of Darlene back in Grecia. She, too, is very social and has made wonderful connections with people.

Finally, the guys return, but Rob is limping into the house with one arm over Ian's shoulder.

"What the hell happened?" I holler.

"We ended up staying in Tamarindo for a little longer than we expected," Rob explains. "By the time we showed up at the mechanic they were closed for the night. I thought I'd take a look inside to see if I could get the scooter."

"I just want to tell you that I tried to talk him out of it." Ian interjects. "It was pitch black in there."

"Anyway, as I was looking for the scooter I couldn't see my hand in front of my face. There were pit bulls running around me; and I could hear the pitter-patter of their feet. It started freaking me out. I tried retracing my steps to find a way out, but the next thing I knew I was falling through the air. I instinctively stretched out my arms, catching myself. It's a good thing I have cat-like reflexes or I would have fallen right into a bay pit."

"Bay pit?" I echo.

"Yeah, it must have been a fifteen foot drop. I nearly cracked my head open and ended up smashing my leg pretty bad." He rolls up his pants and shows me his shin. It looks awful—possibly broken—but Rob insists that he is fine. "I just need ice and a few anti-inflammatoires. Maybe I should elevate it for a while too. But first let's enjoy this pizza."

"I *told* him not to go in. Your husband is nuts," Ian sighs, a little shaken by the incident. I now know for certain I will never see Ian or Sandy again. I feel like showering them with streamers while yelling "Bon Voyage." They should leave as quickly as possible before Boy Wonder has any more stupid ideas. I wave to them as they drive away. It was good while it lasted.

"I really wanted that scooter and I didn't want to wait until morning. Oh boy, it's starting to throb pretty good."

"Are you sure it's not broken?"

"It's not broken; I can put weight on it." I take a look at his shin. There is huge dent and a big circular black spot about three inches in circumference. The epidermis is completely crushed, and surely the layers underneath must be as well. I used to work at a wound maintenance ward in a hospital and I know we will need to clean this wound out or it will become necrotic. It's going to be ugly, but I don't tell Rob this disturbing information yet. I'll save it for tomorrow morning.

"Look on the bright side—in the end I got the scooter, and I'm glad if anything happens to you I can get you out of here." Rob positions himself on the couch and asks for fresh pillows, ice, the remote control, and another slice of pizza.

The Pen is Mightier than the Kayak

"I've been thinking," Rob announces as he hobbles into the living room. Three words I don't want to hear early in the morning. "If we can't get that water letter, I've come up with a few alternatives." The worst thing about Rob being laid up is not the constant need for ice packs or sandwiches; it's the crazy schemes that pop into his head. "We can dig our own well."

"How far will we have to go?"

"Unfortunately, about a zillion miles," he confesses.

"So now we're digging to the center of the earth. Great."

"Okay, scratch that one. How about a cistern? We could collect enough water to last us all year."

"Where would all that water go?"

"Into an underground tank. Of course with that much stagnant water we would need to devise a plan to keep it clean and make sure bacteria doesn't build up. Oh... and it'll cost us about sixty thousand dollars."

"Next."

"Now don't say anything until I'm through. We pee in the woods..."

"No!"

"Wait, I haven't finished. We design a water system where we use gray water for the garden. It'll be a great source of nitrogen for the tomato plants."

"The tomato plants that we eat?"

"Yeah, what do you think?"

"Rob, I think you have officially lost your mind."

"A waterless toilet?"

"We already put that one to bed. And quite frankly, the waterless toilet was never on the table to begin with."

While Rob is contemplating sanitation schemes, I search CNN.com and find the article—it has just posted. I forget all about Rob's urine-enriched garden and stare at the page. There we are, Rob and I, standing in Darlene and Frankie's yard. The reporter wrote about us quitting our job and even mentions *Happier Than A Billionaire*. My book is on CNN. It's hard to believe.

"Rob, the article is out and it's awesome. Look, there's a picture of us at the beach!" I shriek as Rob stands over me.

"This is big, Nadine. Look at how many people "liked" the article already. Did you see the comments? People are already chiming in."

"I don't know what to say. I mean, this is crazy!"

"I'll tell you what we do… get on Facebook and post this link. This is it. Tweet it, use every social media to get it out there. If anything is going to happen with your book, it's going to be now."

Rob has been quietly cautious of this process until this moment. He realizes this could be the big break every writer hopes for, and being on CNN's radar is invaluable. I immediately send the link to all of my friends and family, write a blog post about it, and link it to my Facebook page.

I Skype my mother and tell her the article is online. She calls my dad over to the computer and I study their faces as they both read the story. Once they are done, my dad sticks his face a half inch from the camera.

"You did it, kid. You did it." It seems like my book is starting to turn him around about my move to Costa Rica.

"Congratulations," my mother says.

"I need to tell some people about this," my dad chimes in.

"I don't want your father bragging to all his relatives. We have to do it subtly." To my mother, subtly means not telling anyone at all.

"I need the addresses of Stan and Vivian. I'm sending a letter to them today. Remember that postcard we got from their damn trip to Ireland? Well, this is better than Ireland. My daughter is on CNN baby. Maybe I'll refrain from a letter. Yes, perhaps a postcard is the best way to go with this. Something simple, but direct."

"Don't you dare, Bill," my mother yells. This good news has suddenly turned into an argument over how my distant relatives—ones that I have not seen since I was seven years old—will learn of my good fortune. My parents are now having a screaming match which quickly deteriorates into one where my dad is being unmercifully blamed for drinking an entire carton of Half and Half.

I say my goodbyes and go back to the CNN article. More and more comments are coming in and I check the stats on my website. They are ten times their usual number and the visitors are staying on each webpage for twice as long as before. This is all very exciting.

"You've done good. Who in their lifetime can say they've been on CNN without committing a heinous crime?" Rob says.

I go into the bedroom to lie down. It's all so surreal. But before I can get too comfortable, Rob calls me back into the living room.

"Just wanted to let you know word is quickly getting around. Our neighbors in Grecia just emailed us to congratulate you. They've already ordered a bunch of books for their family back home."

Every ounce of blood drains from my face. "Which neighbors?"

"The kayaking ones that used to live next door. Oh Lord, Nadine. Please tell me you didn't write about them."

Here's the thing: Rob has only read parts of the book. He may be surprised to find out what's inside.

Part III

No Apology Left Behind Tour

So my book made it on CNN. I should be popping champagne and sharing a private jet with Mick Jagger to Monaco. Instead, I'm on the worst book tour ever.

"You have to copy what you wrote and send it to our old neighbors. It's been a week and it's just not right," Rob reprimands.

"But I don't want to. Maybe they won't even notice it."

"It's about when Harry asked me to break his brother's legs. How many kooky kayakers have we lived next door to that asked me to throw people a beating? For crying out loud, he's sending the book to all his family members in the states."

"Yeah, I guess that's probably a bad idea."

"Can you imagine what Christmas dinner is going to be like over there when the family reads it?"

I acquiesce and email the couple, word for word, the passage concerning the infamous broken leg powwow. Maybe they'll think it's funny? I'll explain that it's just a characterization of them, hoping there's a good chance they'll laugh at the whole thing.

We get an email back from the wife who says not to worry about it. She thinks it's hilarious and giggled while reading it. But just when I think I'm off the hook, I get an unpleasant email from the husband:

Once there was a guy called Harry who asked a city slicker for a contact to take care of a situation. Next thing Harry knows the East Coaster tells his wife something Harry said in confidence. Now Harry is sick of Costa Rica and thinking about moving back home to get away from these North Easterners.

"Okay Rob… I guess he took it a little hard. But it was way too funny not to write about. Anyway, why should I feel bad that he asked a guy he hardly knew to break his brother's legs?"

"Don't worry about him. I'm glad you apologized. Now check this out: after I posted the CNN link to Facebook, a lot of people started chiming in saying they were buying the book. My old girlfriend somehow caught wind of all this and she just wrote me saying she bought one too and is going to recommend it to her book club.

"Did you say your old girlfriend?"

"Why are you looking at me like that? You got to be kidding me. Please tell me you didn't write anything about her."

"It's not actually about her. Well… sort of. I wrote about how important it is for people to be good travel partners, and how you wanted to go to the beach while she was content to stay indoors and do arts and crafts."

"And that's how you wrote it—just like that?"

"No… I gave it a little humorous twist, just for effect. I might have mentioned macramé friendship bracelets in there somewhere."

"Let me read it," Rob barks. I hand him the passage, and after a thoughtful read he puts the book down and glares back at me with a furrowed brow. "It's snarky, Nadine."

"It's not my fault. Why didn't you read the whole book before I uploaded it to Amazon?"

"Now you're blaming *me*? Copy this passage and email it to her before she tells more of her friends to buy the book."

"No way, I don't even know her. It's too embarrassing."

"You know what's more embarrassing? Recommending a book to your book club that has a snarky paragraph about you written inside."

I wonder how many apologies I'm going to have to make today. When did my city-slicker husband become my moral barometer? The emotional high I was on just moments ago now has me feeling terrible. I didn't mean to hurt anyone's feelings. My big mouth (even in the written word), has got me in trouble once again. The lady on the airplane was right—I should sit down and shut up for the remainder of my life.

"Your old boyfriend just emailed. He also bought the book. I'm not even going to ask if you wrote about him."

"I think I called him a jerk," I confess.

"He wrote that he's up to the Swiss bank story. Maybe he read it already and you're off the hook."

"No, he's in the chapter after that. I think I need to lie down, I'm not feeling so good."

"I wouldn't be feeling so good either."

"I think I have moon pain," I groan.

"Nope, full moon is *next* week. You have apology pain. Now go walk the plank."

This is humiliating. Now I'm apologizing to my old boyfriend? I never thought anyone would read the book, no less people from my past. But ever since that CNN article came out, my plans of remaining an incognito author have been replaced with being a public apologizer.

Aside from the apology tour, my email box is flooded with emails. Most are from people asking me questions about moving here, but I also have a good number of emails from people either requesting a condominium rental or a ride from the airport.

The best one by far is a guy from the Middle East who contacted me to replace a souvenir he had lost while vacationing in Costa Rica a few years back. Apparently, his wife never forgave him. He wants me to find the souvenir and mail it to Dubai. I find this message particularly fascinating because he doesn't describe what the object is.

It could be a postcard, a hammock, or—for all I know—a poisonous dart gun.

"There's no way I'm running around Tamarindo looking for a souvenir," I snapped after reading it.

"Stay calm. I think you should do it."

"Why on earth would I?"

"Why? Because honey, you have no idea… no idea at all… what hoops a man will jump through to get his wife to stop bitching at him." Rob looks at me in a manner that would suggest he has suffered from this horrible malady on more than one occasion during our married life.

I should probably have sympathy for Dubai Guy. Maybe this is the big elephant in the room, the wife berating her husband at every Ramadan about his carelessness. Then again, perhaps this guy deserves it. The wife was probably carrying the diaper bag *and* pushing the stroller around Tamarindo while he was off licking frogs. I can come up with a thousand different scenarios why I should dislike this guy, but it's becoming obvious that I am just taking out my aggressions on this poor, henpecked hubby.

"Okay, I'll try to find it, but he's going to have to describe what the item is and send me the money first. Shipping to Dubai is not going to be cheap."

I log off my email account and check out a popular chat room about living in Costa Rica. There's a good chance someone came across the CNN article. I read a few entries—it's a firing squad.

This girl's a phony. This whole CNN piece is a sham. How come she doesn't talk about the varying residency categories foreigners have to jump through to retire here? Perhaps she's hiding something??
DrunkinTraveler

Look at this jerk. He photoshopped an ocelot on his back. This is straight from the mouth of the tourism board. Don't believe it.
BeachGringos

I'm a phony? I'm hiding something? I go from annoyed to angry in five seconds and type a steaming reply:

Dear DrunkinTraveler,
Very perceptive, and I can see you wear your screen name well...

What am I doing? I don't want to participate in this. I hit the backspace key and delete every single word to DrunkinTraveler. I have to learn to let it go and not care what anyone says. This is not going to be easy.

"Hey, my mom called, and my uncles just bought the book," Rob says from across the room. "They're so excited for us. You didn't write anything about them... right?"

I pick up the phone and start calling Rob's uncles. At the rate I'm going, this apology tour is going to sell out Madison Square Garden.

No Alternative for our Alternator

The mechanic calls and informs us our alternator is busted and needs to be replaced. This should be an easy fix; simply swap out the bad alternator with a new one that matches the make of the car. The reason we bought this type of car in the first place was because we saw so many on the road in Costa Rica, with the theory that parts for our vehicle will be easy to find. I love living in "theoretical world." It's an effortless place where Xerox machines are plentiful and toilet seats can be found in every bathroom.

After a week of the mechanic fiddling with our car, it's fixed and ready to be picked up. Before heading out on the scooter, Rob bandages and applies fresh ointment to his leg. He's been taking really good care of it since the fall. I explained that we had to get rid of all the dead tissue out of his shin or it would turn gangrene. Rob perked up pretty quick after that. It is truly a horrible thing to go through.

I want to help Rob but I don't have the best work history in regards to this procedure. Back when I worked at a hospital, I was asked to assist a diabetic man in the hydrotherapy room. The therapist had to leave for a few moments and asked me to help the man remove his foot from the whirlpool. I briefly glanced down at the open gash in-between his toes, and had a feeling that all the blood was draining from my face. I ran out of the room and fainted next to a guy doing leg extensions for a torn meniscus.

The situation rapidly deteriorated from there. The diabetic man was so freaked out by my reaction, he too looked down at his wound; consequently, passing out and falling straight into the water in front of him. Through my haziness, I watched three therapists jump over me to save this poor guy from drowning. I was reassigned to cleaning the exercise mats after that.

Rob took all this to heart and started picking out the dead tissue himself and packing the wound every day. He's the toughest guy I've ever met, especially since I almost passed out again while watching him do it.

We get to the mechanic, pay a reasonable sum, and I drive the car back home while Rob follows on the scooter. As I climb the last hill to our house, I push my foot hard against the accelerator. The car takes the abuse and doesn't stall once.

"It's running great," I tell Rob as he pulls into the driveway.

"Pop the hood, I want to see the mechanic's work." Rob disappears in front of the car and starts to stick his hands in the engine. "Mother fu…"

"What's wrong?"

"It's gigantic!"

"What's gigantic?"

"The nuclear reactor that he attached to the side of my engine. Look at it—he hacksawed the base off this alternator to make it fit. He *hacksawed* an alternator. What kind of asshole would do something like that?"

"Measure twice, hacksaw once. That's my motto."

"You're hilarious, Nadine, but it's all wrong. Get back in the car. We have to go for a ride and see how it sounds going up and down hills." I'm fairly confident the car will sound fine. I drove it home and didn't hear any unusual noises. However, after fifteen minutes of driving the car begins to make a funny noise.

Weeee… Weeee

It's rather girly, and nothing like the rugged, masculine SUV sounds it made before.

"Come on. I can't drive around with the car like this. What the hell did he do?" Rob grumbles. I think my husband is more embarrassed of the sound than anything else. If the noise was clickety-clack, or something equally as manly, Rob would surely drive around until the wheels fell off.

"I happen to like the cute noise," I add. As we drive faster, the *weeee* sound becomes so loud it turns heads as we pass people waiting for the bus. It makes me so happy I feel like hanging out the window with a pinwheel.

"We're taking it back. This sound is going to make me crazy."

Seventy dollars and three days later, we drive the car home from the mechanic. In his latest effort to fix the girly noise, this guy replaced it with a grinding one. We once again return the car, presumably so he can hacksaw the entire front end off. It's only a matter of time before our SUV transforms into a tricked out Yugo. All of this leads me to believe being a mechanic may be the most lucrative job in Costa Rica.

We get the car back and all the noises are gone. It's a small victory. Still, I can't help but think about all the problems we've encountered since moving to the beach. The first couple years in Costa Rica were a major adjustment, but I eventually got to a place where I thought most of our headaches were over. Then we move to the beach and Rob's either having surgery or falling into a bay pit. I'm fighting to get a water letter for a piece of property that already has water, while being faced with the task of explaining to my parents why there is an abandoned house filled with African bees next door. I'm searching for the light at the end of the tunnel and, at his point, would even settle for a monkey in my window. I've tried tossing a few melon rinds in the trees, but they still haven't made it to my side of the street yet.

"I can't believe what we are going through just to replace an alternator. It's practically the easiest thing to fix on a car," Rob says. "But at least it looks like it's working now. Oh shit...," Rob points to a little dial on the dashboard that I never noticed before.

"What's that for?"

"It's a voltage meter. It measures how many volts the alternator is putting out. Wow... it kicks out sixteen volts instead of twelve. Now look... quick... look at the needle now." The red indicator pings all the way to the right, past any numbers, struggling to blast straight off the dashboard. Our car is turning into The Hulk.

My Parents Are Coming

My parents are planning a five week visit to Costa Rica. We immediately start looking into places for them to stay. Rob calls several realtors and makes a list of affordable options. I need to make sure whatever accommodations I find has reliable internet since my dad can't live without it. I can't imagine them staying in our house that long without one of us losing our minds.

Every morning my father types *Nadine Pisani* into a search engine to see if someone is talking about the book. He shares what he finds, leaving out anything negative. He is my biggest supporter and has assigned himself the role of public relations coordinator at *Happier Headquarters*. I no longer Google my name because I never know what I'll find. Recently, I came across a guy announcing to the world he would run as far from me as possible if we were ever at a party together. It was touching.

When I think about Party Guy, it makes me wonder what lengths he would go to in order to avoid me. I mean, what type of party are we talking about here? A barbecue? That would be easy; he could duck inside the shed and sharpen the hedge clippers while waiting for me to leave. But what if it's in a studio apartment? I fear he might leap out a ten-story window just to avoid being on my Pictionary team. It appears my social inadequacies cause hysteria rarely seen since the daring escapes from East Berlin.

Rob experiences this same type of delirium after I mention my parents want to visit Costa Rica for over a month. He all but digs an escape tunnel out of our living room.

"A whole month? Don't you think that's a little… uh… long?"

"They should get away in the winter. It is too cold for them now that they are older. And don't worry, my dad doesn't want to stay at our house for five weeks. He sent this email yesterday."

Nadine, this is daddy. We are coming to visit for five weeks. As you are well aware, I'm not at the age where I want to be sharing space with other people. Your mother might, but I have a routine I like to keep and would rather not stay in your house. You tell me you live in a tourist area, so I assume there will be a wide variety of accommodations to choose. I will allow you to do the leg work on this matter.

"I don't mind your parents staying here. I love them, but even in the best of situations a week is usually enough for guests. I know what I'll do. Since that CNN article came out, and we've been getting a lot of people asking us to write posts about their hotels, why don't I see if we can get a stay for them at a reduced cost? Four Seasons has been sharing pictures from our Facebook site. I'm going to contact them and see if they will give us a break on the price. Can't hurt to ask."

"Wow, could you imagine if we got them into the Four Seasons? It would be so exciting for them." I'm already picturing myself snorkeling with George Clooney and palling around with Brad Pitt. (They'll think my loud voice and flailing arms are cute.) "We have to make that happen."

While Rob is trying to figure a way to contact them, I call my mom and tell her our plan.

"I will absolutely not stay there!" she screams into the phone. It's as if I just suggested bunk beds at a hostel. She has clearly slipped into the final stages of dementia.

"You don't understand. What if we got a decreased rate, Mom? What if they let us in for free? Don't you think that would be fantastic? It's the best hotel around." I hear my mother put down the phone. She proceeds to share this horrid news with my father.

"Listen here, Nadine," my father barks into the phone. "I'm not sure what's going on, but I have no intention of packing a suit and tie. I threw them out the day I retired. I'm not sure why at this stage in the game you want to put your parents through this charade." As my father continues to berate me, I can hear my mother scream in the background.

"I'm not packing fancy shoes. I have heel spurs and I can't wear anything except my sandals. I was only planning on taking a carry-on. Jesus Christ, why did you do this to us?"

I hang up the phone and reach for a bottle of rum. Unfortunately, it's a temporary fix for what ails me. "What did they say?" Rob asks.

"They're excited." Just as I'm about to hit the bottle, my sister calls.

"I want to let you know, full panic mode in the Hays household thanks to you. Mom just called and screamed something like you booked them a month someplace where she has to wear heels and dad has to wear a suit for dinner? What's that all about?"

"Stacey, I didn't book anything. I was thinking out loud and wondered if I could get a decreased rate if I write about their hotel. For heaven's sake, it's the Four Seasons I'm looking into."

"Wait a second, back up. You're trying to get them into the Four Seasons hotel. Like, terry cloth robes and champagne on ice Four Seasons?"

"Yes."

"Our parents have lost their minds. They called me screaming that you ruined their vacation. Listen, if you can make that happen, just book it. Drive them there, drop them off in the parking lot, and take off. I'm not about to feel bad because they get a chance to stay at one of the best hotels in the world. Right now I'd settle for a quiet room with blackout curtains."

"Yes, the mommy vampire special. I'm sure I've heard of it."

"Exactly, the one where there is a bottle of wine stashed behind each potted plant in the corner. I don't even need glasses, plastic cups will do. Now that I think about it, it doesn't even have to be a bottle—boxed wine is fine," my sister adds. "And skip the cups. I'll drink it right out of the box."

"Would you also like a chauffeur available in case you want to run to the border?"

"You're reading my mind, Nadine."

I don't bother calling my mother back. I'll let her imagine all of the loathsome conditions she will have to endure: the six hundred thread count sheets, Jacuzzi tubs, and ocean views. My parents are driving me crazy and they haven't even boarded the plane yet.

Deep Thoughts

Dad, this 1 star review just came in… it's horrible.

NOT ABOUT ECUADOR, JUST ABOUT STUPIDITY

"This somewhat funny treatise of a couple, who pulled up stakes and moved to Ecuador without any preparation is a keystone cops like read. Unfortunately it casts them as another of the "Ugly Americans", who expect foreign nationals to behave like us. Anyone who moves to a foreign country without even trying to learn the language and then complaining because the people don't speak English is not laughable, it's stupid. These two chiropractors are obviously educated beyond their common sense. I am happy that I only wasted $3.00 on this piece of trash."

I got a 1 star review because the book was not about Ecuador. He read the entire book and couldn't figure that out half way in?

Oh brother… is this how it's going to be, Dad? I don't know if I can take it.

```
From: Dad
To: Nadine
3:35AM
RE: 1 Star Review
```

I find this disturbing. He has the makings of a sociopath, and we must never, ever assign a conscience to a sociopath.

Went to Burger King today and got our senior discount. The place was filled with old people… the stench of death was in the air.

Daddy

Soap, Underwear & Bungee Cords

I eavesdrop as Rob calls over a dozen hotels in the area, "Maybe we could share your story in exchange for a discounted price," my husband explains. "Who am I? I'm *Happier Than A Billionaire*. You've never heard of us?"

This is exactly why I can't make these calls. Once I sense any hesitation, I get nervous and drop the issue. Rob actually enjoys that uncomfortable feeling, and will make you uncomfortable right along with him.

"Yes, I understand the ocean view rooms go for a lot of money, but my wife will put you on her blog. It's a win-win for everybody. Hello... is anyone there?"

"No luck, Rob?"

"That guy just would not budge on price at all, and the Four Seasons hotel said they don't give discounted rates in exchange for publicity. You know what? Jackson said his friend owns a place in that other fancy resort down the road. Let me give him a call and see if we can get a deal there."

Jackson is a handyman the landlord uses to do maintenance on the house. He was here the other day and mentioned that he has a lot of friends in that resort. They have every amenity you can imagine: spa, gym, multiple pools, and a golf course. All of it borders one of the prettiest beaches in Costa Rica. We have tried numerous times to get in but always get turned away. Rob even used the line, "See my wife sitting here, she's *Happier Than A Billionaire*." The guard glanced into the car like he was expecting to see Selma Hayak wearing a bikini; disappointed was an understatement. I can't blame the guy; I, too, am disheartened that I'm not Selma Hayak.

It's extremely embarrassing when Rob does this. "We have to try, sweetie. People don't get anywhere in this world if they don't speak up," he insists. "I once made five hundred dollars a day working a ride at a fair where a person gets flung like a slingshot. Do you know how hard it is to convince someone to be shot up in the air a hundred feet? But I was still able to gather a crowd around me and talk people into doing it. Didn't you ever have a job where you had to hustle like that?"

"I was a waitress throughout college, but all I had to do was upsell the potato skin appetizer."

"One day they are going to let us in that gated community and I'm jumping straight into that big pool."

While Rob is waiting for his response from Jackson, time is ticking away. My parents' flight arrives in two days, and we still haven't come up with an alternative plan. We are getting down to the wire.

"Maybe they can stay the first half of their trip with us," I tell Rob. "We can then find them someplace else for the other half."

"Think positive. I'm going to get them somewhere for the entire month. Trust me on this; your father does not want to stay here. For all of our mental health, we should get them a place where I know they are safe, happy, and can have all the privacy they want." I've never seen my husband so focused on a task before. The dining room table looks like he's campaigning for public office. Brochures are strewn everywhere and he has both the landline and cell phone up to his ears at once. I'm all but ready for a press conference. Nothing like the threat of having your in-laws stay for a month to light a fire under your keister.

"Aside from your parents, we need to figure out what to do with the car. That voltage meter is peaking all the way to the right now."

"Is it okay to drive it around like that? Is the car going to... I don't know... blow up?" I live with a deep-rooted paranoia that at some point in my life, something will explode. This may stem from my Nana, who believed that one day someone would toss a stick of dynamite into the neighborhood mailbox and blow everyone's utilities bills to smithereens. Because of this, she'd drive across town in her Mustang to drop her mail off at the Post Office. This must have left a lasting impression on my mother whose lifelong Easy-Bake Oven ban has had me believe that I'm one epidermis layer away from being blown away as well.

"Umm... I'm sure it'll be okay." Rob tries to look confident, but I can tell he is as concerned about the car as I am. I'm beginning to question my husband's mechanical skills; perhaps he is not as knowledgeable as I once believed.

Exhibit A: Six months ago Rob asked me to hand him a new bar of soap while he was fixing a squeaky belt in the car. I thought it was to wash his hands so I handed him a lovely jasmine-scented bar infused with therapeutic oils. Before I had time to react, he shoved the soap into the engine block.

"Wait, that was expensive."

"See, that's all you have to do to fix it. I've done this plenty of times with my older cars. Watch, it won't squeak anymore."

Rob seemed pleased with his hillbilly fix until the soap shot out of the engine like a bullet, barely missing our faces, and disappeared into the outer limits of the atmosphere. While staring up, I came to the conclusion that this object, if not already circulating the earth, will surely come falling back down. We both stepped back and watched the soap crash onto the roof of our house.

"Now, you have to expect a couple glitches when you perform this maneuver," Rob confessed while removing soapy splinters from my hair.

"We could have just paid to get it fixed, Rob."

"Pay? That's the difference between you and me. You throw money at a problem when a little elbow grease is all that's needed. When I was a teenager, I had to be creative when my car broke down. One time my fender got bashed in and it destroyed the housing for the headlight. Did I whine because I couldn't afford to fix it? No. I did what any guy would do when he depends on his car for work. I took a few bungee cords, connected a new light from the junkyard, and aligned it by stuffing underwear behind the housing in order to angle it correctly. I drove around like that for over a year. I called it my "underpants headlight stabilizer" and it passed inspection twice with flying colors. When I was fourteen, I even took a broken moped out of the trash, fixed it up, and rode it around for an entire summer."

I heard about this infamous moped from Rob's mother. Determined to get it up and running again, Rob installed a new spark plug and patched the flat tires. However, the cable for the throttle was broken. In order to fix it without putting out any money—and channeling the vast intelligence that we all know fourteen-year-old boys possess—he connected a bungee cord directly to the carburetor. He held onto the handlebar with one hand while the other hand pulled on the bungee cord to accelerate.

Since this was such an ingenious way to ride around the neighborhood, Rob decided to go the next logical step and wrap the bungee cord directly to the right handlebar. It worked out fine as long as he went straight, but once he made a right hand turn he would lose power. Left hand turns were equally problematic since the cord prevented him from veering in that direction, so straight and right were his only options.

One night while pulling into his driveway Rob tried to kill the gas, but because the cord had snagged around itself, the moped continued at full speed straight into a brick wall. The back wheel came off the ground from the momentum, and Rob's face softly kissed the brick house before the moped crashed back down.

A good portion of my married life has consisted of listening to long examples of Rob's enterprising problem-solving skills. I've done some calculating and seventy-five percent of Rob's solutions always involve bungee cords or duct tape. The other twenty-five percent include underpants.

This most recent soap incident makes me question whether Rob is sane enough to determine if this alternator is going to destroy our car. But I have to give him some credit. Rob's DIY soap fix stopped the squeaking for two weeks and—quite pleasantly—had the car smelling like jasmine for a month.

"Rob, if we have an alternator that is too big, isn't it producing too much electricity?"

"It's a strong possibility."

I get an uneasy feeling and fear that our car is going to die precisely at the time my parents are coming to visit. And I doubt there is a bar of soap, pair of underwear, duct tape, or bungee cord, that can fix this problem.

The Gated Community

"That sounds great, Jackson. I'll shoot him an email. I owe you man." Rob hangs up the phone with a big smile on his face.

"What's that all about?"

"Jackson's friend owns a condo in that fancy resort and it might be available. The guy read your book and thought it was hilarious. I'm going to ask if we can get your parents in there."

"I'm afraid it will be too expensive. I'm also afraid that my parents will think it's too fancy. They completely wigged out on me when I mentioned... just *mentioned*... the Four Seasons hotel."

"People never know what they want until they see it. They're going to be here tomorrow. I'm jumping on this." Rob immediately sends an email to the owner explaining the situation. I decide to turn in for the night, pessimistic about Rob's crusade.

"Hey, you still up?" Rob asks while nudging my shoulder.

"Huh? What's the matter?"

"Nothing is the matter, in fact, everything is looking pretty good. We just got an email from the owner of the condo. He said your parents can stay there."

"That's nice, but it's still too expensive, and my parents are going to fight you all the way," I argue before pulling the blanket over my face.

"Wait, there's more. He's letting us stay there at a *really* reduced price. All we have to do is pay for the monthly HOA fee, the housekeeping, and utilities. For what it all comes out to, your parents basically have the place for free. And if that doesn't make your dad happy, I don't know what will."

I rip the blanket off my head, "What do you mean by *free?*"

"Just what I said; we pay for the upkeep of the place for a month, utilities, etc., but that's it. Now your parents get to stay in the fanciest, most secure community, with all sorts of amenities. They are going to have a great time, and I still didn't tell you the best part."

"What's that?"

"It's a penthouse."

My parents are going to be miserable.

"Once we unpack, I want to go to the grocery store," my mother orders as I load her bags into our trunk. She is barely off the plane and has an uncontrollable urge to buy cold cuts. "I need to get some food in your house so your father doesn't get grumpy. Your dad doesn't care for the food you eat."

"We'll do whatever you want, Mom." She recently broke a rib, so I place a small stool on the ground making it easier for her to hoist herself into my towering SUV. We get her into the back seat, where she instantly transforms into Jessica Tandy from *Driving Miss Daisy*.

"Do I need to go to the bank and exchange money? Maybe we should do that now and get it over with. Will they take one hundred dollar bills in the supermarket? I made a list while on the plane and we have to make sure we can find coffee creamer. Your father likes

Half & Half, not that one-percent you kids drink. All it does is turn the coffee gray. We hate gray coffee."

We stop at a supermarket and I patiently follow her as she shops aisle by aisle. She handles every product on the shelf like she's taking inventory. Somebody should hand this lady a nametag and put her on the payroll.

"Can I ask you something, Nadine?" my dad says while I'm searching for his creamer. "Do you think it's possible since I'm staying with you for a whole damn month that I can eat something other than cold cuts? It looks like you and your mother are buying enough ham to last a nuclear winter." Clearly, my father is suffering from nitrate poisoning.

Luckily, I find the Half & Half. I grab as many as I can. "How much it that going to cost?" my dad asks.

I do some quick math and realize it costs close to four dollars a pint. When I explain this to my dad, he shouts as if I just tried selling him a timeshare in Detroit. "I'm not going to get ripped off. I can get that same carton in the Dollar Store back home... for a dollar, Nadine!"

"Stick the Half & Half in the cart," my mother yells from behind. "I'm not drinking gray coffee."

"This is criminal, Diane. I won't allow it."

"I'm buying it, Bill." My parents spend a good five minutes fighting over the creamer. I watch my dad take it out of the cart while my mom puts it back in. This, of course, has drawn a considerable amount of attention and I imagine bookies are already taking bets. My mom is favored ten to one. In the end, she gets her creamer while my dad sulks in the cookie aisle.

Two Excedrin later, we're back on the road, and after a short drive we pull up to the gated community. "What is this?" my mother asks. At this point my parents still believe they are staying at my house.

"We're going for a ride in here." The last thing I want her to do is start yelling at me in front of the security guard. I've already disappointed him once before with my very un-Salma-Hayek-like cleavage. The guard lets us through, but my father is oblivious to where we are; he's too busy staring out the window, presumably brooding over the big-ticket creamer he'll be boycotting.

"What are we doing here?" my mother asks. "I don't want the food to spoil. Is this really the best time for sightseeing?"

"You'll see," I reply. This is a big place. It sits on a huge amount of land, and getting to our condominium takes us along a scenic drive. The landscaping is so beautiful it makes Rob want to jump out of the car and steal hundreds of clippings.

We finally pull up to a parking lot where Rob parks and opens the trunk. My parents are confused as they follow us, carrying their suitcases into the elevator. I can see a small smirk on my dad's face; it's tiny, just on one side but it is definitely there. We get to the top floor and put the key into the penthouse door. For all of my mother's worrying, for all of her inability to enjoy being anyplace nice, you would never know it at this moment. Her face immediately lights up as she heads straight to the balcony to stare out at the ocean view. As if choreographed, two sailboats coast across the sea directly in front of us.

"Okay, what's going on? Why did you bring us here?" she asks.

"This is where you are staying," I announce with a big smile across my face.

"But..."

"Wait Diane," Rob interjects. "Before you have a coronary, you should know we got a great deal. It's yours for the month. Enjoy."

"But how did you do it?" she giggles. Suddenly, the idea of her staying in a place other than a Howard Johnson doesn't sound so bad.

"It all came together in the end. Sometimes you have to put yourself out there and just ask. This is how we found the house we rent now, and it's exactly how I found you this place." When my mother explains all this to my dad, we are greeted with a reaction that makes the Half & Half altercation seem tame.

"Are you sure we will not get thrown out?" my dad panics. "I don't want my old ass woken up in the middle of the night by some security guard, and I'm not sneaking around this place for an entire month. You know your mother broke a rib, she can't handle any stress. This was supposed to be a relaxing vacation for us." I spend the next ten minutes reassuring him that he is allowed to be here.

My mother checks out the kitchen and opens the refrigerator. She inspects all the compartments as she puts her groceries away. She starts a pot of coffee while my dad goes upstairs to check out the three bedrooms. The master has sliding glass doors that open onto a private balcony. The view is spectacular with White-Throated Magpie-Jays already sitting on the railing. It seems every room in this penthouse is built to take advantage of the views; even the bathroom has a wall that opens so you can stare out at the ocean while soaking in the Jacuzzi tub. This, by far, is the fanciest place they have ever stayed.

"I'm making your father a sandwich," my mother yells. "They didn't serve any food on the plane. Did you know it costs eight dollars for a snack box. *Eight* dollars, Nadine. They nickel-and-dime you for everything now." She makes a ham sandwich and hands it to my dad once he's back downstairs.

My parents are finally unwinding from their flight and kick off their shoes. "When are we going to see your property? I hope it's like this development," my mother says.

"We'll go, Mom, after you and dad are settled in." If my dad had a conniption about the Half & Half, wait until he sees the African Bees.

Cheating Golfers

My father has never concerned himself with high fashion, or from what I've seen today, embarrassing his family. Since he never passes on a bargain, he recently bought eight blue mechanic shirts for eight dollars at—do I even need to say—the Dollar Store. They each have a name stitched on the front; one says Gabriel, while another reads Charlie. My dad looks like he works at Jiffy Lube.

He wears these blue shirts while taking his morning stroll around the development's golf course. It's not meant to be a walking path and guests are instructed to stay off it unless they're playing golf. Since my dad looks like he's planning to fix the pool pump, everyone just thinks he works there. Sometimes the golfers stop him to order hamburgers or martinis. My dad nods his head as if deeply concerned with their request before swiftly abandoning them, thirsty and hungry, on the ninth hole.

Aside from his daily five mile walk, my dad enjoys standing on the balcony and looking down at the golfers below. When one misses a shot, he shakes his head in disgust. Mind you, my dad has never played a game of golf in his life. I asked to try it when I was a kid and his response was, "That's a rich man's sport," and then he promptly handed me a bag of rubber bands. My dad was convinced that seven-year-old girls could easily (and more cheaply) entertain themselves with office supplies. If rubber bands did not do the trick, he would grab a bucket of nails, a few scraps of wood, and I'd spend an entire summer's day mindlessly hammering nails into a board, mastering my carpentry skills for the possibilities of a job in construction. I am certain if you dig deep enough into my parents' garage, you can still find my handy woodwork propping up cases of RC Cola.

It's not only that my dad is cheap. The man just can't pass up anything that is free or—in most cases—discarded. He can't see anything go to waste. Once at Newark International Airport, I wanted to buy a newspaper. My father reacted as if I'd bought an eight dollar in-flight snack box. He ordered me to sit back down while he searched for an abandoned newspaper. The man cruised around British Airlines, got lost at Air India, and most likely went out on the tarmac to wave a few planes in before bringing back four different newspapers, and a bag of rubber bands. "I worked in New York City for thirty-five years and never bought one goddamn newspaper," he said, slightly winded from the impromptu excursion. Where he found these papers I do not know (the men's room comes to mind, and possibly the ladies' room as well), but I had enough reading material to last me the entire flight.

"See that woman sitting in the golf cart?" my dad says while pointing over the balcony. Every day when I visit my parents, this is the exact position I find my father in, hanging over the balcony. "She waits there while her husband plays golf. What a vacation, following that horse's ass around all day." I look out and see her reading a magazine, her feet propped up over the dashboard.

As one golfer prepares to putt, a family of coatis waddles out from behind the trees. These are cute, docile animals that resemble raccoons with the most adorable faces, narrow upturned noses, and tiny ears. They're rarely bigger than large house cats and have long tails that often point straight up. This posture helps the pack identify each other while walking through thick vegetation, similar to the tall orange flags tour guides use in crowded cities. Whenever I see one of these creatures, I can't help but smile.

When the woman notices the coatis, she tosses her *Vogue* magazine in the air and starts screaming as if they are wielding machetes. The golfers scatter in every direction and one even manically swings his golf club in case one sprouts wings, going for his throat.

"Do something!" I hear magazine lady tell her husband.

"What the hell do you want me to do?" the horse's ass yells from behind a bush. "They look rabid." I don't think the man has to worry; his plaid pants alone could scare away a herd of elephants.

"What a bunch of amateurs," my dad laughs. "I pass these animals everyday on my walk... dozens of them. They don't even look up at me."

Maintenance workers are frantically radioed to shoo them away. They drive up in a beverage cart, hand out drinks to the bewildered guests, and like Pied Pipers, march the coatis back into the forest. Once all is clear, the golfers resume their game by missing every shot. Not one player gets his ball in the hole. They eventually give up and pick up their balls.

The moment the last golfer steps off the green, the next group of men are teeing up. "You see the guy in the yellow shirt?" my dad asks. "I watched him cheat the other day. When his friend wasn't looking, he kicked the ball at least five feet closer to the hole." My dad describes this information in excruciating detail, certain it can be used later as valuable blackmailing material at the all-you-can-eat buffet. "The guy looked up and caught me watching him. I made sure he saw me take my notebook out and record his indiscretion... you know... to make him think I'm going to report him to law enforcement."

I look in his notebook and discover a log of bad behavior that has been occurring on the golf course. My dad has been taking notes on people who not only cheat, but litter, drive their cart on the grass, and urinate in the woods. Dolores the Dog Lady would have had an entire binder to herself if she lived here.

"And it's not the first time I've witnessed someone cheat. You'd be surprised how serious the men take this game. Funny thing is, the best golfers I've seen so far are women. They are quick and methodical. They make their shots, then get the hell out of there."

While listening to my dad recall other unseemly incidents, White-throated Magpie-Jays land on the wrought-iron railing. I already know how this is going to play out, and in a matter of seconds they dive down and attempt to pillage the snack mix out of my hand. They are tyrants stuck in tiny bird bodies. Even though I'm being attacked, I can't help but be impressed that this massive development is home to such an abundance of wildlife. Yesterday, Rob and I walked to a large pond where Roseate Spoonbills searched for fish and Great Blue Herons majestically soared over the water like Chinese kites. Everywhere I go I am witnessing something marvelous.

"You know what, Nadine?" my dad says while looking through a pair of binoculars, "This is the best vacation I ever had." He pauses while he focuses in on a few new golfers. "Aha! Another one cheating, he pushed his ball at least ten feet. I gotcha, you son of a bitch."

Yes... I think this might be his best vacation. Perhaps not so much for the golfers.

German Mechanic & Lots of Balls

Our car is acting wacky; the radio and headlights turn on and off by themselves and the overhead lamp flickers like a strobe light. *That's weird*, I think as I glance at the voltage meter. It's wildly swinging from left to right. Rob assures me not to worry but I think we may have a big problem here. However, I like the idea that my car is a beast full of unbridled power.

On the way home from the supermarket, I notice sparks flying out of the dashboard. I hit the accelerator and suddenly the interior of the car turns into a dazzling fireworks display. If electricity bolts weren't skimming past my head, I would lay a blanket on the back seat and start humming "The Star Spangled Banner." This is, by far, the best way to watch your car detonate and I would recommend it to anyone looking for heart palpitations. I coast into my driveway and leave the car smoldering while I carry our groceries inside the house.

"Houston, we have a problem that is going to take more than a bar of soap or a pair of underpants to fix," I announce to Rob. He is not happy with the news.

"I knew it," Rob grumbles. "We need a new mechanic. We're already three hundred dollars in the hole with this guy and worse off than when we started. I'm calling Ian to find out who he uses."

Ian recommends Claus, a German mechanic whose prices are fair. He can get the job done in a reasonable amount of time. Rob calls him and Claus graciously comes to our house to look at the car. He's bald, stands 6'5", and towers over both of us. A Camel cigarette dangles from his mouth as he digs his hands into the engine.

"Ah," Claus mumbles as cigarette ashes fall to the ground. "For me... you connect this wire. You have no... how do you say..."

"Ground?" Rob asks.

"Ja, ja... ground. Let us connect jumper cables to the negative and then to engine block." Remarkably, the car starts. This guy is a genius.

"I can't thank you enough," Rob cheers. "Now I can drive it back to your shop so you can take a look at this monstrosity of an alternator this knucklehead put in. All the major problems started with that."

"For me... I would replace it with the correct part. I will order it but it can take weeks. In Germany I have it in a day. In Costa Rica, much longer. For me... no pura vida."

I notice Claus has an interesting way of prefacing each sentence; he always starts with the words "for me." I continue listening as Claus lectures Rob about the superior craftsmanship in Germany. "Parts are made to last in my country," he says. It appears nothing breaks down in Germany, not a car or a refrigerator. It sounds like a magical place.

After we drive our car to the mechanic's garage, Claus drops us off at the local car rental agency. The only vehicle they have left looks as if it was designed for the lollipop guild; it seems impossible that it could accommodate four people. My dad's head will be bouncing off the ceiling with every pothole and just getting in the car will aggravate my mother's cracked rib.

"We don't have a choice, we'll have to make it work," Rob says. "Why don't we take them out to dinner and then show them our property after dessert? Maybe even catch a sunset up there."

"Oh brother. I don't know if I'm ready yet. Plus, do you think this car can drive up a hill? It's like a tin can with a toy engine. For me...

I would rather not take my parents up there." I wish Claus was coming with us so he could use his magical German fingers to fix this situation. But I doubt any amount of German engineering could make this foreclosed house disappear. "Okay, I'll bite the bullet. Let's take them to a nice restaurant on the beach. Maybe I can liquor them up first."

As I walk into my parents' living room, I notice golf balls. Everywhere. They are on the kitchen table, piled high in vases, and even placed on top of the candle holders.

"What in the world?" I whisper to Rob.

"See what I go through? This is what your father does every morning. He finds lost golf balls and brings them back to the house," my mom explains.

My dad walks into the room with a big smile on his face. "Come here kids. I have to show you something." We walk out to the balcony and he hands me a pair of binoculars.

"You see that ravine straight ahead. I noticed something interesting. Every hour at least three golfers lose their ball in there. I did some math. Let's just be conservative… if two are lost each hour… eight hours a day… that would be over a hundred a week. It's a gold mine down there. A golf ball gold mine."

I imagine my father trying to retrieve these golf balls, precariously dangling by his rubber band rappelling gear over this twenty foot drop. No doubt, he'd be wearing his janitorial blue Dollar Store shirt labeled Señor Carlos. When his rubber bands snap and the emergency crew comes to rescue him, everyone will wonder who the hell Mr. Carlos is and if he really works here.

"I start my walk every morning before dawn hitting several hot spots where I know I will find dozens of balls. Look around. Isn't it fantastic?" I have to admit, it's an admirable collection of golf balls. It's nice to know my dad did not leave his eccentricities at home, but I have to wonder why a man who has never played a round of golf in his life would need all these. Somehow all this craziness warms my heart, reminding me of old times. I'm even thinking of asking him to play the Burglar Game tonight.

"Although I love what you've done with the place, let's get out of here. Rob and I want to take you out to dinner."

"Your father doesn't want to go to dinner. He just wants to have a sandwich at home." A few moments later, my dad turns to Rob and asks if we can go out to eat.

"My wife keeps pushing these cold cuts on me. Can't I get a normal dinner in this country?" My mom has made every decision for my dad, including every meal the man has eaten for the past forty years.

"Don't pressure him," my mother says. "Let's just get in the car and see your property."

Amazingly, my mother is able to squeeze into the back seat. My dad is in the passenger seat with little room for his legs. Unfortunately, this will have to do since we have no idea when the alternator is coming. Like Claus said, it could take weeks.

"I love these trees," my mom remarks as we drive into the development. "It's so shady and cool. Oh look, monkeys." We glance up and see howlers sleeping on branches above us.

"There are a lot of them here. Deer too," I explain as we drive up the hill. The car struggles, but Rob manages to keep the tires from slipping. We pass the first boarded up house—my mom and dad don't notice. I try to convince myself that they won't notice the big foreclosed one either. *Just keep talking, Nadine, keep them distracted*, I think to myself as we round the bend.

"What the hell happened here?" my dad asks. "It looks like someone stole every damn window and door off this place. Even the roof tiles are missing. This doesn't look at all like the picture you sent us."

We pull into the driveway and the bank's guard waves from the second floor. "Come inside and take a look," I urge. "It was a nice

221

house. The owner ran into some financial difficulty so it's a foreclosure. I'm sure someone will buy it for cheap and fix it up."

While Rob talks to the guard, my parents walk through the house. I warn them to stay away from the pool and African bees. They both are silent as they climb the staircase to the second floor. Even with no doors or windows, you can't deny the fact that this house has a spectacular panoramic view of Flamingo. You can almost imagine what it was like sitting on the terrace and enjoying a cold drink while watching the boats sail by.

"Take a look at the master bathroom," I say as I stand in the shower stall. "They used to have French doors here so you could shower and be outside at the same time. Cool right?" My parents don't say a word.

Once we're done poking around, we get back in the car just to drive another two hundred feet up to my lot. They get out and walk to the edge of the property. The view is even better than at the foreclosed house. "Rob, come here," my dad yells. "Is this where you are going to put the… what the hell do you kids call it? The never-going-to-end pool."

Rob draws where the infinity pool will go in the dirt. It doesn't surprise me that my dad wants to know about the pool. To him, that's the big time; a house with a pool is something that he always dreamed about. We even show him the part of the property where we would like to build a guest house, which of course, would be for them when they visit.

My dad walks around some more and calls me over. I prepare myself for the bashing that is about to happen. If only there were a ravine full of golf balls up here to distract him. But I have no choice but to suck it up. My stomach is in knots as I brace myself for the lecture.

"It's going to be beautiful," he says. "I'm very proud of you, Nadine. You have a lot of guts to do this." I couldn't be more surprised by his reaction. "Don't worry about that damn house over there. I love that you have so much privacy. I've been living next to people my whole damn life. On this lot, you could water the lawn in your underwear. I've wanted to do that for forty years but your mother won't let me."

I thought for sure my dad would be disappointed, but once standing on the lot, admiring the view, and dreaming about watering the lawn in his underwear has made him abnormally optimistic. Maybe this crazy idea of building a house here will work out in the end.

"I'm hungry," my dad says. "Let's get the hell out of here and get something to eat before your mother tries to unload thirty pounds of liverwurst on me."

With that, we shoo away an African bee and drive away.

Runaway Horses & Three-Day Weekends

It was great having my parents here for a month. They even got used to their luxurious accommodations and hope to have the same experience next year. I'm not sure if we can get another deal like that, but you never know with Rob's perseverance. My dad even left with a few golf balls as souvenirs for my nieces.

"You know, you and Rob should have some fun and play a round of golf every so often," my dad says while I'm dropping him off at the airport. It seems that he has softened on the rich man's sport. Either that or he wants me to continue recording the lengthy misdeeds of the players. Nothing would make him happier.

On the way back from the airport, we pass horses grazing along the road. You can rarely turn a corner in Guanacaste without seeing one either tied to a post in front of someone's house or running across a field. Even while living in Grecia I saw a few. Sometimes you find groups of them hogging the road, creating a traffic jam. Other times they just show up on your doorstep.

One morning in Grecia, our motion sensors started beeping. I cautiously opened the curtains—partially concerned there was an intruder, and partially concerned that Dolores was out there tinkling on my lawn. I was surprised to find a horse staring back at me. She was the color of chocolate, a little skinny, and had round, shiny eyes that reminded me of black buttons on a winter coat. And because I am the queen of bad ideas, I immediately wanted to keep her. "It's fate, Rob. You know how they say cats adopt you. Maybe it's the same for horses."

"You don't know anything about horses. You can't even ride one without becoming hysterical. I've never ridden one without it taking off on me."

"I know, but this could be a win-win situation. She eats grass, so I don't even have to feed her, and she will help mow our lawn. She'll poop somewhere in the woods, and even if she doesn't, it will make great fertilizer for your plants. Anyway, I've already named her Sunshine."

"You named her? Don't get too attached. This horse obviously belongs to someone and he will eventually come and get her." Realizing Rob was making too much sense, I immediately stopped listening to him and emailed all my friends, telling them that I now owned a horse. I grabbed a few carrots out of the refrigerator and went out into the backyard to feed her. She sweetly ate them out of my hands while I stroked her face. We couldn't have made a better team; I was smitten.

The next day, I woke up to find Sunshine still living in my backyard. Only this time she was eating Rob's string beans. Knowing that this would upset Rob, I ran outside and coaxed her to the other side of the house.

"What happened to my string beans?" Rob questioned a couple hours later.

"I don't know honey. I bet it's that crazy kinkajou that keeps coming around."

"I know who did it. It's that horse. She's going to destroy my garden."

"Well, I'm keeping her. I love her, Rob. I wake up in the morning and can't wait to see her."

In a desperate attempt to save the rest of his string beans, Rob sprayed an organic garlic bug repellant all over every plant, trying to make them as unappetizing as possible. The next morning Sunshine ate every plant in the garden, delighted over the latest seasoning that appeared overnight. Essentially, all Rob did was make a gourmet salad dressing for this horse.

To show how much she appreciated me, Sunshine continued hanging around the house, destroying ornamental grasses, trampling the shrubs Rob had just planted, and taking midnight craps right on my terrace. It seemed there was a glitch in my plan for adopting this horse. To rectify this, I began sketching out a structure we could build to keep Sunshine confined.

"We are not building a barn, Nadine. This is not our horse, and if someone doesn't come soon and take her away, she is going to destroy everything." Just as Sunshine set her sights on Rob's scrumptious tomatoes, the owner comes and escorts her away. To this day I wonder where she is and if she's enjoying any dressing on her string beans.

Now that I live on the coast, there is no shortage of horses. They are everywhere, sometimes walking right past my house. Even at the beaches you can't avoid them. It's always fun to watch as the horses ride straight into the ocean, cooling off before continuing on their way.

At one beach, a woman frequently rides her horse up and down the shoreline. The horse has furry feet like a Clydesdale, a braided mane, and a tail so gloriously long and bouncy it looks like he just came from the salon. It appears this woman lives here and uses this specific beach to practice.

The woman wears full equestrian gear and handles the animal as if she's preparing for a competition. She controls every movement the animal makes, cantering at first before sending him into a full gallop. She sits straight up in her saddle, a posture that seems impossible to keep while sprinting across the beach. At times she has a little girl (also in full equestrian gear) with her. The child rides a pony and follows the woman up and down the beach.

I have never actually seen a pony outside of a petting zoo. The girl looked so cute on the one she was riding, I can't help but want to join her. I thought about introducing myself but didn't want to disturb their practice. Instead I sat back on my towel and watched them ride up and down the coast, the waves rolling in alongside them.

Riding horses has never been my favorite pastime. My first attempt was when I tried to ride up a mountain during my first visit to Costa Rica. I had absolutely no idea what I was doing. Of course our old realtor, Martin, set that up. I'm sure if he was around today he'd have us skydiving into the jungle to check out the "awesome deal" he just found. But after watching this mother and daughter have so much fun, I consider taking lessons. The whole reason I moved here was to try new things. Unfortunately, there is too much on my mind to begin lessons right now. We're still concentrating on getting building permits which is becoming an uphill battle.

Today we are going back to the municipality to follow up on progress on our water letter. They state that if we can get a letter from the "big guy" at AYA, they will give us a permit. Does this guy even have a name? "Big guy" is not a very nice moniker for an oversized man and it makes me wonder how many people call me "short broad" behind my back. The longer we continue this endless crusade the more I worry about building this house. We are living in an awesome place and pay so little in rent it doesn't make much sense to build. I'm starting to believe that the universe is trying to tell us something. Perhaps it has a different plan for me. Maybe this is just not the right time to do something that on all accounts seems so impossible.

On the way back from the municipality, we take the only paved road into town. It's a fun one, and what I mean by fun is that there is a healthy number of potholes to jiggle you out of your seat. We cruise at forty miles per hour and enjoy the breeze. It feels good to roll down the windows and let my hair fly in my face. I don't know why I ever stopped doing this. I began rolling up the windows and using air conditioning as I got older, the breeze feeling more like an annoying distraction than a welcome escape. But things are different now; I feel young in Costa Rica. It could be my new healthy diet or maybe my change in attitude. All I know is I'm having a lot more fun than ever before. It took me a while to get to this place, and now that I'm here, I don't want to go back to my former tumultuous self.

Someone recently asked me what this adventure feels like, wanting to know if it really was so different. The best way to describe my new life in Costa Rica is to say that it feels like a three-day weekend. It's similar to that distinct moment on Monday morning when you wake up and realize you don't have to go to work. Lying in bed knowing you have the whole splendid day to yourself is one of the best sensations in the world.

As we cruise on down the road, we see a bunch of horses running toward us. Rob slows down as fifteen horses gallop at full speed toward our car. It's common to see cattle do this, but this is the first time I've witnessed horses so out of control in the middle of the road. We notice two young men on a dirt bike following them. Without even slowing down, the kid on the back suddenly flies off the bike.

"Oh my God! He fell off! Pull over, pull over!" I scream. But as we slow down, we realize he didn't fall off, he jumped off. This kid isn't even wearing sneakers. He jumped off a moving dirt bike wearing flip-flops. Costa Ricans are a tough lot and are unyielding in any situation. I get embarrassed thinking about how I recently sprained my ankle after getting out of a chair. I was even wearing sneakers when I did it.

We watch as the young man runs after his horses. He succeeds in simultaneously lassoing one as he leaps on top of it. There is no doubt in my mind he will collect the rest of the runaways. It wouldn't surprise me to see him later today. Now that I think about it, maybe it was his horse I witnessed dashing wildly down the street with a terrified tourist in the saddle.

It's a common sight, a group of amateur riders galloping on the beach and riding horses into the ocean. The animals always appear to behave and everyone looks like they are having a great time. This is why we were so surprised to see a horse with a tourist riding it gallop past us and run straight into a busy soccer game in Brasilito. The kids scattered while the horse paused for a moment, looked around, and continued down the road. It was a runaway horse.

In a split second, one of the barefoot boys playing soccer—a boy no older than twelve—ran as swift as Achilles after the horse. I have never, ever, seen a boy, or a grown man no less, run this fast. He sprinted across the field and down the street, his bare feet kicking up a storm of gravel and dirt. The boys stopped their game, all of them watching their brave friend charge after the horse.

The boy eventually caught up and gallantly grabbed the horse's reins. He turned the horse around and escorted him back to the beach. He was met with a round of applause. The tourist was in a state of shock. I am sure the horse was just trying to get back to his stables; nonetheless, it was a scary moment.

When people ask me if Ticos are really as friendly as I say they are, I tell them this story. It's not only the adults but the children who have a steadfast kindness and strength. Whether it's in flip-flops or bare feet, jumping off a dirt bike or racing down the road, they will eventually catch that runaway horse.

It's now that I'm realizing this may be the first place I've lived that I truly love. I hope these "three-day weekends" last forever.

Korean Sandwich Maker

Claus finally found the correct alternator and fixed our car. "For me... what the last mechanic did was bullshit. That part was fucking bullshit." Claus takes his job seriously and gets offended by shoddy work by other mechanics. By the amount of gringos' cars in his driveway, there is no doubt he must get offended all day.

He takes us around to the side of his garage and shows us a Pathfinder SUV that was dropped off this morning. "I have to fix this today. It didn't pass inspection because the last mechanic replaced the muffler with one from a Volkswagen Beetle. For me... it's bullshit, Rob, fucking bullshit. You would never see that in Germany."

I met someone who left their car at our old mechanic's garage for a simple fix and the guy charged him two thousand dollars. When he wouldn't pay the bill, the mechanic kept his car hostage at his shop. It's been sitting there for over a year, chained to a steel beam until the guy ponies up the money. Coincidently, this is the same mechanic who installed the Space Shuttle alternator in our car. With all that in mind, I don't care if Claus drives my car to Venezuela as long as he can get it fixed and doesn't hold it hostage.

Once back at the house, I call my friend Benjamin for advice about an email I received from a Korean editor expressing interest in my book. She wants to translate it into Korean and publish it. It's all very exciting, but I have no clue what to do. Benjamin is the brother of my girlfriend and is an uber-smart guy. If he can't answer my question, he always knows someone that can. He has become the go-to person for Rob and me.

In fact, Rob says he is the smartest person he knows; unfortunately for Benjamin, that's not saying too much. Tommy Walnuts called yesterday from Atlantic City and asked to borrow three hundred dollars. I could simultaneously hear the slot machines in the background and the imminent fight Rob and I were going to have if he loaned Tommy the money. Rob remarkably had the same premonition and decided it was a wise decision not to invest in Tommy's Texas Hold'em business venture.

In comparison, Benjamin has never called from a casino floor asking for money. Instead, he gives us great advice on the foreign currency market or why commodities are not a good investment this month, all of which I don't understand. Rob hopes to return the favor one day. I'm not sure how that's ever going to happen unless Benjamin needs three hundred dollars at two in the morning or advice or how to make U-turns on one of the busiest bridges in the country. But if he does, Rob's got him covered.

"I have a good friend that is a literary agent. In fact, she used to work for a major publishing house in New York City. Emma's the real deal. I'll ask her if she'll read the contract," Benjamin offers. As always, he's got a connection for me.

"Thanks. It's all very confusing. They are willing to give me a tiny advance, but after that I'm not sure if the contract is in my favor. I'm not even sure if it's for real. There is a part where they need my address and bank account to wire the advance. It can easily be some naked guy in a La-Z-Boy recliner yanking my chain."

"Yes, I suppose it could be. Those recliners are quite comfortable. Did you Google this editor?"

"No, not yet."

"Hold on, I'm doing it right now. Hmm... that's interesting."

"What?"

"Nothing that looks really bad. It's just that this lady is listed as an editor and a sandwich maker."

"Come again?"

"See for yourself, I'll email the link to you." Benjamin is right. She lists her occupation as an editor and sandwich maker.

"Nadine, I'm not saying that it's a bad thing. She could be working hard and has a second job at a deli. There is nothing wrong with that. I would just be a little careful with this."

I imagine her reading my book over a pastrami sandwich in the break room; choking on coleslaw after laughing about Rob macing himself in the face. This is not how I thought my foreign publishing career would begin. I imagined being whisked away to Paris, invited to dinners with buttery entrees and talking shop with the most recent bestselling authors. But I don't get any invites to exotic lands, just an email with a side of pickles.

"Listen, what's most important is having Emma look over the contract. She will know what to do. Don't sign anything and definitely don't give them your bank account information."

After a couple days, Emma gets back to me and points out the many things that don't sound right to her. She is incredibly helpful, especially since she didn't ask for any money and is doing this as a favor for Benjamin. Before emailing her, I did look her up and found she is a successful photographer and agent. As far as I can tell, she is not moonlighting at Subway.

"At the very least, your name should be on the book. It should say that in the contract," Emma advises.

"I actually have to specify that my name will be on the cover? Isn't that implied? I'm the author."

"Nadine, you have no clue how many things need to be in this contract. Sure, they can put someone else's name on the book. Why the hell not? I'm not an expert on Korean contracts, but from the looks of it there are things I'd be concerned about."

"Would you be concerned if she is an editor and a sandwich maker?"

"A what?"

"She lists both on her resume. Does that raise any suspicions?"

"I can say, in all my years in this business, I have never been asked that question. Are you sure?"

"Yes, Benjamin pointed it out to me."

"Maybe she just works a second job. But let's not speculate. First we need to send her back the changes and see what happens." I take Emma's advice and send over the corrected contract. There's nothing to do but wait and see.

The reactions I get are interesting when I tell people I wrote a book. Just the other day I mentioned it to a woman who then went down a laundry list of the many reasons I wouldn't succeed, "It's useless unless you know someone... you have to be in the right circles... you're not writing what's selling." It seems that my project is getting a lot of the same reactions as moving to Costa Rica did.

Sometimes they share their own stories about lost opportunities in a field they were passionate about. "The position was low paying," one woman said after getting a job at an art gallery. "I quit after a year and took a job in accounting. Better salary, but I always wondered what would have happened if I stuck it out."

These long lost dreams come at me from every direction, whizzing past my ears like stray bullets. I notice the sparkle in their eyes as they remember their passions, and the pain that follows after revealing they quit trying. Their pain was ultimately not caused by the failure to succeed, but from their own resignation. I too have encountered this fork in the road. I remember standing in my office thinking if I didn't move to Costa Rica would I always wonder "what if" and if it would be too high of a price to live with. Harriet Beecher Stowe once said:

"When you get into a tight place and everything goes against you, till it seems as though you could not hang on a minute longer, never give up then, for that is just the place and time that the tide will turn."

I think often about that quote. I'm learning that there is intrinsic value that comes from staying in the game. Any given opportunity can change the path of your life. Unfortunately, that path is also littered with insecurity and rejection. But these are small hurdles when compared to the satisfaction one receives when they continue following their dreams.

These self-doubts remind me of *The Wizard of Oz*. The wizard hides behind a curtain operating imaginary levers and only has the power you willingly relinquish to him. And isn't that what criticism is, imaginary levers someone else is controlling?

Ms. Stowe was a brave lady. She wrote *Uncle Tom's Cabin*, a subject that infuriated many at a time when women weren't even allowed to vote no less add their opinion on the moral consequences of slavery. My book may not be one of great social change; quitting my job will not garner me a Pulitzer Prize, but it does mean something to me. I wrote a story about following a dream, and now I need to see how far I can take this project. Maybe it all starts in Korea and this is the first part of the journey.

Or maybe it's like trying to put a Beetle's muffler on a Pathfinder. It might look good at first, but eventually it all goes up in smoke.

Deep Thoughts

From: Nadine
To: Dad
2:33 PM
Subject: 1 Star Review

Dad, another 1 star review. This one particularly harsh:

Trying WAY too hard to be funny - not!

"I was excited to get this book after all the great reviews on Amazon. My husband and I took it on retreat as we are planning a trip to Costa Rica. We started reading it together and I thought - it has to get better. After three pages my usually optimistic husband said, who wrote this drivel? I had to agree. The author is trying (and trying is the right word) to be funny and fails miserably. Self-indulgent might be a good way to describe the author's writing style. This is painful to read. Whoever compared this to "A Year in Provence" is way off the mark - this book is not at all in the same caliber. All I can say is this book is a huge disappointment."

It seems as if I really ticked off some lady from Boulder Colorado. I guess I just have to get used to this, but it's hard when people seem to REALLY hate me. Her husband supposedly read the book over her shoulder and thought it was drivel. Wow… this one didn't hold back. ☹

```
From: Dad
To: Nadine
1:35 AM
RE: 1 Star Review
```

It has always been sad for me in life to see or witness a woman who so obviously has lost her identity, attractiveness and self-esteem. And frankly it is kind of pitiful when a woman cannot even write a book review without bringing in her stuffy husband for emotional support.

God help this wimpy man if he disagrees with this overbearing harridan. I have taken books on vacation, not one of which had anything to do with my wife. So off they go to their retreat (God only knows what that means, perhaps the latest apparition in a cloud or pane of glass) and the most important thing they bring is a book by Nadine Pisani that cost them a small fortune. So the both of them, joined at the hip, concentrate their entire attention on you.

This woman has lost the capacity to laugh and even more, both of them have lost the ability to love. They are both as emotionally destitute and empty as a rusting oil drum caught in the mud tides of Bayonne, New Jersey.

I see you put a sad face at the end of your message. I want to learn how to do that but not if it requires me to sign up for Facebook or that thing where you do tweeting.

Daddy

Illegal License

I love my scooter. Some of my best memories include riding it to Poas Volcano to eat breakfast at a restaurant nestled into the side of the mountain. At eight thousand feet above sea level, I felt like an eagle spying down on the world. It's one of my favorite views in Costa Rica, but I never know when I'll turn a corner and see one equally as spectacular. I look forward to more of these hidden treasures with my arms tightly wrapped around Rob. Even when the road kicks up dirt in our faces, I'm never happier than on the back of that bike.

Riding on it keeps you closer to your surroundings and you can easily spot little crabs darting back and forth across the road or iguanas sunning themselves in nearby trees. You also get a chance to wave at people while they're standing in their front yards. I don't remember waving at people while living in New Jersey. I'm all but certain Rob didn't in Brooklyn.

It's nice to live like this, where people wave for the sake of waving. I wish it was more like that everywhere, but people are busy and usually in a hurry to get to their next destination. For example, my sister is usually taking the kids to music lessons, horseback riding, or play practice. If I were to suggest she slow down and wave at a guy watering his lawn, she might just throw me out of the car. And when

I mean throw, I mean physically kick me out of the passenger-side door and straight into traffic. She might even back up over me a few times depending on whether my niece forgot to tell her about a diorama that is due the next day.

I can understand her position. There is a small window in which to get all of her errands done; unfortunately, this lifestyle makes for a hostile environment where the only thing on anyone's mind is getting from point A to point B. This is a shame because it's between these points that we find the best parts of life. I'm learning that happiness tends to be sandwiched in places that are often overlooked.

I also enjoy the fact that we've never been pulled over on the scooter by police... until today. It looks like a typical traffic stop with other cars pulled over as well. We have nothing to be concerned about since our scooter has been inspected and we are up to date with the marchamo (registration). These stickers are prominently displayed on the front of the bike so the police will know right away if there are any violations. Rob doesn't waste any time and hands the officer his residency card and Costa Rican driver's license.

"No good, Señor," the man says as he hands back the license.

Rob looks down at his license and proceeds to explain in Spanish that his license *is* good, it is not expired, and he is handsomely smiling in the picture with the rosy glow of someone who has survived a stint at San Jose's motor vehicles department. Rob even recreates the smile while holding up the card. The cop is not amused.

"This is not a scooter license. You are not legal to drive with this. Necessita motorcycle license." Then the officer drops the bomb. The fine is:

Six.

Hundred.

Dollars.

I could buy another scooter for six hundred dollars. What kind of hot tamale justice is this? I heard Costa Rican driving fines went up this year—even parking illegally can get you smacked with a multi-hundred dollar fine. This is not only hugely exorbitant in American standards, but outright impossible to pay if you are a Tico. However, Rob remains calm as he does in every situation. I'm already considering selling my eggs to a fertility bank.

"Okay, I will get the license this week and come back to show you. I will not drive the scooter until I get the right identification. I'm sorry. I love Costa Rica and want to respect the law."

While the officer considers my husband's plea, Rob slowly putt-putts away, smiling and waving as we go. The officer takes pity and yells, "Go straight to motor vehicles. Nuevo licencia."

I'm always surprised how many times Rob is able to talk himself out of a situation. He never raises his voice, always apologetic, and often gets a nice response in return. He's good at not jumping to the defense, something I unfortunately have a hard time controlling.

I ask Sergio about the license and he says getting it will be simple. Just go to MOPT (Costa Rica's motor vehicle) and they will give you a new one with a letter stamped on it showing you are legal to ride a scooter. We will not even have to get a medical exam this time. Before leaving, I also ask Sergio if he can fix the internet line. "Maybe mañana," he says. I look up and notice monkeys sleeping in branches over his house At this point, I'd have better luck asking them to fix the line.

The closest MOPT to our house is located about an hour away. I'm relieved I don't have to drive six hours back to San Jose. We'll get this done tomorrow and not have to worry about getting a six hundred dollar ticket. It should be a cinch.

The next morning we start out on our quest; I pack a book and toilet paper just in case we'll have to wait long. I leave the toilet seat at home; I don't want to give the impression I'm a motor vehicle diva. We pass the MOPT several times before realizing it's the government building we are looking for. San Jose's motor vehicle might as well have been Windsor Castle compared to this place. I squeeze the toilet paper against my chest. I'm sure it's a hot commodity here.

Dozens of people are sitting under an awning hopelessly fanning their faces. A guard sits at a desk, his revolver tucked inside a worn out leather holster. I instantly get the impression that this guy is going to be a hard nut to crack. Rob approaches him and asks how we should go about getting a scooter license. He replies in rapid Spanish then rolls his eyes when we ask him to repeat it again. As far as we understand, we'll need to do a number of things:

1. Go to the Bank of Costa Rica and pay for something
2. Get copies of Rob's residency card and passport
3. Return with these documents and wait in line
4. Forget about this being a cinch

It's not like this comes as a great surprise. Government agencies do not accept any cash or credit cards so you must pay at the bank and return with the receipt. I never, ever understand what I'm paying for. I could be putting a down payment on a banquet hall for someone's quinceañera for all I know. All I can do is smile like an imbecile when the teller hands me the receipt.

We find a Bank of Costa Rica down the road. We explain exactly what we need to the teller but she is having problems entering Rob's license number into the computer.

"Problemo," she says. Apparently, the license number is not valid and she can't proceed with the transaction. She tells us to go back to MOPT and explain that there is an issue with Rob's license. I'm sure the guard will be overjoyed to see us.

We return to motor vehicles and sit under the awning with the rest of the crowd. After a half hour the guard calls Rob's name and allows him inside. For unknown reasons, the man stops me. I cannot join my husband and enjoy the air-conditioned building. I show him my prized roll of toilet paper but he's not amused. The guard and I are hitting it off splendidly.

It isn't long before Rob walks back out. "You're never going to believe this. They took my driver's license because they said it's illegal."

I'm completely startled by the news. Of all the things that I imagined happening today, I didn't see this one coming. "How can it be illegal? The Costa Rica government issued it to us. Did you show them the shiny watermark on it?"

"You and I know we got it legally. They said I could get in big trouble because I've been driving around with a fraudulent license."

"That's not good."

"Wait, it gets better. They also confiscated my residency card."

"Why did they take your residency card? We need that for everything."

"They told me I have to go back to the bank, pay for another license, make copies again, and return. If mine is illegal, so is yours. Let's try to figure out if I can get mine fixed today and we will deal with yours another time. We have to hurry because the banks are closing soon."

We rush back to the bank, pay another fee, go around the corner to make copies, and return with our documents. Rob is let back inside and the guard once again tells me to sit. It's mercilessly hot and the only relief comes from a breeze that stinks of sauerkraut. I can't help but feel nostalgic since I'm quite used to breezes that smell like a dirty water hot dog truck.

I grew up in an area of New Jersey where the air often had the pungent aroma of rotten eggs. The likely suspect was a massive oil refinery in town, but hey, I'm no Sherlock Holmes. Sometimes the refinery would explode and rock half the city. In a good year, the local pharmaceutical company would explode as well. This might have upset the adults, but the suburban children found the fiery sky incredibly exciting. I have to confess, there is nothing more fabulous than playing a game of hopscotch and having the ground rumble under your feet. It was almost as much fun as dodging the asbestos chips that rained from our gymnasium's ceiling. As far as I know, no ill effects came from living in this chemically-enriched environment; however, it might explain why I was a puny kid with a speech impediment.

While waiting for Rob, I watch a teenage girl nervously buckle her seatbelt as she prepares for her driver's test. It appears that the test requires one to drive fifty feet forward only to back up an equal distance. I root for her as she starts the car, puts it in reverse, and backs over an orange cone. I can only imagine what will happen if the instructor makes her parallel park. She'll likely take out the entire group of people sitting under the awning.

I notice a woman standing off to the side; she appears to be the mother of the girl. A crease deepens between her eyebrows as she watches her daughter plow over another cone. I've come to the conclusion that within two months, this girl will smack into a parked police car while texting her boyfriend. It's as if I can see into the future. Based on the hysterical crying that is occurring behind the steering wheel, it looks as if she failed her test and will need to come back and try again. I have never seen a mother look more relieved.

Rob exits the building with a big smile, residency card in hand as well as a new driver's license. However, they did not give him a scooter license. The day ended with fixing something we didn't know needed to be fixed and us not getting the actual thing we came for.

"Now I remember why our licenses are screwed up," Rob says as we walk back to the car. "The day we renewed them the electricity went out right as they were about to enter our numbers into the computer. The man scribbled the numbers in a Charlie Brown notebook and said he would enter them mañana. I guess mañana never came."

"I'm glad that's fixed, but what are we going to do about the scooter license?"

"Oh, I forgot to mention what the man told me. To get the scooter license, I have to take a written test in Spanish. I can't imagine how I'm going to pass that."

I wouldn't say this morning presented the best side of Costa Rica. There were no vistas from atop a volcano or rock formations jutting out of the ocean. But strangely this perspective at motor vehicles has made me glad that I'm living here. Life moves along in Costa Rica. It may be at a ridiculously slow pace, but it moves along nonetheless. Once I get past the frustration these situations create, I can really acknowledge how much my life has changed. I am no longer looking into this country as a bystander. I am fully engaged and participating in all the same ups and downs that Costa Ricans do. I am becoming a Tica.

At this very moment, all around the world, there are teenage girls crying because they failed their driver's exams. Their mothers are relieved knowing their daughters won't be behind the wheel anytime soon. Sometimes it's ordinary everyday life that helps you obtain a deeper understanding of the people around you.

We drive away knowing it won't be long until we return to get that scooter license. Rob turns on the air conditioning as I lean my head back against the seat. "But I do have some good news," Rob says as he adjusts the vents so cool air blows across my face. "There *was* toilet paper *and* toilet seats in the bathroom."

The diva in me smiles. Now that might be the best news of all.

Thunderdome

"Look at these brackets! I think someone tried to break in," Rob says. I look at the tiny metal hinges on the sliding glass door and don't see a thing. "Over here, see that? It's been tampered with."

I lean in closer and realize the brackets do look bent, but bent in a way that would suggest someone was trying to break out of the house, not into it, which is precisely what I'm about to do if Rob doesn't stop obsessing about security.

Since he hasn't been able to work out, my husband is concentrating on—no surprise—a massive security campaign to keep himself busy. It now includes driving around the neighborhood and studying other houses. There is one mansion in particular that he always returns to; it's surrounded by a wall with chards of broken glass fixed into the concrete. Rob is so in love with this wall that I fear, if we weren't already married, he would propose to me right in front of it.

"This is what we should do," he declares while parked in front of the house for the second time this week.

"It looks crazy." I pop another gummy bear in my mouth and flip through a three year old *People Magazine*. I have learned from previous reconnaissance missions to pack lots of snacks and reading materials. This could take all day.

"I like that it looks crazy. Who wants to jump over that wall? Just think. If the owner is demented enough to do that, who knows what's waiting on the other side?"

I turn to my husband and wonder if the rumble theme from *West Side Story* plays a continuous loop inside his head. But instead of the Jets versus the Sharks, it's probably more like two monkey gangs dancing around up there.

"You know what else I would do?" he adds.

"I can't imagine, Rob."

"I'd put an electric fence around the top too. Between the broken glass and the fence, it's practically a guarantee that no one could climb over it."

"Wow, sounds like paradise. You know it would also guarantee a graveyard of dead birds. We've been through this before. How are you going to feel when every little creature that lands on the wall gets zapped?"

Rob doesn't answer and continues to ogle the wall. Before driving away, I catch him smile while taking one last glance in his rear-view mirror. Nothing makes my husband happier than zapping a burglar with ten thousand volts of electricity. It's almost as good as jerry-rigging a moped.

I remind Rob that we have to get going; soon the owner's son will be visiting with his family for their annual Costa Rican holiday and we have to get the house in order. Owen works for the government and Macy is an elementary school teacher. They have two small children and save up all year for this vacation. It's the first time I'll meet them and I want to make a good impression. I wash all their bedding, scrub the floors, and make cute origami towel animals for their children. On the other hand, Rob's idea of making a good impression is installing a barbed wire fence around the property.

"It's not electrified, but I'm sure the landlord will appreciate it," Rob grunts while digging a hole for another post. The last time they were here there were no motion sensors, fences, or cameras. I'm not sure what they're going to think of all this. To offset Rob's craziness, I make a dozen more origami swans, turtles, and monkeys with every available towel I can find. After I'm done, I realize I turned their bedroom into Kenya National Park. I look about as insane as Rob.

This morning we pick Owen and his family up from the airport and make small talk on the way back to the house. "Have you started building yet?" Macy asks.

"No," I reply. "We've been working on getting this water letter, but it's taking longer than we expected."

"You don't have water?"

"No, we have plenty of water. It's just red tape, but it has pushed us back from building this year. It's just another one of those nutty things that comes with living here. You run into a problem and everyone sends you someplace else to get it fixed. In the end, things get done, but not necessarily on your time."

"Well, it's nice that you're taking care of our house," Macy says. "We feel great knowing we have such good people living here."

I smile hoping she keeps that sentiment as we pull into the driveway. I can see the surprised look on Owen's face when he notices the barbed wire. "Wow, you did a lot of stuff."

"Let's bring your bags in and then I'll show you what I've been working on," Rob says. Once inside, the children notice the towel safari in the bedroom.

"I love them! I love them!" they scream as they tackle the animals. I'm glad that we start out on a good note before Rob takes them on the Thunderdome tour.

"I just finished the barbed wire fence, and as you can see there are bougainvillea bushes around it. It's practically impenetrable." As Owen and Macy walk around the house, they are completely silent. I plan to check Craigslist for apartments tonight. We are definitely getting kicked out of this place.

They continue parading around the property when Rob stops to show them the eight cameras and fifteen motion sensors he installed.

"This camera is my favorite. The monitor sits next to my bed and I can see *and* hear anyone who pulls up in front of the house. Not even a whisper gets past me. It's the best." Owen just nods as Macy inspects the cameras. Neither says a word. Once back inside, Rob teaches Owen the complicated procedures for arming all the motion sensors. He punches in half a dozen numbers and explains terms like "bypass central station" and "command mode override" to a confused Owen. No doubt there are keypads at the Pentagon that are easier to program. Macy and I sit at the dining room table where I'm convinced I'm about to have a very awkward conversation.

"I can't thank you enough," Macy exclaims. "I absolutely love it. I'm always a little nervous bringing my kids down here. Everything your husband did makes me feel so much more secure." She then gets up and gives Rob a hug. "Thank you so much for doing this for all of us."

"So you like it? My wife thought for sure you would kick us out."

"Kick you out? The exact opposite, I never want you to leave."

I did not, for one second, think this was the kind of response Rob would get.

"Do you want to see more?" he asks.

"Absolutely," Macy replies. They walk outside where I watch Rob impersonate an intruder and try sneaking around the house. The motion sensor instantly sets off the alarm. Macy then tries it herself. I think I've found Rob's security soul mate. Wait until he drives her up to the house with the wall of broken glass, they'll probably pop open a bottle of champagne and watch the sunset together.

"Macy's dad is a cop," Owen explains. "She is very, very security conscious. It's how she was raised. Rob's a little over the top if you ask me, but I don't' think you could have made her any happier. And that makes me happy because I don't want her concerned about the house."

"I have other ideas if you want to hear them," I overhear Rob asking Macy.

"What do you have in mind?"

"Booby traps."

"I'm listening."

"You see what I mean," Owen whispers to me. "By the end of the trip, Macy and Rob are going to have a secret tunnel dug from the laundry room to the front gate. It's a match made in heaven."

Over the next couple weeks, Rob and I stay in the downstairs apartment while Owen and his family enjoy their vacation. They are out most of the day, enjoying boogie boarding or surfing. Since Rob and I go to bed early, Owen is responsible for setting the alarm every night. This means that not only the outside motion sensors are armed, but the ones inside the house as well. Once you step out of the bedroom, if you do not hit a button on your keychain, the alarm will go off. So the first person who gets up in the morning has to make sure they turn off the indoor alarm sensors.

Tonight I hear Owen pull into the driveway after a long day at the beach. Ten minutes later I swear I can hear him apologizing into the camera, but I'm in a dreamy state so I don't pay much attention to it. *He must just be sorry he's making so much noise coming home,* I think before rolling over and going back to sleep. For all of Rob's super security measures—the ones specifically designed to hear if an intruder is coming—the ones meant to protect us from the bandidos that will soon take over the house and hold us hostage—he doesn't even wake up. He sleeps through the whole thing.

Early this morning Owen knocks on the door and comes downstairs. "Did you hear me last night?"

"I think I did but I was sleeping. Did you need something?" I ask.

"I had to make a really important phone call but you guys had the receiver down here."

"I'm sorry, but you know you could have come down to get it. It was on the living room table."

"Nadine, do you really think it's a good idea to sneak down into your apartment with Mad Max around? I'm afraid he'd shoot me twenty times before I'd hit the ground. So I stood in front of the outside camera repeating, *I'm sorry... I have to come downstairs... please don't kill me."*

When I think about Owen's predicament, and how my husband sets booby traps, owns a gun, uses a machete, and sprays bear mace, I wouldn't want to be sneaking around here either. I also wonder if Sergio heard Owen's pleas last night and perhaps this is the incentive he needs to finally fix our internet line.

"So I'm quietly walking downstairs, keeping my head low when Macy opens up the sliding glass doors upstairs. I thought for sure it was Rob coming out of the room. I ran back upstairs and had to take a few deep breaths."

"Did you eventually come back?"

"Later I army crawled across the floor and got the phone. But let me tell you something, it scared the hell out for me. I thought at the very least I was going to get bear maced in the face."

Once Rob wakes up, I tell him the story. "Don't you think it's a little much? Now we have the landlord crawling across the floor of his own house."

"What's the big deal?" Rob asks. "The guy didn't get hurt, did he?"

In the end, Owen had a wonderful time with his family and Macy slept well every night knowing that a zillion motion sensors and cameras were monitoring the house. I enjoyed sharing time with them and Rob enjoyed sharing his security ideas with Macy.

It's awesome how moving to this side of the country has introduced me to such a great couple. Not only are they giving us a great deal on their house, they've become close friends as well. I'm not sure why it is easier for me to make friends here, perhaps it's because I am more relaxed and, as a result, easier to get along with. I know that when I worked, I was short-tempered and more concerned with my busy schedule than taking the time to make connections with people.

After they leave, I wash their sheets and make a few extra origami towels. I place them on their bed, a nice reminder of this lovely family who trusts us with their vacation home. And I'm extra thankful that Rob found a buddy who enjoys talking about Tasers and tear gas as much as he does.

This morning I wake up early and realize that Rob left the keychain with the alarm clicker on our couch. I curse him under my breath while army crawling across the floor, narrowly missing the motion sensors' beams shooting two feet above my head.

My life will never be boring while living in the Thunderdome.

My Mother-In-Law Is Coming

My mother-in-law, Joanna, is coming to visit. This will be her first trip out of the country. She has the usual anxieties of most newbie travelers. What's my gate? Where do I get dropped off at the airport? Will I be human trafficked across the border into Mexico? I can tell this is going to be a blast.

I'm not sure why she thinks she is the ideal candidate for sex trafficking. I'm not being snarky; I don't think I'm on the short list either. But she saw a movie about it, and for her, it must be a legitimate threat. She recently rented *Taken* and has come to the conclusion that she'd better kidney punch anyone who approaches her at Terminal C.

I've been through this with her before. After watching *Wrong Turn*, she convinced herself that inbred Appalachians were hiding at every rest stop along the highway. It didn't matter that she lived nowhere near the woods. In her crazy head, genetically-challenged marauders were lurking along the Brooklyn Queens Expressway.

Maybe this phenomenon has something to do with aging. My father watches *Court TV* and follows every heinous crime as if his family has fallen victim to each. This channel, or some variation of it, appears to be the only one in his cable subscription. It has not been turned off in thirty years. It plays a continuous loop of grisly murders committed on unsuspecting young women. You can see where I get my sense of humor.

Maybe it's because my dad has two daughters and three grandchildren (all girls), that he gets such a visceral reaction. I frequently hear him yell out as each guilty verdict is announced, "You deserve it you son-of-a-bitch!" Occasionally, he'll pause to cut the turkey at Thanksgiving, but by the time the pumpkin pie is served, he has already turned up the volume on the television and high-fived us as some lunatic gets sentenced to death row.

I'm actually looking forward to this form of dementia as I get older. Since it is inevitable, I hope mine is more along the lines of a shark week or noodlin' obsession. For those who don't know what noodlin' is, please skip over the next paragraph because you can never go back to the innocent time before this useless information craps all over your temporal lobe.

Noodlin', or hillbilly hand fishing, is when someone sticks their arms in murky water in an effort to catch a gigantic catfish... with their bare arm. That's right. It's so stupid just writing about it makes me want to smack myself in the face with a catfish. Why people watch shows about this is also a mystery. Surely, it must be the same people who watch programs about finding Bigfoot or aliens making mysterious crop circles with lawn mowers.

When I was in fifth grade, I did a report on aliens and wrote to every kook around the world who publically declared they saw one. I'm not sure if my mother knew I was writing to these people, perhaps she was too busy stock piling enough baloney and mayonnaise sandwiches to last through the Carter administration. Either way, I started to get bizarre responses back.

My favorite was from a cult in California that believed they had sex with aliens. This classy brochure—something that looked like it was printed in Kinko's while eating a greasy gyro—came with crude drawings of bellybuttons, alien faces, and people involved in full-blown sex acts. Lots of it. Pages and pages of triple X alien lovemaking. At ten years old, I was a little taken back by the literature. What was all this? Mrs. Fields just wanted a double-spaced book report, but perhaps this investigative journalism would launch me into that highly sought after A+ grading territory. I planned to rubber cement them to blue construction paper, but before I did, I decided to show my mom first. She was a teacher and could give me insight into whether this material was book report worthy. Lucky for me—and for Ms. Field's heart condition—my mom immediately took the pages away. She never said another word about it.

That's what was great about growing up in the 1970s, complete avoidance of any provocative topic. She didn't go all Geraldo Rivera on the creepy sex cult. Instead she made me Jiffy Pop Popcorn, the go-to therapy in my house. And it wasn't that wimpy microwave stuff kids eat today. This was Tupac style; it had to be shaken over a hot flame, adding the thrill that someone was about to suffer first degree burns while holding the flimsy metal handle. (That person was usually me.)

Witness your best friend crash her Big Wheel head first into a telephone pole? Enjoy some Jiffy Pop while she's scraped off the pavement and shoved into a waiting ambulance. Crazy neighbor tosses a stink bomb in your house? Have some Jiffy Pop while your dad runs him over with his Chevy Impala. Get creepy drawings from a sex cult in California? Heat up some Jiffy Pop and feel the gratification as you watch the aluminum bag expand like a hot air balloon. That—and a can of grape soda—could cure anything back then.

It's not like I'm the only one to fall victim to shady individuals. My friend Loretta wrote to her pen pal "Katie" for a year when she was a kid. She got the name from an advertisement in the back of a teen magazine promising: *your best friend is just one letter away.*

"Katie" said she was going to call that Friday so Loretta eagerly waited by the phone. When she answered, "Katie" sounded more like Christopher Walken than a sweet twelve-year-old girl who loved

Davy Jones and waterfalls. Needless to say, when Loretta's mother found out about this, "Katie" learned he was one phone call away from sharing a cellblock with a very un-tween like pen pal, who did not enjoy Davy Jones or waterfalls. No Jiffy Pop was served.

But in the scheme of things, after witnessing the neurosis that crime programs have created for my father and mother-in-law, watching noodlin' shows seems like a perfectly acceptable way to spend my older years. Sure, it's not Masterpiece Theater, and a little more redneck fare than I'm accustomed to, but it will create the lobotomized trance I hope to induce as I succumb to my twilight years. And if I'm anything like my father, I'll yell, "You deserve it you son-of-a-bitch," at the poor putz who just lost a hand to a supersized catfish. Someone's got to keep my dad's tradition going, it might as well be the flake that quit her job and moved to Costa Rica.

I check the computer and see my mother-in-law's plane is on time. I hope she is having a good flight and that no one tried fondling her while she dozed off. I don't want her to arrive in a bad mood because if she is in a bad mood, she will tell me my house is dirty, which it is by her standards, but I don't need it pointed out to me. I'm still getting over my parents' visit which has drained the mitochondria out of each and every cell. I feel lifeless and I could use some time to get my act together. I have about fifty emails from people wanting to know how to move here, the best places to visit, and if I can spot them a few thousand dollars while they try to find work. I'm not going to be able to answer all of them if Joanna keeps telling me the milk belongs on the top shelf of the refrigerator, which is the exact thing she does when she arrives.

Eyelashes & Boogie Boarding

Aside from inspecting the cleanliness of my produce drawer, Joanna is easy to please. She wants to swim in the ocean and tan on the beach. That's it. Since she's Italian, tanning comes relatively natural for her. She's from an era where coating your skin with baby oil and lying in the sun for hours was perfectly acceptable. And if that didn't provide the bronzed look one was hoping for, many went so far as to use reflective pieces of metal (much like a Chevy bumper) around their faces to attract more ultraviolet rays.

I enjoy the beach too, but that usually means dressing like I'm going for a stroll in Saudi Arabia. Every part of my skin is covered. The sun is so strong in Costa Rica, it's not uncommon to see tourists walking around with wicked sunburns. I've even seen people with second-degree burns on their feet, the only place they forgot to apply sunscreen. I take all this very seriously, thus, my burka-like beach style.

"All I want to do is relax, do some surfing, and soak up the sun," Joanna says. "I don't care where we do it."

"You want to surf or boogie board?" Rob asks.

"I want to ride some waves. Is that a problem?" she replies. Oh boy, I can already see this argument coming.

"Ma, you're not exactly a spring chicken. I don't want you out there getting knocked around. There are strong rip-tides that are hard to fight."

Since she beat breast cancer, Rob is always pestering his mother about losing weight and getting in shape. She blames her weight on being Italian. "We love food, it's in our blood," Joanna often says. In fact, she loves food so much she is the only woman I know that didn't lose weight while doing rounds of chemotherapy. This lady refuses to pass on the joy of eating a fresh cannoli. She embraces life to the fullest—maybe a little too much—and all of this makes my husband furious. He's been on her more than ever to eat fruits and vegetables, but I happen to like her resolve and her ability not to care what anyone thinks about her image. Meanwhile, I'm always wondering if my thighs are too fat.

"You don't have a clue how to eat right. You eat way too much meat," he nags.

"I do not."

"Okay, so tell me what you ate last week."

"Pasta… Monday, Wednesday, and Friday."

"And what did you have on it?"

"My red sauce."

"Your red sauce has a ton of sausage and chopped meat in it."

"I *know* Robert! But it's mostly pasta."

"I swear Ma, why do I even have this conversation with you? You want to swim in the big waves, where lots of people drown, but you don't even bother to try and get in shape before the trip."

"I'm a floater. This fat keeps me alive. There is absolutely no way I can sink. So stop worrying about me and worry about your skinny wife." She points in my direction and puts her hands on her hips. "You really should eat something, Nadine. Look at her Robert, it's ridiculous." She makes a face at me like I'm Karen Carpenter. If my mother-in-law had her way, I would be drizzling olive oil over my Cheerios every morning.

256

As Rob and Joanna argue, I can't help but notice her eyelashes. They are thick and curled up like a Hollywood starlet. "I love your eyelashes, Joanna. I didn't realize they were so long." I'll say anything at this point to take the attention off my emaciated body.

"These aren't mine. I got them done at the beauty parlor."

Rob crinkles his eyes and inspects her face. "Ma, you actually paid for eyelashes?"

"The Vietnamese lady glues them to your existing eyelashes. It's fantastic, you don't have to wear mascara at all."

Rob shakes his head. "I think that's a huge waste of money."

"I like it," I add. "They look pretty."

"Since I beat cancer, they grew back thinner. Now I have thick eyelashes again. So what's the problem?"

"How much did it cost?" If Rob is not hassling her about being overweight, he's hassling her about her spending habits. "Please don't tell me you spent fifty dollars on that."

"Okay, then I won't tell you they cost me one hundred and fifty dollars."

"You're out of your mind. And look, they're all over your face."

"No they're not."

"Take a look in the mirror." Rob's right. Joanna's eyelashes are sprinkled across her cheeks.

"Well, if more come off I'm going back there and have the lady redo it."

"If you go boogie boarding, there is no way they are ever staying on. I'm pretty sure you're not getting your money back."

As Joanna and Rob continue their deliberation about eyelash warranties, I load the car with all the things we'll need for the beach. We are headed to Playa Negra, one of the best places to boogie board on the coast. I want the first beach we visit to take her breath away. I've never been to this particular one, but I hear it's incredible and rarely crowded. I toss lots of suntan lotion in the car hoping Joanna will change her mind about baby oil and lather up.

After a half hour drive, we turn down a dirt road and into a small parking area. A man is sitting there wearing his reflective vest. It's like that everywhere in Costa Rica, people in vests asking for money in return for a secure parking space. The man asks for two dollars. I've seen people argue with these guys, not wanting to pay. However, I've also seen back windows broken out and radio antennas ripped off of cars. So I smile and pay the man. It's hot and I already feel bad for him; I would not want to be sitting out in this heat all day long. We even give him a small tip in addition to the two dollars.

The beach is about a few hundred yards from the car. The walk leads you down a narrow, paved path that leads to the water. It's lined on either side with mango trees, their branches reaching over our pathway and providing shade. This canopy, with the ocean sparkling in the distance, might be the most spectacular entrance onto a beach I've ever seen.

"This is unbelievable," Joanna whispers in a reserved tone, as if she's walking down a church aisle to receive communion. I've seen this before with other guests. One doesn't feel out of place or in a strange land here; instead it's all fabulously familiar. Your mind works to remember, straining as if you can somehow recall being in this exact spot before. It's not Déjà vu, but more like a comfortable place where you instantly feel at home, a place you've always known.

I have yet to invite a guest that didn't want to return. Even with all the potholes and unreliable utilities, Costa Rica makes you feel really good. You can imagine being a better version of yourself here. There is so much to be discovered, whether it is watching a family of coatis running by or enjoying quality time with your spouse. The calming environment forces you to take a deep breath and remember what's most important in life.

I'm sure other people have experiences like this when they travel to foreign lands. For example, I read about a unique condition that occurs when people travel to Israel called Jerusalem Syndrome. People get so excited while on their trip they briefly become psychotic. Their symptoms include: anxiety, the desire to split away from groups, and the need to shout. Sounds like my dad at Disney World.

I'm glad that Costa Rica syndrome seems to create the opposite effect. People become ultra-calm and want to drink a lot of piña coladas at sunset. Plus, who want to waste time shouting when there are righteous waves to catch.

We make our way to the beach and the sand is amazingly hot. I can almost hear my feet sizzle. In the distance I spot a shady tree and command everyone to follow. Joanna's trance ends when she realizes she has to walk a quarter of a mile so that her malnourished/melanin-deprived daughter-in-law can find shelter under a tree. I run to the tree, the sand already burning through my sandals. Rob and his mom mosey along as if they are window shopping. They are the slowest walkers I've ever seen. It's an argument Rob and I have all the time; my stride is at least twice as fast as his. I'm glad they have each other because there is no way I'm slowing down.

Once settled, I set Joanna's chair in the sun while Rob goes out to check the water. There is a perfect channel to boogie board with few rocks. I watch as he catches a wave and rides it into shore. This is going to be a great day.

"I can't wait to get in that water. I've been thinking about this all year," Joanna says while watching Rob ride another wave.

"So you've gone boogie boarding before?"

"No. But it doesn't look so hard. If Robert can do it so can I." I look out and watch as a huge wave breaks over his head. A few seconds later, he pops out of the water. I don't see how this is the best activity for a sixty-two year old woman wearing fake eyelashes.

Rob returns and they both head out together. Joanna easily battles the waves as she moves farther and farther into the ocean. It's impressive how strong she is as she fights each wave crashing on top of her. Every time I think she might be stuck underwater, she rises to the surface like a rubber ducky. There is nothing that can make this lady sink. I guess Joanna was right, she could float all the way to Nicaragua if that circumstance should present itself. And with some luck, she might come across a Chevy bumper and tan her way out to sea.

I notice Joanna having a hard time getting on the board. For all her floating ability, she has no dexterity to maneuver herself into the right position. Rob physically manhandles her onto the board and waits for a wave. When the time is right, he releases her and she shoots out of his hands like a bullet. Consequently, the wave flips Rob to the bottom of the ocean. Each time he sets her up for a wave, she takes off screaming in delight while he inhales a gallon of saltwater. I am all but certain he is going to drown. However, I have never... ever... laughed so hard knowing I could be a widow within the next ten minutes.

After an hour, they drag themselves out of the water. Joanna's adrenaline is pumping and she wants to go out again. Rob's face is covered with seaweed.

"That was so much fun!" she giggles while shifting her chair to face the sun.

Rob spits up some seawater and collapses on his towel. I don't think he's ready just yet.

Playa Grande

I like having Joanna here. I get to sit back and watch her fight with Rob over the most ridiculous things. Now I know how my husband felt while my parents were visiting.

"Robert, you should rinse out that glass before putting it in the dishwasher."

"Worry about yourself, Ma."

"Robert, you should put the laundry detergent in the water first, then add the clothes."

"Worry about yourself, Ma."

It goes on and on. But in-between the badgering, Joanna also loves to tell stories about how smart her son is; a bona fide genius.

"When he was a toddler, he walked around the house with a coffee can on his head all day long. He would take it off from time to time, grab a couple of pencils, and play it like a drum. Sometimes he would tap it while it was still on his head. We just loved it. We all *knew* he was gifted after that." I nod my head in agreement, although *gifted* would not be the adjective I would use for a kid who plays the drums on his head.

"He was such a happy baby. Never cried, always smiling. I always *knew* he would be successful. A mother just knows."

I listen to her stories and think about my parents. I never hear glowing reviews about my academic superiority, no cute tales about science projects or adorable habits. All Rob had to do was stick a Chock full o' Nuts coffee can on his head and his mother was already inducting him into MENSA.

My parents had other ideas on how to raise their kids. At four years old, my father started showing me various pictures of Rome. He taught me the names of Roman emperors, described ancient aqueducts, and then proceeded to show me horrifying pictures of people entombed in ash at Pompeii. I remember one in particular, a cast of a seated woman with her hands over her mouth. It was about the most horrifying thing one could show a four year old. A close second would be the bloody drawings he showed me of the Christians being thrown to the lions.

"This is what happens when kids don't eat their mother's pot roast," he'd say. Well played dad.

When I listen to Joanna's stories, I can't help but laugh at the differences. It appears Rob has been showered with praise from a very young age. Me... not so much. But what I can say, for all the unorthodox parenting methods my father used, I've never plunged into a bay pit and bashed my shin open. Now knowing the Chock full o' Nuts story, perhaps Rob was walking around that garage wearing a coffee can over his head when he fell. I never thought to ask.

She continues her stories over breakfast while I find a few clean towels. Today we are going to Playa Grande, a beach with even bigger waves. This a bad idea. A *really* bad idea. Although Playa Grande is lovely, it is more suited for surfers than sixty-two-year-old women who want to practice their boogie boarding skills. I am against the idea.

"Can't we take her to Sugar Beach, or how about back to Playa Negra. The water can get so rough at Playa Grande. It's too dangerous."

"Did you not see her the other day? She'll never take no for an answer. If she wants bigger waves then I'll give her bigger waves."

This morning is particularly hot as we unload the car and walk toward the beach. I find a picnic table under a shady mango tree next to a stand selling food. There are five stools in front of the counter, all of which are taken by hungry surfers discussing the conditions of the day. They are tan and unintentionally flexing their ripped abs as they talk. Even the women are rocking a solid six pack. Surfing must be the best cardiovascular exercise, and for a brief moment, I consider getting out there. That is until I turn around and look at the waves. They are big. And judging by the time of day, they are only going to get bigger. This doesn't faze Rob or Joanna as they head out with their boogie board. Rob runs quickly across the burning sand into the water. Joanna wisely brought her water shoes; she sashays across the sand like she is in a *Sport's Illustrated* swimsuit shoot.

They settle in an area where waves are rolling in from opposite directions. Rob makes his way out but Joanna is having a difficult time. One wave crashes into them from the right, another one hits from the left five seconds later. One smacks Joanna so hard it sends her back ten feet causing her to land on her backside. She tries to get onto her knees, but appears to be stuck in the sand. She keeps rolling back and forth, unable to get her legs underneath her. She ends up just sitting there laughing while stuck in a sandy hole that keeps getting deeper. I look around for the surfers but they have already finished their drinks and ran out to take advantage of high tide.

Robs finally gets to his mother, drops his boogie board, and grabs her hand. She is unable to get to her feet and just sits in the water as each wave slams into her. As the last wave recedes, I can see that she is being sucked back into the ocean. Joanna is now in the middle of a rip tide. "Get up!" I hear Rob scream.

"I can't! Let go of me!"

"Ma, I'm not letting go. Try to get on your feet."

"I could if you would stop pulling me."

"The riptide is going to suck you out. Listen to me and get the hell up!"

I briefly go over the physics lesson my mother-in-law taught me the other day, *I'm a floater. I can't even get to the bottom of the pool.* But if she starts out at the bottom of the ocean, I am all but certain she will stay there. And Rob better do something quick to get her on her feet.

Finally, a strong wave barrels in, pushing Joanna further into shore. It rolls her onto her belly and she's finally able to get up. Rob sprints back out to catch up with the boogie board that has floated a quarter of a mile down the beach. They walk back exhausted and defeated. Not one eyelash survived.

They order a drink from the food stand and collapse at the picnic table. Joanna is worn out; the very first time I've seen her exhausted on this trip. I don't know where she gets her energy from. She is a great example for anyone who is under the misconception that growing old means sidelining their adventurous spirit. It's exactly the opposite for her. She wants to get the most out of life. I'm not sure if this is a consequence of her struggle with cancer—maybe it makes her value each day in a way that most of us don't. All I know is she is not afraid to try new things and doesn't care what others think. Joanna proves a little bit of fearlessness goes a long way.

Before going home, we sit and watch the surfers in the distance. They are patient, waiting for the perfect wave before paddling and jumping up on their boards. Their moves are as sophisticated as professional figure skaters. Some fly high into the air before crashing into the water. Others get lucky and ride within the tube of a wave. I imagine how this must feel, completely surrounded by water, speeding through like a locomotive. It must be such a rush. I can see why surfing is more than a sport—it's a lifestyle.

Some of the surfers must be on vacation and will end up going back to work later in the week. It's hard to imagine this group stuck in an office all day, but I bet they are already planning their next visit, and dreaming of what it would be like to make it their profession. I admire the people who do just that, who come here and open surf shops. Somehow, they turn the thing they love the most into a way of making a living. I'm sure people told them they couldn't do it, just like people told me I would ruin my life by moving to Costa Rica. Whenever I start to doubt what I can accomplish, I'll remember the people out there who are taking control and designing their own life. For these surfers, that means finding a way to catch as many waves as they can while they are healthy enough to do it.

It's Joanna's last night here so we take her to an extra special restaurant for dinner. It is one of my favorites. It has the best ocean views and the most delicious cuisine. It's not uncommon to see crowds of people sitting upstairs with a drink in one hand and a camera in the other. They are all trying to capture the bold, golden hues that spread across the sky at sunset. It's unfortunate that people often turn around once the sun plunges below the horizon, missing the best part of the fanfare. This is the moment I love the most, the backwash of color that floods the sky with pink and lavender. It's nature's encore performance when the colors swirl around like cotton candy clouds. Eventually, darkness washes away the portrait like rain to chalk drawings on a Paris sidewalk. And even though I get to watch this whole production again tomorrow, I don't take this one for granted. Every one of these sunsets is as precious to me as the one before.

Joanna orders a Mojito and takes in her last moments in Costa Rica. We talk about her favorite parts of the trip and are happy that she has had this chance to experience a piece of our life here. She's already planning to come back next year to tackle a few zip-lines. My husband just shakes his head; there is no use arguing with her. I'm sure this woman will be flying through the jungle in twelve months' time.

Our dinner arrives and everything, from the tuna to the shrimp, is perfectly prepared. I've always been guilty of overcooking fish, making it rubbery and unappetizing. It makes me wonder how these chefs always know how to get it just right.

The dessert, coconut ice cream, is equally as delicious and served inside a halved coconut shell. As we enjoy our last bite of creamy goodness, I notice many tourists gathering to lean over the railing. Instead of looking at the ocean, they are twisting to look back toward Flamingo.

"Wow, that is a big fire," I hear one of them say. I don't pay much attention since many times these fires are started in order to clear brush.

"Should we be concerned?" another tourist whispers to her husband. I get up from my table and take a look.

"I wouldn't worry about it," I offer. "It's not uncommon to see this type of thing here. It looks like a raging forest fire, but it is actually a controlled burn." But as these word leave my lips, the wind picks up and carries the flames across the mountain. In a matter of minutes, our view looks like a lit charcoal grill. Rob leans in next to me to assess the situation.

"It's okay, right?" I ask. "I mean, we've seen this dozens of times."

"No, I don't think so. This looks like a wildfire."

Not only is it a wildfire, but the fire is completely engulfing the mountain where we own our lot. From this decadent view, I feel like a fiddling Nero watching Rome burn.

Fire on the Mountain

After dropping Joanna off at the airport, we head back home to switch our car for the scooter. We figure if there are any fallen trees blocking the road to our lot, it will be easier to navigate around them on two wheels than four. The scooter has come in handy many times, and today is no exception.

The closer we get into town, the stronger the smell of burnt leaves. The air has a thick, dirty quality—more like Los Angeles than pure rainforest air. I look to my right and notice the fire has skipped over a neighborhood up high in the mountain. Only the trees at the very top are smoldering. The colorful bougainvillea bushes that adorn the entrance are unharmed, as are the palm trees that line the road into the community. If you didn't look up, you would never know last night ever happened.

I hope for the best as we approach our development, but it quickly becomes clear that the fire was as bad as it looked from the restaurant last night. It bounced across our mountain, destroying mature trees in some areas while only igniting the underbrush in others. The long, shady drive past the entrance is littered with fallen trees, some precariously leaning against others while one completely blocks the road. A couple of men are already there with chainsaws slicing into the wood. They break apart the tree and pull a heavy branch to the side so that we can pass.

"I just can't believe it," I say. Gray spirals of smoke rise off the debris, forming tiny tornados before disappearing into the breeze. Some trees and plants survived while the ones right next to them perished. It's this randomness that scares me the most. I think back to the news footage of canyon fires in California and wonder how those people continued to live in those areas. Did they love the place so much they didn't hesitate to rebuild?

The first thing we do is stop and visit Mike, the owner of a house down the road from our lot. He battled the fire alongside Luis, the caretaker of the community.

"Man, I feel like I smoked two hundred packs of cigarettes. That was the scariest thing I ever lived through," he says.

"Did the abandoned house make it?" Rob asks.

"Yup."

"Damn it. I was hoping to see a pile of ashes."

"Amazingly, none of the houses caught fire. Every last one of them survived."

"Did you stay here all night?"

"Had to." Mike replies. "The water lines started melting so Luis and I ran around sealing the geysers to ensure we would have the water we need. We worked all night trying to save the water system. All the while, flaming debris was flying around our heads. I don't know what would have happened without Luis here. I believe he saved this whole development." This caretaker continually delivers on a job that few would handle. He has that kind of toughness that Ticos who grew up in this area possess. He can handle the suffocating heat and work a full day in the sun. I don't have a tenth of the stamina this man has.

If the water lines had all melted, the job of fixing them would be immeasurable. Our dreams of building a house would be on hold for quite some time. I give Mike credit for sticking it out and not running away. I can't imagine how frightening the whole ordeal must have been for two men alone here in the dark. I don't think I would have had the courage to stay.

I'm glad to hear the water lines are safe. But that's the extent of the jubilation. I start to get a sick feeling in my stomach. We can't catch a break with this land and it seems there is always something going wrong.

"Do you have electricity?" Rob asks.

"Yes, can you believe it? The electric company came while the fire was still whizzing around our heads. I know everyone complains about how slow things are done here, but these guys have been fantastic. It hasn't been twenty-four hours yet and they've fixed every line. I'm glad because it's going to be a scorcher today. And the wind has no plans of dying down either. There will be more fires, maybe not here, but somewhere for sure. I'm going to soak everything around my house just in case."

Rob and I drive up to our lot and pass the abandoned house. Like Mike said, it's still there, killer bees and all. It turns out the fire skipped right over it.

We stand on our land and stare out at the ocean. It's the same beautiful views that makes me—for a moment—believe this fire never happened. I'm sure those same people from the restaurant who were worried about the fire are now relaxing on Flamingo Beach or enjoying a dune buggy tour. They have the right idea. They don't have to worry about broken water pipes or smoldering land. They're just visiting while I packed up and forfeited my career to live in Costa Rica. I'm going over the obstacles we've encountered so far: permit delays, empty houses, and wildfires. The more I think about it, the more I wish I was one of those tourists right now.

"It's all so discouraging, Rob. It's like someone keeps telling us not to build. Like there is a larger force making it impossible to move ahead with our plans. It used to be something I wanted, something I was looking forward to. Now I feel like it will never happen and we are just wasting our time."

"Don't think like that. You're only looking at the negative. You want to know what I see? I see that we escaped unscathed. We considered building only a short time ago. All of our construction supplies would have been on the lot and they would have all burned. Can you imagine the cost of that? We would be so far behind in our budget we definitely couldn't have finished building."

"Well… okay, that's good news."

"And yeah, the abandoned house didn't burn down, but someone will buy it. It's a five thousand square foot house with an ocean view. It's not like it's a four story walk up in the Bronx. Anyone would be lucky to be standing here right now looking out at that water. Don't get wrapped up in all this drama. Concentrate on the positive. Our dream is still alive and we still have the ability to make it work. Look, that's a huge yacht out there in the distance. Imagine waking up to this every day."

He's right; this isn't the worst thing that could happen. I look out across the horizon and listen for the sweet sound of howler monkeys. It's completely silent.

"But it's so quiet up here. Where are the monkeys, Rob?"

"Don't worry. Give it some time and all the animals will come back. It's Costa Rica. Once the first rains come everything will turn green again." He looks around the property, turns to me, and starts laughing.

"What are you so happy about?"

"I was going to clear the lot with my machete this week. I just realized I don't have to, the fire took care of that for me."

As Rob walks the ashy perimeter of our property, I sit in the car and turn on the air conditioning. I check my phone, and remarkably, it has reception. It's one of the best things about this development. There is a cell tower within the project providing a decent connection and internet bandwidth. At least I know that if I build here, I will have reliable internet... hopefully.

I log onto the internet and check my emails. I open one from the company that prints my books:

Today we received an email from a publishing house in China. They are interested in translation rights to your book. We included the information so you may contact them yourself.

Today didn't turn out so bad after all.

The Turtles Are Coming

A remarkable event is about to happen in Costa Rica. People are discussing it in the supermarket and tour operators are already advertising this excursion. "Are we going?" I overhear a couple say to each other while sharing a plate of nachos in Tamarindo. The turtles are coming, and no matter where you go, people are eager to witness this migration.

There are a number of species of turtles that come ashore to lay their eggs: Olive Ridley, Leatherback, Green, Loggerhead, and Hawksbill. It's the Olive Ridleys that are now making their way to Playa Ostional in an event called the big "arribadas." Thousands of these turtles return to the place they hatched. Once they land, they use their limbs to crawl through the sand, looking for the perfect spot to lay approximately one hundred eggs. I can't think of anything I want to do more than share this miraculous experience with Rob.

We waste no time and wake up early for the trip. The dark, sandy beach is only an hour and a half drive from Tamarindo and I've been informed by a friend that the dirt road is in good shape. Of course, there will be a couple of rivers to drive through. Back in the states, I used to complain about the New Jersey Turnpike—now I talk about forging rivers.

There are varying degrees of difficulty when crossing a river and the advice given is usually broken down according to the vehicle you may be driving. There are three categories. The first: If you are driving a compact car, you may just get the compact car answer. "Don't be a schmuck… you'll never going to make it." The second: If you own an SUV, you may be advised to pack extra equipment. "Make sure you bring along some cables just in case you get stuck in the middle." And the third: If they lean in and demand to know if you own a car snorkel (a large tube that prevents water from being sucked into your engine—something I didn't even know existed until I moved to Costa Rica) you might as well discontinue the conversation unless you want to take your car SCUBA diving. The river we will be passing through gets the compact car seal of approval, which means our SUV will have no problem crossing over.

I grab a beach bag and search for supplies: bug spray, plenty of water, and a large brimmed hat to protect my face from the sun. I also fill the camera with new batteries in case we actually do see a turtle. I positively don't want to miss the chance of getting a shot.

We enjoy the cool morning air as we drive along shady roads to Playa Ostional. Howler monkeys are already awake and active in the branches above us. These adventurous drives are my favorite, filled with anticipation of what's ahead. It's why I always recommend renting a car in Costa Rica. At any moment, something fabulous is happening a short distance away. A ten minute drive in either direction from your hotel will usually take you to deserted beaches with spectacular views. And like today, maybe hundreds of turtles landing ashore.

We come across a small river and pause. It appears to be shallow so Rob goes ahead and slowly drives through. At the deepest point, the water creeps up to the middle of our tires but slowly recedes after that. The advice we received was perfect; even a compact car could cross this river. When we first moved here, Rob used to get out and toss a stick in the water to determine its depth. Most of the time the stick just floated down the river, but occasionally Rob would get lucky and it would pierce the bottom like a javelin. Eventually, we skipped that altogether after noticing Ticos driving their little Nissan Sentras around us. They must think it's hilarious every time they witness a gringo sprinting toward the edge of a little river and tossing a stick as if they are preparing for the Olympic Games. It was one of the first things our realtor, Martin, said when we considered moving here, "If you want to live in Costa Rica, you better get used to driving through a river every now and then." It's one of the few things he was right about.

The drive takes us straight into Ostional, a tiny town with a few hotels built on the bluff above the town. The road borders the sea and we find a place to park under a palm tree. We both look out across the water and can't believe our eyes. Hundreds of turtle heads pop out of the ocean like submarine periscopes. It resembles a well-planned naval offense; a platoon of Olive Ridleys gunning for land. This invasion is not just happening in front of us, but continues down the beach. Everywhere I look, turtles weighing upwards of one hundred pounds pepper the horizon. We came at the perfect time.

"Rob... I can't... I can't believe this. It's one of the most beautiful things I've ever seen." The turtles closer to shore are aggressively tossed into a final wave before they're spit out onto land. And that's just the beginning of their day.

Up and down the beach, we see tire-like impressions in the sand. These turtles use their paddle-like appendages to dig in and propel themselves forward. It appears to be an unfortunate design flaw; forelimbs perfect for swimming but counterproductive for movement on land. However, this doesn't stop them from pushing ahead inches at a time in-between stopping for prolonged periods of rest. Sometimes it takes hours before they find a suitable place to nest.

"I knew it was going to be incredible, but I'm speechless. I'm so glad we didn't miss out on this," Rob says before running off with his camera.

Eventually the turtle finds a spot, turns around, and begins laying her eggs. I stay a good distance away and let her have her privacy. I admire her impressive heart-shaped carapace (shell), two feet in length. These shells are grey when the turtles are born but change to an olive color when they mature.

These eggs are thought to be an aphrodisiac and are highly sought after by people of Costa Rica. It appears this close-knit community has struck a delicate balance between preserving the turtles for future generations and maintaining the culture of the people. I learn that so many turtles arrive with each new wave that they trample and destroy the nests that were laid the night before.

The town participates in a program that allows collection of up to five percent of this first wave of eggs, which are likely to be destroyed by the turtles themselves. The remaining nests are left to hatch and hopefully make it back to the sea. But even with these measures, the turtles are still decreasing in population. Many perish after being trapped in the large nets used for fishing. Costa Rica, for all its beauty and grace, constantly reminds you how precious and delicate our ecosystem is, and how quickly we can lose the things that are the most beautiful in this world.

The turtles who have already laid their eggs begin the long route back to the sea. It's hard to watch as they struggle, going a few inches before collapsing from exhaustion. Labor and birth have taken so much energy from these mothers that they look as if they want to call it quits and take a nap. But every time I think they are through, they thrust themselves forward another foot. It takes all their strength to return home.

I watch one as she makes it to the foamy edge. Cool water washes over her body giving her a much needed second wind. She reaches her neck up and gulps two big breaths into her lungs; her home is only a few more feet away. After a couple of minutes, she looks straight into the cloudless sky as if to ask for help from above before completing the last leg of her journey. I am so overcome by this event I don't even realize I'm tearing up.

I feel something shift in me, a clarity that rushes through my body and fills me with immeasurable appreciation. I see how wondrous all of it is, that today I'm here to witness this mother struggle her way back into the water. I'm watching turtles come back to the place where they themselves were hatched. I can't help but reflect on the years that have passed, and that maybe things aren't as random as I always believed. This journey that I'm on is beginning to make more sense. Maybe in a way, we all return to where we started. I think I've come home.

Another wave moves in and momentarily lifts the mama turtle. This gives her enough buoyancy to thrust her body further into the ocean. A couple more waves wash through, completely submerging her. All at once her four appendages burst into a quick paddle. I'm prepared to watch her swim away, but with lightning speed, she's already gone.

Warning: Never Ask Rob for the Coffee

"Today is going to be great," I tell Rob while on the road to meet Ian and Sandy for a little kayaking trip.

"We'll do some snorkeling too. You know me, I never pass up a two-for-one excursion," Rob adds.

Ian is excited to introduce us to his new neighbors, Ryan and Lisa. They just moved in next door and they've become close friends. It doesn't surprise me; Ian is the most even-tempered person I know. Nothing seems to shake this guy. Maybe Rob falling into a bay pit startled him for a few seconds, but other than that, he is the most even-keeled person I ever met. I always enjoy spending time with him.

We drive to Playa Minas where Ryan and Ian are already unloading three kayaks off the top of their cars. When they put them on the ground, I notice they are not the hard, fiberglass ones but more like flimsy, inflatable rafts.

"Ian, how far out are we going?" I ask.

"You see those rocks?" he says while pointing out in the distance. They are so far away they look like two tiny dots on the horizon.

"In these kayaks?" I gasp.

"Yup."

"Where did you find them?"

"Someone gave them to me," Ian says proudly. "Didn't pay a dime."

I nudge Rob and whisper in his ear, "Isn't it a little risky to paddle out in the middle of nowhere in this thing? Do I really want the only thing between us and a crocodile to be an inflatable kayak?"

"Don't be silly, there are no crocodiles in the ocean. It'll be fine. What's the worst that can happen?" You're right, Rob. Why should I worry? I've already run into them while kayaking through mangroves and hiking a bat cave in Panama. And aside from that, experience has taught me that putting Rob in charge of anything inflatable is always a bad idea.

Ian, Ryan, and Rob each grab a kayak and drag it to the water's edge. There are two, two-man kayaks, and one that can only fit a single person. It looks like someone has to sit out. I mention this to Sandy.

"Oh no, someone will swim behind," she explains. Swim all the way out into the ocean? Are these people nuts? Everyone volunteers to swim and not wanting to appear like an inflatable kayak princess, I volunteer as well. They look at me like I'm one cough away from being admitted to a consumption sanatorium. No offense is taken; I've come to terms with my noticeably lackluster upper body strength.

"I'll swim," Ryan volunteers. I learn he's a surfer and is very comfortable in the ocean. Lisa feels confident that she can paddle the single kayak and we are given one of the two-seaters. We only get one paddle since there are not enough to go around.

While I'm busy putting our camera and phone into Rob's perfected waterproof pack (a few plastic Ziploc bags), the gang takes off. I store the bag in the bulkhead while Rob places the huge sack of snorkeling gear between us. He drags the kayak into the water where

I proceed to gingerly step inside. Once I'm settled, Rob climbs in and immediately flips us over.

"Do you have the camera bag?" Rob yells while I float to the surface. A second later, so does the pack. Remarkably, not a drop of water has leaked into the bag. We try the whole process again and this time we are successful. I look out and notice our friends are at least a quarter mile ahead of us.

"How did they get out there so quick? Come on… let's catch up," I order.

"I'm trying but I can't seem to get this kayak straight." The more Rob paddles, the more we spin in circles. "Can you scoot down? I need more leg room."

I scrunch my knees up to my chin while Rob stretches out. I have essentially wedged myself into a space totaling ten square inches.

"I can't believe we have to go all the way out there," I say while pondering which leg will be crippled first by the inevitable Charley horse.

Rob continues paddling but it takes twice as long to get half the distance the group got only minutes ago. "I know what the problem is, there is no rudder on this stupid thing," he says. The boat maneuvers through the water like the last scene in *The Perfect Storm.* We fight the tide as every wave splashes buckets of seawater at us. I am wedged so tightly in-between the plastic, I can't even put my arms up to block my face. I bravely spit out every mouthful of saltwater. This is, by far, the worst kayaking trip ever.

"Uh… Rob… we have a problem," I state after noticing a big bubble rising off the right side of the kayak. It's like a huge inguinal hernia that tilts us thirty degrees to the left.

"Holy shit! Lean to the right, lean to the right!" Rob yells.

"I can't move. I'm stuck."

"You better unstick yourself or we're going over." Rob positions himself so he is sitting on the bow which only crushes the back end of the kayak and sinks him into the water. I free my body and hang myself over the right side like a sand bag, in which I have found I have quite the natural talent for. With my ass in the air, our kayak steadies and we continue our journey out to sea.

We finally meet up with our friends and everyone is already snorkeling. Ryan swims over and tethers us to the other anchored kayaks.

Rob and I jump in the water and start putting on our snorkel gear. "Don't forget to wear your floaty," Rob demands.

"I don't want to, it's embarrassing."

"I'm going to be nervous knowing that if I turn my head for a minute you could be drowning, which is exactly what happened in the Caribbean."

"But I feel more confident in the water now."

"Nadine, you're already drifting away. Just wear it." In front of everyone, Rob straps the device around my chest and now I'm the big dork floating upright while everyone swims around me.

I put on my mask and stick my head in the water. Ian was right, the fish here are amazing. There are angels, tangs, parrot, and butterfly fish swimming underneath us. After floating around for twenty minutes, I notice Rob has disappeared. I look up and find that he's sitting on a rock about fifty feet away. He is all alone except for a couple curious pelicans darting over his head.

"Is your husband okay?" Lisa asks. "He looks a little green." For all Rob's love of snorkeling—for all his passion of anything fish related—he gets seasick quickly when out on the water. I swim over to him to see how he's doing.

"Why are you sitting on a rock? Come back to the kayak."

"I just need to be on solid ground for a minute or two."

"How long do you think we're staying out here? I'm concerned our kayak won't make it back."

"I've been thinking about that. We'll tie the kayak to the back of Ian's. At least his has a rudder on his. It will keep us straight as I paddle. I'm not as worried about that as you floating away out here."

"If you haven't noticed, I have a blue piece of Styrofoam strapped around my body. Where could I possibly go? Every time I try to put my face in the water, I pop back up like a jack-in-the-box. It's really quite demoralizing."

"My stomach is already feeling a little better. I think I'm going to get into Ian's kayak. I'll meet you over there." Rob slides into the ocean and swims around for a few minutes before jutting his head out of the water.

"Hey guys, there's an adorable octopus over…" he calls out. Rob sticks his head back in the water but suddenly panics and swims toward us. "Holy crap! I just got attacked by an octopus. I was checking him out when he started scurrying up the reef. He was coming straight at me."

"That's so awesome. I saw a tentacle before, but it was hiding under a rock. I'm going to check it out," Ryan says.

"I don't think that's a good idea. He's really ticked off."

"He was probably just curious of you. They're really quite awesome sea creatures. They completely blend in with almost anything—even a clear piece of glass."

"Yeah, they're really cool until they grab you by the face and hold you down on the ocean floor," Rob says while escaping into Ian's kayak.

After hearing there is a killer octopus on the loose, I scramble back into my kayak. Even though it is now tilting at least forty degrees, I love having the whole thing to myself. The extra leg room is luxurious.

"Would you like a cup of coffee?" Ian asks.

"Here, have a scone and some fresh fruit," Lisa adds. Wow, these guys have come prepared. Now that I'm caffeinated and have a pastry in hand, things don't look so bad. In fact, it's utterly delightful out here. From this vantage point, the area looks completely uninhabited. The lush vegetation hides any signs of people living on the coast.

"What a wonderful place," I say after taking another sip of coffee. I watch as the waves wash over the rocks creating miniature waterfalls that empty back into the sea. "It was a little hard getting out here, but I'm so glad I came." I reach over and Lisa hands me a skewer of fruit. I'm having breakfast with a group of friends out on the ocean without a care in the world.

"Do you have any more coffee?" I ask Ian.

"I have another thermos in the bulkhead," he replies. "Rob, do me a favor and reach in there and grab it for me."

As Rob pulls out the thermos, we are greeted with a pronounced, *Psssssssss.*

"Holy shit. Holy shit! There's air escaping." Rob yells.

"What did you do?" I scream.

"I don't know!"

"It looks like we're going down," Ian says while calmly pouring himself another cup of coffee. "You must have knocked the plug out."

"Stick it back in!" I shriek. "IT'S THE GOOD KAYAK." Rob looks around for what I can only imagine is either duct tape or a pair of underwear.

"Would you like a refill, Nadine?" Ian asks. Is this guy serious?

"I really don't think it's Rob's fault. It could have happened to anyone. Those plugs are tricky," Lisa says while passing another skewer of fruit.

I watch the kayak slowly deflate while Ian and Rob sink further into the ocean. By the time Rob secures the plug back inside the hole, the kayak has lost half of its air. To make matters worse, I look around and realize that we are not in the same position we were fifteen minutes ago. It appears we are drifting out to sea.

"Look," I shout. "The current has us—we're drifting."

"Hmm… I guess my anchor didn't work. Honey, can you pass me the coffee?" Ryan asks.

"Sure, and here, have another scone," Lisa says. What is this, *Breakfast at Tiffany's*? Don't they realize we're down two kayaks, drifting out to sea, with a killer octopus on the loose? I'm about to have a heart attack while still wearing my stupid blue floaty.

I pull out my cell phone and find that I have one bar left. Do I call Sergio? Nah, he won't come looking for me until "mañana." Maybe I should call 911 and ask for the Coast Guard. Crap, how do you say Coast Guard in Spanish? Costa Seguridad?

"Guys, how far do we plan on drifting?" I ask. "I'm pretty sure I can see Panama from here."

"I guess we should start heading back. Too bad, I was hoping to spend a couple more hours snorkeling," Ian replies.

Sandy jumps in behind me while Ian ties his boat to mine. Ryan is happy to swim while his wife stays in her kayak. Surprisingly, we rip through the waves twice as fast as before. Sandy paddles behind me like a champ as I sit up front leaning on the right side to keep it from flipping. Rob was right, as long as my kayak stays straight, it moves fairly quickly.

"Hey guys," Lisa calls from behind. "I've got a great waffle recipe. Why don't you come to my house for lunch?"

While racing back to shore as storm clouds threaten us from above, I revisit the three things I learned about this trip:

One: An inflatable kayak may be a good idea. And a free kayak sounds great. But when someone presents you with a free, inflatable kayak you may want to be the one who volunteers to swim.

Two: You don't want to mess with an octopus, unless you want one attached to your face.

Three: Nothing—I mean absolutely nothing—alarms Ian, not even a sinking kayak drifting out to sea.

We make it to shore and the day ends with an invitation to our new friend's house for waffles. For all the predicaments we faced, this was by far the most exciting Monday morning I've had in a long time.

And I'm happy that for once our two-for-one-excursion was crocodile-free.

Baby Turtles & Scary Hotels

After the six week incubation period, we return to Ostional hoping to witness baby turtles scurry off toward the ocean. We are advised to come just before dawn since the babies hatch in the middle of the night and are guided by the moonlight reflecting off the water. The few that hatch after the sun comes up are at a bigger risk to predators and the punishing heat. It's never been more important to be an early riser than today.

We walk the beach and find it littered with broken egg shells; they are scattered everywhere. This overnight activity has caught the attention of lurking vultures. They wait in trees while others are in groups on the sand. It's a chilling sight and warrants the turtle's quick sprint to the sea. We continue up the beach until we spot tiny prints in the sand. I follow them and find a nest of turtles busting out of their shells. However, I'm not the only one that notices; the vultures also perk up, turning their heads toward the turtles.

The tiny babies sprint across the beach, their little paddles flinging sand onto the top of their shells as they go. In the moonlight, these specks resemble tiny flakes of gold glitter, turning their grayish shells into sparkling pendants. It's as if someone has overturned a jewelry box.

I've been warned to resist the urge to pick up the turtles and carry them to the water—they need time and exercise so their lungs fill with air. Without this workout across the sand, they will ultimately drown. As with most things in the animal kingdom, the turtles must do this journey on their own. All I can do is chant, "Go turtle, go," as I protect them from the predators overhead. *This one will make it*, I say to myself as I shoo the vultures away. I watch as the baby finally reaches the surf. His little appendages paddle rapidly once hitting the water. In a split second, he disappears into the darkness of the ocean like his mother did six weeks ago.

Since we came this far and it's still so early, we want to explore further south and see what other beaches are along the coast. We set our course on visiting Nosara, one of the prettiest towns on the Nicoya Peninsula. Not long into the drive, we come to the bank of another river. This one is exceptionally wide.

"Whoa. You need a bridge to cross this, Rob."

"I think there was one. Look up." Iron support beams rise out of the water, but there is no bridge attached to them. "I don't know what happened to the bridge, but I sure wish they had finished it." This unfinished, abandoned, or collapsed bridge gives me little confidence as Rob gets out of the car and tries to judge the shallowest part of the river.

"Look to your right. I think people cross over there." I point to tire tracks that lead twenty feet away and then disappear into the river.

"Honey, I think you found the perfect place to cross. And by the looks of it, I'm pretty sure we only have one shot at this."

Rob starts the car and drives to the edge. He slowly moves into the water and we watch as it quickly rises up the tires, then over them, and quickly makes its way up to our doors.

"Oh boy… oh boy," I squeak. We are smack in the middle and I hear our car begin to putter. I prepare to bail and make arrangements to toss my body out the window. This way I can enjoy both sightseeing and Grade 2 whitewater body rafting, a new sport I just invented that I can't wait to try. Like most people who are adrenaline junkies, I, too, have always wanted to know how many skull fractures I can sustain before dipping into the peaceful sanctity of unconsciousness. Combined with a light lunch and an emergency CAT scan, this plan would fit perfectly into Rob's uniquely budgeted two-for-one excursion deal.

Of course, Rob doesn't panic. He continues through the river as I watch as the water sneaks closer to my window. After a couple tense seconds, the water recedes and we make it to the other side. I look behind me and see another car at the river's bank. The passengers get out and struggle with the decision on whether or not to cross. I give them a thumbs up before continuing on. I like that we are now the thumbs-up people instead of the other way around.

There is nothing more bucolic than a morning in Costa Rica. The air is cool and infused with what I like to call "happy molecules." This time of day always reminds me of joyful memories. Right now I'm recalling how handsome Rob looked when I walked down the aisle at our wedding. If there is any place for good mental health, it's on a morning drive through the rainforest. It's nature's Prozac.

Nosara is an active community with houses nestled under shady trees giving it a homey feeling. I love how the town is woven throughout the jungle, and I wish more areas had adopted this layout. Here you feel as if you are a guest of the forest.

We find the road to the beach and stop to walk out onto Playa Guiones. I have the same reaction as when I found Pirate's Bay; it takes my breath away. Miles of white sand borders a powder blue ocean while behind us lies rich vegetation. I flip off my shoes and let the warm sand spill between my toes. No wonder people travel to this area for yoga retreats. Everything about it makes me want to inhale deeply and perform a morning salutation. This is heaven on earth.

I look out across the beach and see a strange, domed cupola rising out of the countryside. I grab my camera and zoom in on the structure. There is a large sculpture of a hand attached to the tippy top. "What do you think that is?" I ask.

"Wow, that's strange. I'm hoping it's a restaurant since I'm starving. Let's check it out."

We drive up and down the winding streets but can't seem to find the place. This beach town has roads that curve, then fork, only to bring you back around to where you were before. But this place is too beautiful to care. I could drive in circles here forever.

We eventually climb a hill and pull up in front of what appears to be a hotel. We park the car and walk up a spiraling, white staircase. Palms reach over the bannister and above my head like a palace entrance.

Once at the top we walk into a circular room with a fifteen foot wide plaster hand coming down from the ceiling. There seems to be a running theme of ornamental hands at this establishment. Its index finger and thumb are pressed together, as if to pinch off the top of the plant sitting below it. Someone had one heck of an imagination when they built this; it's by far the most peculiar thing I've ever seen.

"Hello... is anyone here?" Rob calls out. A man wearing gardening gloves walks into the lobby and gives us a big smile. We ask if there are any ocean-view rooms available and he nods his head. We follow him as we walk past a gorgeous white pool. This place seems pretty amazing so far until he takes us to the back of the property and opens up a small cabana. It looks like it hasn't been cleaned in years. However, if a room goes unattended for even a few days in Costa Rica, it can easily look this bad.

There is a spare room at my house that I didn't go into for two weeks. I finally opened the door and it was if I just rolled the dice in *Jumanjii*. Dozens of geckos were scaling the walls and scores of scorpions were crawling around my feet. For a moment every critter paused, their beady eyes staring at the lumbering intruder who just invaded what they thought was a gated community. They then scattered and the room turned into one big bug emporium. Noises emanated from the air conditioner, and in my heightened state of panic, I might have seen an armadillo in the corner. I can't be sure about that since shock was setting in and I was getting tunnel vision. I screamed for Rob who bravely entered the room with only a broom as his weapon. I'm not sure what happened in there, but he reappeared an hour later with a distant look in his eye.

"I've seen things," Rob mumbled. It just goes to show you that you should never let your household chores lapse in Costa Rica. Maybe my mother-in-law was right about me and my laissez-faire attitude toward domestic duties. That milk probably should go on the top shelf of the refrigerator.

The man walks over to the window, props it open, and tells us to look out. It's a panorama of Playa Guiones and Playa Pelada. I can even hear the tide rolling in below and it's the perfect spot to watch the surfers. I couldn't imagine a better view. It might not have all the bells and whistles of Four Seasons, or even the amenities of a Motel 6. However, it does have this vista and that beats out a mini bar or Jacuzzi tub any day.

"Is there a room with air conditioning?" Rob asks.

"Lo siento. No, just the fan," the man says. We turn on the fan but it barely moves, rusted from years of neglect. Between that and the sheets that feel like sandpaper, we tell him that we're sorry for wasting his time. The man smiles and says we can look around if we want.

There are no other guests in sight. I've come to the conclusion that this place used to be a hotel but is now someone's residence. They probably let people stay here if they are willing to deal with the less-than-stellar accommodations. If the rooms were a little better maintained and had air conditioning, I would definitely consider it. Although its features are strange, I can't help but admire the eclectic design of this place. You have to give the owner credit; the cupola rises so high in the air it's an instant tourist attraction. One can never accuse this hotel of having the same cookie cutter appearance as a Hampton Inn.

We dip our feet into the pool before walking back down the spiraling staircase to our car. I make a mental note to come back here one day. I love that Costa Rica still has mom and pop businesses that look different from anything else I've ever seen. In New Jersey, as you drive down a busy street, it could easily be one located in Wisconsin. All the franchises, fast food chains, and large box stores make everything look like a carbon-copy of everywhere else. Maybe that's why there are so few Xerox machines in this county. Who wants to be a clone when you can be the only one with a hand atop a deluxe cupola in the sky?

It's not even eleven o'clock when we stop by a café for breakfast and start to run down all the great things we did this morning. The longer I live here, the more time seems to stand still. It doesn't rush by me anymore, stealing away precious moments. The clock now resembles a patient traveling companion.

I've witnessed many incredible things, but nothing compares to this day. Watching turtle eggs hatch just reaffirms how lovely this world really is—a planet that will dazzle you if you take the time to be part of it. I will never be the same person I was before this event and long to visit more places: the Sloth sanctuary on the Caribbean coast, the Scarlet Macaw rehabilitation center near San Jose, and the Monkey Park just fifteen minutes from my house. All over this country there are wonderful people doing great things to preserve the environment.

I now understand that I have a purpose for being here and it is far deeper than just quitting a job. My life is unfolding in ways that are extraordinary but familiar all at once. I had to push through many challenging experiences in order to become a better version of myself. My reflection is the same, but the road I'm on is remarkably different.

Today, this new road has taken me to Ostional beach. Under the cover of night, I witnessed precious baby turtles dig their paddles into the sand to chase the moonlight's reflection. It's the only light they have ever known, but they trusted it nonetheless. I also got the chance to drive through Nosara, a place so beautiful it brought back a lovely memory of Rob at our wedding. That image reminds me of all the great qualities that I adore about him. I never want to forget that time when we were once young, carelessly in love, and everything seemed possible.

My journey continues to grow in ways I could never have predicted. It may not always be perfect, but I know I will never be left stranded. I've learned to follow my own beacon, one that is not a carbon-copy but is uniquely suited for me.

And like the baby turtles, even in darkness, I'll trust this light, dig my paddles into the sand, and follow wherever it leads me.

Deep Thoughts

From: Nadine
To: Dad
1:13 PM
Subject: The Worst Book He Ever Read

I got a one star review today. He said it was the worst book he ever read:

"I'm halfway through and struggling to finish it: it is simply one of the worst books of any genre that I have every tried to read. Nadine, in particular, is what would be called an "ugly American" by many ex-pats living in Costa Rica (or other foreign places). Instead of appreciating and blending into the culture, she appears as a bull in a china shop in nearly every chapter.

My wife and I are contemplating a retirement move to Costa Rica (or the Caribbean). My father built a house in CR in 1995 and we have made many trips to the country. Likewise, the Caribbean where I have almost thirty years' experience as a visitor. Trust me, this book has almost nothing serious to offer the person seeking good information of making such a move. It is a serious undertaking, with many pitfalls that will happen to you if you don't understand the culture..."

And it doesn't stop there, it goes on and on and on. He practically wrote a book about how much he didn't like my book.

Seriously Dad, the worst book of any genre? Is it the worst book in any language in the world? How about the worst book in every universe on every Starfleet?

Because if that's true... it sounds like a pretty shitty book.

From: Dad
To: Nadine
2:45 AM
RE: The Worst Book He Ever Read

This misanthropic bastard has lots of time on his hands and completely misses the point of your book, which is a narration of a young couple, who for varied and serious reasons, decided to begin a new life free from the stresses and strains of the old. The book was not intended to be a Frommer's Travel Guide on how to blow your nose in San Jose. And of course it helps this sans-culotte to have a Daddy who has a home in Costa Rica, which makes it ever so much easier for him to go down there on his great adventure.

He speaks as an expert on many things, Swiss banks, the IRS, his thirty years' experience traveling, boring the hell out of his wife and companions with his encyclopedic knowledge. Mr. Perfect never made a mistake, speaks of 'blending with the population' and makes generalizations all of which are false and at times insulting.

It's obvious to any discerning individual that this constipated couch potato will never make it past the TV, and do anything that even comes close to the courage and audacity of the author and her husband. He will sit there, eating his Fritos and blending with the culture. It is obvious to me that this book DISTURBED HIM, and it disturbed him for obvious reasons. *Happier Than A Billionaire* awakens him to his manifest failure and he can only justify himself by lashing out at those who fulfilled their dream. He knows everything about moving EXCEPT ACTUALLY MOVING. His advice???? Sit on a couch and write long angry letters to hide the miserable failure of his life.

I trapped three squirrels in three days. I brought Mom to release Number one, I released two and three. I will fill you in another time with my success as Jeremiah Johnson mountain-man trapper.

Daddy

293

When One Door Closes

I just got great news; one of the big publishing houses in Manhattan may be interested in my book. "I can't promise you anything," Emma says, "but your sales and reviews speak for themselves. I'm going to have lunch with them and I'll pitch your book. So be prepared for a possible meeting in New York City this week. And I haven't forgotten about those contracts from Korea and China. Don't sign anything until I read over them." This couldn't have worked out better since I'm already in New Jersey visiting my family. It occurs to me that if I do get this meeting, the only thing I have to wear is yoga pants and an oversized T-shirt. I doubt my pajama fashion will go over in trendy New York so I enlist my sister to drive me to the mall.

"What's the deal with dad and the squirrels? He was outside this morning with a pair of binoculars searching for them in a tree," I ask her while checking the price tags on blouses. Everything seems so much more expensive now that I no longer partake in retail therapy.

"He thinks they're looking at the house funny," she replies.

"Who's looking at the house funny?"

"The squirrels."

"Oh jeez, I'm afraid to ask why."

"When dad fixed the hole in the aluminum siding, it stopped the squirrels from getting into the attic. But he swears the same gang is still out there staring at the house... you know... devising a new strategy for another home invasion. Now he puts traps outside, captures them, and takes them to a park five miles away."

"So his master plan is to relocate all the squirrels in our neighborhood?"

"Apparently. Now mom and dad are fighting because mom wants to drive them to a park across Route 1. She feels there needs to be a more significant buffer between the house and the park. Makes you want to move back home, right?"

"Route 1 is a *six-lane* highway. I've got to hand it to Mom; she's very Stalin-esque in her squirrel removal." This all sounds ludicrous until I consider my own obsession with coaxing the monkeys to my side of the street. I briefly thought about trapping them but Rob gave the kibosh on that plan, largely because I volunteered *him* to set up the cages and release the hysterical monkeys into our yard. Now that I'm watching my dad stare at crafty squirrels through binoculars, I can foresee my future. There is a whole lot of crazy in it. To all appearances, the banana does not fall far from the tree in my family.

"Forget about the squirrels," my sister says while pulling a pencil skirt off the rack. "Remember, you'll be speaking with professionals in New York City. Put your game face on and don't say anything stupid."

"I know. *Believe me...* I know. Me not saying something stupid has become a full-time job."

"Seriously, I think you should let Emma do all the talking. I'm convinced you'll pronounce something wrong and make a jerk out of yourself."

"I got this far, haven't I? And there is no way I can change my personality in the next seventy-two hours."

"Just trying to help. The other day you pronounced the Palace of Versailles, "Ver-sail-ees." And whatever you do, don't tell them any vomit stories. I'm still recovering from the last one about the Vatican."

A few years back, I went to Rome and toured the Vatican museum. It was insanely crowded, and we had at least thirty people in our group. Some were teenagers who just happened to be from a town in New Jersey that is... let's just say... a little hoity-toity and gives out tickets for backing into parking spaces.

Our informative Vatican guide was describing a technique called "change of perspective" as we walked past a wall of Italian Renaissance tapestries. Instead of two-dimensional woven designs (as was common in medieval tapestries), these had a three-dimensional quality to them. It was fun strolling down the long corridor and watching how the faces of these characters followed us along. I suppose this wasn't as much fun for a hung over teenager in our group, since after staring up at The Apostles' roving eyeballs she proceeded to barf—in a display reminiscent of a scene in *The Exorcist*—all over the marble mosaic floor.

What I found so intriguing about this event was not that she ruined her Coach sneakers or that she would now have to spend the majority of her life in confession, it was the response from the Vatican security. Five men in sunglasses and three-piece suits advanced on the scene and contained the mess as if it was a biological weapon. Soon another group of men lugged over red velvet ropes (similar to ones seen on the red carpet). They cornered off the Limoncello regurgitation and stood guard as if they were protecting the pope himself.

It was the most impressive display of vomit removal I've ever witnessed, and I wished they were around when I hurled all over the cafeteria table in elementary school, resulting in me being shamefully escorted to the first graders' coat room by Mrs. Engle. Undoubtedly, those stockpiled baloney and mayonnaise sandwiches finally caught up with me. No guards with velvet ropes appeared, only a disgruntled janitor with a bucket full of sawdust.

"I stand behind that story. Everyone who goes to Rome insists on boring you with their play-by-play description of the Sistine Chapel. I gave you an insider look into behind-the-scenes action."

"Like I said… don't tell that story."

I purchase an outfit that makes me look like I work at an advertising agency, which is precisely the look you want when meeting a publisher. I'm even considering getting a spray tan and gluing eyelashes to my face. It's all very intimidating.

"Don't get so stressed out about it," Rob says over the phone. "It's not as important as you think."

"But it's a publisher. The real deal."

"You see, that's the thing. You already did it. Whether they want to represent you is not going to make a difference. The only important thing is the readers. If they enjoy the book, that's the final say, and that's all you care about anyway—to write something that people enjoy. Remember when you said you wanted someone to laugh while on the subway reading your book? You just got an email from someone who said exactly that. It made her day."

Rob is right—I'm stressing myself out. I'm so grateful that people are reading my blog posts and purchasing my book. Why am I so concerned what this publishing house thinks? Once again, I'm looking for other people to decide whether I'm worthy enough. And it was this exact thing that almost stopped me from self-publishing my book in the first place. It's amazing the power other's opinions have on you. They're a formidable opponent.

A few more days pass and I finally get a call from Emma. "I'm sorry, they passed. They said the genre you're in is not a big seller."

"How can that be? My book is selling really well. I have more reviews than people who are on television."

"It's just business. Don't take it personally."

I hang up the phone, angry. If the whole reason you print books is for readers to purchase and enjoy them, and you have one on your desk that people are purchasing and enjoying, why would you use the excuse "the genre doesn't sell?" Why aren't you listening to what readers are saying instead of just making an assumption on what they want to read? I call Rob and give him the news.

"Like I said, Nadine, it's not a big deal. You did all of this on your own, without anyone's help. If they can't acknowledge that, fine. People like it, that's all that matters. You don't need some big shot in a Manhattan skyscraper to decide whether your book is good enough."

"Thanks, I guess I just got caught up in the whole thing."

"Good, now that you are feeling better I need you to go to Walmart and buy me three soaker hoses, four regular garden hoses, and a couple of sprinklers. And do you think the airport would let you pack barbed wire?"

"I'm not packing barbed wire."

"At least bring the hoses and sprinklers."

"No."

"I really need them. They cost a fortune down here."

"My bag is going to weigh two hundred pounds, Rob. I'm going to hurt myself trying to lift it."

"Come on. Your suitcase has wheels. Just do it for me; I have about a thousand bougainvillea plants that I have to water every day. I'm getting exhausted over here." I'm getting exhausted just thinking about schlepping that bag through the airport.

Once back in Costa Rica, I wait for my oversized bag to come around on the Liberia airport baggage carousel. I'm silently debating on where I want to get my future hernia surgery performed when someone taps me on the shoulder.

"Excuse me, are you Nadine?" a woman asks. For some reason, all I can think about is that I'm in trouble for smuggling a suitcase full of hoses and sprinklers into the country. *Thank goodness I didn't bring the barbed wire*, I think to myself while preparing myself for an uncomfortable back room interrogation.

"Yes, I'm her," I cautiously respond. The woman is not an employee of the airport. She turns out to be someone who enjoyed my book. I am completely dumbfounded and look around to see if this is some sort of practical joke. This causes a small stir and others standing around me start whispering, *Wow, someone famous was on our flight... I sat next to her and had no idea.*

The person who sat next to me on the plane approaches me and asks who I am. I tell him I am the author of *Happier Than A Billionaire,* an answer that produces the level of excitement rarely seen outside the oral hygiene aisle at Walgreens. He should have known I was not famous since I flew coach and was too cheap to buy the inflight television/movie package. This resulted in me catatonically staring straight ahead for five hours like Robert De Niro in *Awakenings.*

I exit the terminal where I find Rob waiting for me. He gives me a big hug. "I missed you so much."

"I missed you too. Get this... you are never going to believe what just happened. I got recognized at the baggage carousel."

"Recognized for what?"

"The book. Someone actually recognized me from the photo on the back cover. It's completely surreal."

"That's awesome. But I have something even crazier to tell you."

"What?"

"We were contacted by a production company in New York City. They want to come down and film us. How about that for good news?"

"Wow... I can't even... I don't know what to think."

"I know what I think," Rob smiles.

"What?"

"I think that publisher made a mistake."

Happier Than A Billionaire

My internet has worked consistently for the past four days. It appears Sergio has finally come through and fixed the line. Unfortunately, I hear two unknown men talking on the phone when I pick up the receiver. They appear to be a jolly pair and I politely ask them to get off the phone before I place my call; there is no reason to be rude. I'll just let Sergio know and I'm sure these new issues will be resolved by mañana.

I start looking over the contract that the production company sent me. "We love your website and your book. You're living a life that most dream about," one producer said over the phone. I didn't mention we haven't had water for two days—it might ruin the romance.

"So, are you going to sign it?" Rob asks.

"I'm not sure. It could be fun. How about you, do you want to do it?"

"I go back and forth. They always say to be careful what you wish for."

"I know, but I'll take a page from you... how bad can it be?"

"Well, I'm definitely not going to stress out about it. My plan is to enjoy my breakfast on the terrace and play my guitar," Rob replies. The phone rings and Rob picks up the receiver.

"That's interesting," he says before taking the call outside.

It's an odd feeling to have a television crew contact you about filming your life. I'm not quite sure what they want to see, me shopping at the farmers market? Rob bungee cording our car back together? At least it's this part of my life they want to shoot; the "pre-Costa Rica" portion was not nearly as interesting.

I look back at it all and think of the many things that have changed. I believed I was coming to Costa Rica to build a house and live a simpler life. It turns out this was just a fraction of what was in store for me. This adventure turned out to be much grander than I had anticipated.

I've driven, hiked, kayaked, and scootered with Rob to every corner of this country. I visited the Osa Peninsula where Scarlet Macaws dropped almond shells on my head, fished for Jacks the color of sheet metal, and jumped out of a boat to trek into the depths of the jungle. In Ostional, I witnessed mama turtles lay their eggs, and later the babies as they hatched under crescents of moonlight.

I've rappelled into ravines and stood at the bank of a turquoise waterfall. I watched Rob jump into the swimming hole and drench his head under the cascading water rich with healing powers. I'll always cherish the memory of his laugher as he looked up toward the sky and reached out his arms. It was as if he was receiving a blessing from above.

I even made friends. New ones that helped me find a pirate's cave and hosted old ones who had the unfortunate experience of getting zapped by a suicide shower. I stuck my toes in black sand and pink sand and every color in-between. Every shoreline was a new frontier, every drop of water splashing against my body an emancipation. It's all been so good, so real, so worth it.

It is true that our plan had called for building a house by now, but instead I built a book. Rather than constructing something brick by brick, I did it word by word. I allowed myself to be vulnerable. Although it terrified me, it was this vulnerability that paved a new path. I'm no longer running away from my life in the states, but instead standing still and relishing the life that is present before me. It turns out I had to let go of it all to rediscover everything that matters.

It's now common to find me sitting under a lavender sky while I coax the bigness of this world through the tip of my pen. Costa Rica helped me realize that I'm a writer and I'm the happiest while typing something on my blog or scribbling down an idea for a chapter. Maybe this is the real reason I started this adventure. Nothing is permanent in life, but maybe my story is the one thing that lasts long after I am gone. This is my purpose, the very reason I'm standing on this planet, and happiness has galloped toward me like a determined, runaway horse. So I encourage others to follow their dream but be ready to grab those reins and hold on tight before another moment passes you by.

If I am lucky, people will continue to read my stories. They'll put their kids to bed, grab the nightlight, and giggle under the covers as they are reminded of all the things they wish to do before there is no more time left to do them. My book once made a woman laugh on the subway and I hope I can make her laugh again someday. I think about her often, wondering what she daydreams about as she walks up the subway stairs and onto that busy street. Does she realize that despite what others might say her dreams haven't expired yet? They have a much longer shelf life than what's printed on the carton.

I'm grateful that I have Rob along with me on this journey. We were out boogie boarding yesterday when the water suddenly became rough. He lifted me over his head so I wouldn't get hit by the waves. He did this over and over again, taking the brunt of the waves while I floated gently over them. And in a way, he's been doing this for me in some form or another since the day we've met. Lifting me up, protecting me, and keeping me safe. With Rob by my side, I'll always have something to write about. Let's just hope it doesn't involve another bay pit or a Winnie the Pooh surgical notebook.

"I got some good news," Rob yells from the terrace.

"What?"

"The foreclosed house sold. The guy who bought it is a developer and he is already bringing supplies there to fix it up. He even got a water letter so I'm sure we can get one too. See, I told you it would all work out. It just took a little more time than we expected."

Knowing this eyesore will be repaired and transformed back into the luxurious mansion it was before is an incredible relief. I'll be sure to take my parents up there the next time they visit. They had such a good time that they plan on coming back next year. God help the golfers who plan to cheat or pee in the woods. My dad will be ready, notebook in hand.

I start thinking about our construction plans, but now I'm much less anxious. We will build one day but there is no hurry. I'm content right now living in the Thunderdome. I'm happy riding my scooter, resting my head against Rob, and waking up at five AM to the sounds of howler monkeys. So I guess a person can learn the same lesson twice; once I stopped looking for more, I got everything I needed.

I glance again at the contract in front of me. I go to the last page of the document and find the place to sign. I place the pen down on the line and...

"Honey quick, the monkeys are in the tree next to the house!" Rob shouts.

I toss the pen, grab my camera, and run outside. There they are; a family of monkeys only ten feet away. They're hanging upside down, tails wrapped around branches while stuffing leaves into their mouths. They are so close I can see the wrinkles around their noses and the darkness of their eyes. The big male looks over at us, makes a light hearted attempt at a grunt, and goes back to eating. One female is carrying a baby on her back with the cutest little face. I've watched them through my binoculars for so long, I actually recognize every one of them like they're old friends. I'm snapping pictures as fast as my camera will take them. I don't want to miss out on this.

Finally, the monkeys are on my side of the street.

ABOUT THE AUTHOR

When not writing, Nadine enjoys watching monkeys outside her window and taking pictures at the beach. Say hello if you see her there.

Read more about her adventures at her blog and Facebook page.

www.happierthanabillionaire.com
www.facebook.com/happierthanabillionaire

31730583R00180

Made in the USA
Lexington, KY
23 April 2014